China, Marxism, and Democracy

D0169113

REVOLUTIONARY STUDIES
Series Editor: PAUL LE BLANC

China, Marxism, and Democracy

Selections from *October Review*

Edited and Introduced by

THOMAS BARRETT

HUMANITIES PRESS
NEW JERSEY

This collection first published 1996 by Humanities Press International, Inc.,
165 First Avenue, Atlantic Highlands, New Jersey 07716

This collection © 1996 by Humanities Press International, Inc.

Library of Congress Cataloging-in-Publication Data

China, Marxism, and democracy : selections from October review /
 edited and introduced by Thomas Barrett.
     p.   cm.—(Revolutionary studies)
   Includes index.
   ISBN 0-391-03923-7
   1. Democracy—China. 2. China—Politics and government—1976–
 3. China—Economic conditions—1976– 4. China—Economic
 policy—1976– 5. Communism—China. I. Barrett, Thomas. II. Shih
 yüeh p'ing lun. III. Series.
 JQ1516.C4526   1995
 320.951'09'045—dc20   95–30166
                                           CIP

Contents

Introduction

In the waning months of 1991 the curtain fell on seventy-four years of what the world has called "communism" in the Soviet Union and Eastern Europe. When the Berlin Wall was dismantled and Boris Yeltsin was put to rout, not only those bureaucrats who would have returned the USSR to the policies of Leonid Brezhnev, but to his reforming predecessor Mikhail Gorbachev as well, the world was gripped by a feeling that a new era of world peace and human rights was dawning. Two years later the reality of ethnic hatreds flaring up into civil war in the former Yugoslavia and into neo-Nazi rioting in Germany has shattered the euphoria that ensued when the red flags were lowered from the Kremlin's cupolas. The American President Bill Clinton supports restrictions on democracy imposed by Yeltsin in Russia. The promise of prosperity that accompanied the dismantling of "communism" has turned into a bad joke, as workers throughout the USSR and Eastern Europe face not only lower wages but—worse—an end to the social services that they had considered basic human rights for generations.

To those following the events in China over the past seventeen years— since the death of Mao Zedong in 1976—the turn of events in the Soviet Union and Eastern Europe comes as no surprise. In a far more systematic and controlled fashion, Deng Xiaoping has been guiding China toward a restored capitalism while maintaining the Chinese Communist Party (CCP)'s harsh dictatorship. He and his associates have seen to it that there will be no free trade union elevating its leader to the presidency (as in Poland), nor artists and intellectuals taking over the government (as in Czechoslovakia), nor certainly the execution of the ousted dictator (as in Rumania). However during the period that Deng has been leading China—whether in an actual governmental post or from an advisory position—China has become more favorable to foreign investment and more fertile for the growth of a domestic capitalist class with each passing year. And though the leaders of the "Free World" may scold the Chinese tyrants in public, they are happy to do business with them in private.

This collection of articles from the *October Review*, a revolutionary social-ist magazine published in Hong Kong, presents and analyzes the economic and political evolution of China since the introduction of Deng Xiaoping's "reforms." The authors explain what Deng's economic and governmental policies have meant to the peasants and industrial workers and to those activists who continue to struggle for genuine democracy. However they are not content merely to comment on events; they are working to change

1

the reality, both in the British Crown Colony of Hong Kong and in the People's Republic of China, to which Hong Kong will be united in 1997. Their mission is to fulfill the promises made to the Chinese people in the 1949 revolution, promises that were cruelly broken.

Why did the Chinese revolution result in bureaucratic mismanagement and totalitarian dictatorship? Was this what Mao Zedong and his associates in the CCP leadership intended? If so, why did the Chinese people follow the CCP's leadership in resistance against the Japanese invasion and occupation of 1936–45 and in the 1945–49 civil war, which resulted in the overthrow of the Jiang Jieshi (hereinafter referred to by the more familiar spelling of Chiang Kaishek) regime? Is totalitarianism and bureaucratic mismanagement the inevitable result of any attempt to create a socialist society as envisioned by Karl Marx and Frederick Engels? These are some of the questions to which the *October Review* gives its answers, and the reader will find their logic persuasive. However *October Review*'s writers often assume a certain familiarity with events in the history of the socialist movement and the history of China that many readers may not have.

WHAT IS STALINISM?

For a period of about a year, the Russian Revolution held out the greatest promise in history for democracy and social justice. The Russian workers, peasants, and soldiers, demanding "Peace, Land, and Bread," overthrew the tsar in February (according to the Julian calendar, which was in use in Russia at that time) of 1917 and elected democratic councils in their factories and regiments. The Russian word for council is *soviet*, and history has since called the "Councils of Workers' and Soldiers' Deputies" by that name. However a capitalist provisional government, which was unable and unwilling to provide "Peace, Land, and Bread," competed with the soviets for power. In October (again according to the Julian calendar) the soviets, led by the Bolshevik Party, which held majorities in a number of important soviets, including in Moscow and St. Petersburg, dispersed the Provisional Government and took complete power.

It was assumed by both the people and their Bolshevik leaders that their revolution was only the first in a worldwide wave of workers' revolutions, which would establish socialism on an international scale. Disastrous defeats in Germany, Italy, and other countries dashed those hopes.

The Soviet government's first act was to negotiate its complete withdrawal from the First World War. After the November 11, 1918, armistice, the United States, Britain, France, and other countries invaded Russia in support of counterrevolutionary forces seeking the restoration of the tsar. In the ensuing civil war, Russia's economy was devastated, and thousands of the revolutionary workers, peasants, and intellectuals, who were the heart and soul of the Russian Revolution, perished in battle.

During the civil war, the Soviets considered it necessary to prevent by any means necessary any popular support to the counterrevolution. They suppressed virtually all newspapers that were not either government—or Communist Party—controlled. They executed the tsar and his family to eliminate any popular symbol for the White Armies, as the counterrevolutionary forces were called. Anyone suspected of aiding the Whites was subject to summary execution without trial. That included those who did no more than express discontent with Soviet policies.

To first win the civil war and then jump start the Russian economy after its conclusion, the Soviet government had to rely on a layer of tsarist military officers and on a section of the vast tsarist bureaucracy. Courage and dedication were not enough: knowledge and experience in military strategy and tactics (in the one case) and management and organizational (in the other case) were also required. The Soviet government had to give incentives and inducements to persuade them to support the Soviet cause.

Vladimir Ilyich Lenin was the undisputed central leader of the Bolshevik Party. He was the party's general secretary and the first prime minister of the Soviet government. The popular spokesperson and activist leader was Lev Davidovich (Leon) Trotsky. At the time of the insurrection, Trotsky was president of the Petrograd (originally St. Petersburg, later Leningrad, today St. Petersburg again) Soviet. Immediately after the October Revolution, he was assigned as foreign minister, with the task of negotiating Russia's withdrawal from the First World War. When the civil war broke out, he was reassigned as war minister, and it was his responsibility to organize an army to defend the proletarian revolution. Trotsky's military policies were a key factor enabling the Red Army to prevail, and after Lenin he was considered the most important individual Bolshevik leader.

During the civil war, the Soviet government had nationalized all industry and expropriated farm products, a policy called "War Communism." It was assumed that collective ownership would be permanent, because the revolution would spread to other more economically advanced countries, who would be able to provide material aid to impoverished Russia. When revolutions in Germany, Hungary, and other countries failed, the Bolshevik leadership recognized that the Russian economy could not grow under conditions of total state ownership and control. A New Economic Policy (NEP) was instituted in 1921, which allowed private ownership and a free market in agriculture and light industry. Shortly thereafter the former tsarist civil servants on whom the Soviet government continued to rely for management of production and distribution were invited to become members of the Communist Party, as the Bolshevik Party had been renamed.

Because of the influx into the party of bureaucrats who had never really been revolutionaries, combined with the death in battle of thousands of the most dedicated worker–Bolsheviks, the balance in party membership shifted in favor of government staff people. Furthermore these "apparatchiks," as they were called, appropriated for themselves special privileges, and they made sure that their needs were met in the event of any shortages. In the inevitable internal disputes that arose inside the party, the bureaucracy found a powerful representative: Joseph V. Stalin, a second-tier leader but nevertheless a Bolshevik of many years' service.

Lenin recognized the danger to the party and to the revolution. However, because he was incapacitated as a result of an assassination attempt, he was unable personally to lead a political struggle against the bureaucracy. Instead he made a personal request of Trotsky that he rally the worker rank and file to reclaim the party leadership and expel Stalin, whom Lenin had come to consider a dangerous opportunist.

Unfortunately Trotsky's popularity with the rank-and-file worker Communists and with the population as a whole was not reflected within the party leadership. Many Old Bolsheviks, especially Grigori Zinoviev and Lev Kamenev, resented Trotsky as a parvenu, having joined the Bolsheviks only upon Lenin's return to Russia from exile in April 1917. They further resented the circumstances by which Trotsky joined the Bolsheviks—Lenin's agreement with Trotsky on the necessity for proletarian revolution in Russia and his sharp displeasure at the conservative course followed by Zinoviev and Kamenev. Trotsky's uncompromising personality was also a handicap. He believed to the end of his days that loyalty to the principles of proletarian revolution transcended all personal loyalties, and he acted accordingly. He thus never developed the knack for hand-holding and feather-smoothing, which is unfortunately necessary for a political leader in our imperfect world. His enemies in the bureaucracy were well schooled in back-stabbing, flattery, and backroom deals, from the tsarist period. Trotsky was unable to defeat them on that battlefield.

For some Communist leaders, however, their personal animosity toward Trotsky was more important than revolutionary principles. They acquiesced in the junking of revolutionary internationalism in favor of the antimarxist notion of "socialism in one country" and its corollary, "peaceful coexistence" with capitalism. Zinoviev, in alliance with Stalin, led the transformation of the Communist International from a world revolutionary party to an instrument of Soviet diplomacy and compromise with imperialism. He also played a central role in transforming the Russian Communists' moral authority in the Comintern to an iron dictatorship. The Comintern took upon itself the authority to impose policies and select leaders in any and all national sections. Comintern dictatorship was to have disastrous results in China.

When the bureaucrat-led party was unable to prevent peasants and businessmen who had grown wealthy under NEP from acting against the economic interests of the workers and poor peasants, revolutionary leaders, including Zinoviev and Kamenev, who had previously supported Stalin, reversed course and joined with Trotsky in the struggle against Stalin.

However the precedent of harsh repression of dissent, which had been established during the civil war, returned to haunt the Communist Party. Stalin combined the methods of the Red Terror with tsarist-style bureaucratic machinations to isolate the Left Opposition, as Trotsky's faction was called, and drive it out of the Communist Party. In 1928 Stalin expelled Trotsky and turned against the wealthy peasants and NEP businessmen, brutally repressing them and killing thousands in a forced collectivization of agriculture. In 1929 Stalin and his supporters expelled Nikolai Bukharin and others who had represented the wealthy peasants and small businessmen in the Communist Party, thus gaining undisputed dictatorial control of the Communist Party and the entire Union of Soviet Socialist Republics.

The rule of a bureaucrat-dominated Communist Party, in which dissent and democracy are brutally purged, is called "Stalinism," and it has mistakenly been equated with "communism" by both its friends and enemies. Stalinism was to have disastrous consequences for China, from the 1920s to the present day.

THE STRUGGLE FOR INDEPENDENCE AND DEMOCRACY IN CHINA

A pernicious myth, which fortunately has lost favor in recent years, holds that civil liberties and democratic decision making in society are essentially Western European—even Anglo-Saxon—concepts and are not relevant to the experience or political aspirations of African or Asiatic peoples or the indigenous population of the Americas. The historical record in China for at least the last century disproves that notion conclusively. Even if some democratic ideals were imported by English and American missionaries, they took strong root in Chinese soil and have survived civil war, foreign invasion, and some of the most brutal political repression ever recorded in history.

In most countries of Eastern Europe, Stalinism was imposed by the Soviet occupation forces in the aftermath of the Second World War. Political commissars from the Soviet Union organized Communist parties in Poland, Czechoslovakia, Hungary, Rumania, Bulgaria, and East Germany. The CCP, in contrast, was founded shortly after the Russian Revolution by young activists who were leading the fight for democracy and national independence in China. They saw in Bolshevism a winning strategy for their own ongoing struggle. The students who filled Tiananmen Square in 1989 were continuing a campaign begun in their great-great-grandparents' day and had far more in common with the CCP's founders than the bureaucratic fossils who rule China today.

The history of nineteenth-century China is essentially a story of humiliation. The Qing dynasty, which had held power since the seventeenth century, was corrupt and oppressive. They had originally invaded from Manchuria and had imposed what many Han (the majority Chinese ethnic group) people considered "barbarian" customs on the Chinese people. Even without Qing oppression, however, Chinese society had become ossified and backward-looking. The entry of the Western Europeans into Asia only brought China's stagnation into sharp relief. Europeans took possession of territories on China's perimeter—the Dutch in Taiwan, the British in Hong Kong, the Portuguese in Macao—and ruthlessly exploited China's population for cheap labor and for consumption of whatever the Europeans wished to import. Possibly the most notorious example occurred when Chinese authorities demanded that the British stop importing opium into China in the 1840s, and Britain responded with military force. In addition the Western Europeans, especially the British, insisted on importing something else into China—their religion and culture. Showing a total disrespect for China's ancient civilization, they sent hundreds of Christian missionaries into the country, reinforcing a sense of humiliation for many Chinese people.

However it was an Asiatic power, not a European one, that provided the catalyst for change in China. When the Japanese made contact with the industrialized West in the 1850s, their response was to emulate Western economics and technology while maintaining their Asiatic society and culture. The Japanese samurai nobility—like the Prussian Junker nobility half a world away—saw in industrialization a means for enhancing their own military power and achieving supremacy on their continent. By the last decades of the nineteenth century, Japan had become a player in the imperialist "Great Game." In 1896 they imposed a crushing defeat on China, claiming a "sphere of influence" in Korea and northeastern China. The imperial family's conduct during the war was justly considered cowardly. The empress dowager and her entourage fled Beijing, compounding the humiliation felt by many patriotic Chinese, who felt that if Japan could become a world power, there was no reason why China could not as well.

In 1900 a secret martial arts society called the Fists of Harmony and Justice (dubbed "Boxers" by Westerners in China) led a revolt against the degenerate Qing monarchy. Though the so-called "Boxer Rebellion" was brutally suppressed, it sounded the death knell for the old regime. In 1911 Sun Yatsen, a martial arts master who was influenced by Western-educated Chinese businessmen as well as Japanese-influenced young anti-Western intellectuals, led a successful uprising, which established the Republic of China

(ROC). The ROC was unable to consolidate its power throughout China, however, and Dr. Sun and his supporters organized a political party, the Guomindang (KMT), to unite republican forces against the vestiges of the Qing and emerging independent warlords in the northern regions.

ASIAN DEMOCRACY AND RUSSIAN MARXISM

The capitalist classes of Western Europe and the United States, having come to power through democratic revolutions during the seventeenth and eighteenth centuries, ruled—and continue to rule to this day—on the premise that their economic system of private ownership of the means of production combined with a government that defends their property rights first and foremost is the essence of democracy. In the dawn of industrial society, the ascendant revolutionary bourgeoisie could earn the loyalty of broad sections of the population by conceding political rights and social mobility, most especially, free ownership of farmland by those who worked it.

The peoples of Asia and Africa—and even Eastern Europe and Russia— saw a different reality. Capitalism in those regions did not evolve naturally from the indigenous society but was introduced from the outside, from Britain, the Netherlands, and France at first and from the United States, Germany, Belgium, and Italy later on. The financiers who invested their capital in mines, plantations, and, in some cases, labor-intensive industries did so for their own benefit, not for the benefit of the indigenous people. In contrast to the revolutionary bourgeoisie of seventeenth-century England or eighteenth-century France, the foreign capitalists who invested in Asia and Africa during the nineteenth century allied themselves with the old despotic ruling classes against the peasants and city workers—or imposed a colonial government of their own if the native rulers proved uncooperative. To the peoples of Asia and Africa, capitalism meant *imperialism*, and to fight for democracy and national independence meant, in reality, to fight against capitalism. Most often, the imperialist officials and financiers understood the threat to their power and profits that the struggle for democracy posed far better than the native nationalists.

Sun Yatsen had little understanding of the complexities of global politics, but he understood it well enough to have a completely different reaction to the Russian Revolution of 1917 than did "democratic" statesmen like U.S. President Woodrow Wilson. He recognized in the Russian workers' and peasants' revolution against tsarism a parallel revolution to the Chinese people's overthrow of the Qing emperor. Dr. Sun congratulated the Bolsheviks enthusiastically and promoted friendly relations between the Republic of China and the new Soviet Republic. In turn Lenin and Trotsky supported Dr. Sun's government against the imperialists and warlords and established a

cadre school, the University of the Toilers of the East, to train revolutionary fighters to continue the struggle that Dr. Sun and his comrades had
started. The KMT sent its most promising young leaders, including Chiang
Kaishek, to the school. Among those trained in the Soviet Republic (and
later the Soviet Union) were the founders of the CCP, including Chen
Duxiu and Peng Shuzhi.

The CCP emerged within the democratic nationalist movement and was
not counterposed to it. Not even the Russian Bolsheviks—including Trotsky—
considered socialism realistic in impoverished and backward China at this
time. There was general consensus within the Third International and within
the Chinese democratic movement that the goals should be the unification
and independence of China, a democratic republican government, and economic, social, and technological modernization. The CCP supported the
KMT government in its conquest to wrest northern China from the warlords
and to lead the entire country out of underdevelopment.

The Comintern's policy in China was consistent with its support for emerging
nationalist republics—or even monarchies—in the underdeveloped world.
Support for the Kemalist republic in Turkey or Emir Aminullah's regime in
Afghanistan was not motivated by considerations of "peaceful coexistence"
with capitalism nor even primarily by the diplomatic concerns of the Soviet
government. The Bolsheviks genuinely believed that the cause of international socialism was best served by supporting governments in the Middle
East and Far East that worked for independence and modernization, even
though they unquestionably represented the interests of the native bourgeois
class. (Africa and Latin America were more complex situations and beyond
our discussion here.)

Even so, however, the Comintern and the young Chinese Communist
leadership recognized that the convergence of interests between the Chinese
bourgeoisie and working class was temporary. The manifesto adopted by the
second CCP congress in 1922 made clear that the Communists insisted on
their organizational independence within a broad united democratic front,
consistent with the views expressed by V. I. Lenin in his "Draft Theses on
the National and Colonial Questions" of 1920.

However within weeks of the second CCP congress, the Comintern reversed its policy. The Comintern representative Henricus Sneevliet (using
the pseudonym Maring) arrived in China with instructions that the party's
members join the KMT as individuals and give up the party's independent
existence. The CCP leaders unanimously opposed Maring's proposal, but
Maring then made it a matter of Comintern discipline, and the Chinese
Communists submitted, against their better judgment.

Unfortunately the authority of the October Revolution gave the Comintern—
and the Soviet Communist Party within the Comintern—virtual dictatorial

power, to use or abuse. The Comintern, led by the erratic Grigori Zinoviev, tended to ignore the opinions of revolutionaries directly involved in the struggle in their various countries. When Communists disagreed, the Comintern felt no hesitation in imposing iron discipline on its national sections. The results were disastrous in all too many cases.

The Comintern's orders to the CCP to dissolve itself into the KMT co-incided with the growing dominance of the Soviet government bureaucracy over the Soviet Communist Party and thus over the Comintern. The bu-reaucrats had no perspective of breaking the Soviet Union's diplomatic and economic isolation by workers' revolutions in other countries; rather they looked to conventional diplomacy with the advanced capitalist countries and trade with the multinational corporations as the exclusive means toward peace and prosperity—which meant peace and prosperity for the bureaucrats them-selves, not necessarily for anyone else. Of course a foreign policy based on "peaceful coexistence" had its price, a price that the Kremlin *apparatchiks* were willing to pay or rather were willing to extract from working people in their own and other countries. Though the Comintern may have had an incomplete and partially erroneous perspective on the Chinese revolution during the 1918–22 period, it was still motivated by genuine revolutionary concerns. From late 1922 and thereafter, its policies were increasingly based on the Soviet government's diplomacy rather than aid to workers' revolu-tions throughout the world.

During 1923 and 1924 the Soviets provided considerable political and military support to the KMT. Its representative Mikhail M. Borodin aided KMT forces in defeating Canton warlord Chen Jiungming. Soviet General Vassily K. Blyukher (using the pseudonym Galen) worked closely with Chiang Kaishek in raising and training the KMT's army, including the establishment of the Whampoa Military Academy. Whenever conflict arose between the Communists and the KMT's bourgeois leadership, the Comintern ordered the Communists to capitulate. Nevertheless the KMT leaders trusted neither the Chinese nor Soviet Communists. Sterling Seagrave, in his book *The Soong Dynasty* (Harper and Row: 1985), quotes Chiang Kaishek:

> The Russian Communist Party, in its dealings with China, has only one aim, namely to make the Chinese Communist Party its chosen instru-ment. It does not believe that our Party [the KMT] can really cooperate with it for long for the sake of ensuring success for both parties. It is the policy of the Russian Communist Party to turn the lands inhabited by the Manchus, Mongols, Moslems, and Tibetans into parts of the Soviet do-main; it may harbor sinister designs even on China proper.

Whatever the Soviets' motivations may have been at this time, the KMT leaders knew that the Chinese Communists' aim was proletarian revolution.

They also knew their own aim: a stable capitalist China in which native Chinese financiers could make enormous profits. Sun Yatsen understood clearly the distinction between the Soviets' and the Chinese Communists' support to his party. Peng Shuzhi, in his introduction to the collection *Leon Trotsky on China* (Monad Press, N.Y.: 1976), quotes Dr. Sun:

> If Russia wants to cooperate with China, she must cooperate with our Party and not with Chen Duxiu [the central leader of the CCP at that time—TB]. If Chen disobeys our Party, he will be ousted.
>   The Chinese revolution has never been welcomed by the foreign powers, which have often helped our opponents [militarists—Peng] in attempts to destroy our Party. . . . Sympathy can only be expected from Russia. . . . It was not Chen Duxiu's but Russia's idea to befriend us.

Consistent with this attitude, Sun had a motion passed by the KMT Central Committee meeting in August 1924 that the KMT review all Comintern resolutions and orders to the CCP.

That was too much for the CCP's revolutionary leaders. They acted to reestablish local CCP units and to renew activity among the urban workers. Led by Chen Duxiu and Peng Shuzhi, the CCP decided to withdraw its members from the KMT and work with it only "from outside," that is, in a united front. In so doing they were in direct violation of Comintern directives.

In early 1925 the Communists led a victorious strike in the Japanese-owned cotton mills of Shanghai. Other workers in Shanghai and elsewhere in China joined in active struggle. The Japanese owners launched a vicious counterattack to break the millworkers' union, and on May 30, 1925, British troops fired on a workers' demonstration, killing seven and wounding dozens more. In response to the "May 30 Incident," workers throughout China rose in open revolt. The second Chinese revolution had begun, a revolution that could have given state power to the Chinese working class but instead ended in complete disaster for the Communist Party, for the workers, and even for the Soviet Union and Comintern.

The KMT was at first helpless in the face of the aroused Chinese proletariat. Sun Yatsen had died in March, and no other leader had his authority. The KMT attempted to ride the revolutionary wave, claiming to be "anti-imperialist" and joining in the population's outrage at the May 30th Incident. However, Chiang was planning his bid for power, and in March of 1926 he staged the first of two coups d'état. The Communists might have stopped him had they not been prevented from doing so by the Comintern representatives, who by now took their marching orders from Joseph Stalin.

Chiang followed his second coup in 1927 with bloody repression against the Communists—whether they had supported Comintern policy or not—

and the militant workers of Shanghai, Canton, and other cities. The Comintern still did not get the message, and instead ordered the CCP to support the "left" KMT, led by Wang Chingwei. Wang joined Chiang in his suppression of the workers' revolution and together the KMT leaders succeeded in defeating the second Chinese revolution. When the defeat was an accomplished fact, when hundreds of worker militants had been killed, imprisoned, or simply demoralized, and when the revolutionary tide had begun its ebb, at that time the Comintern ordered the CCP to stage an armed insurrection! Of course, abject defeat was a foregone conclusion, and what was left of the Communist Party retreated on the famous Long March.

Rather than admit that its policies had been disastrous, Stalin and the Comintern leadership attempted to find a scapegoat. They pinned the blame for the disaster on none other than Chen Duxiu, who, along with Peng, had opposed the Comintern's false policies from the beginning. Trotsky, who had supported Chen's and Peng's position since 1923, used the Chinese experience to prove how disastrous Stalin's policies were for the Communist movement and for the Soviet Union itself.

Trotsky drew another important conclusion from the Chinese experience: in 1906 after the 1905 Russian revolution, Trotsky determined that because of Russia's rapid industrialization with imperialist financing, the Russian bourgeoisie was no longer capable of leading the democratic revolution against tsarism. In his book *Results and Prospects* (Pathfinder Press, NY: 1972), Trotsky argued that the Russian working class would carry out an uninterrupted—or "permanent" revolution—combining socialist and democratic objectives and that the bourgeoisie was incapable of fighting against tsarism or imperialism. When Lenin embraced the essence of Trotsky's theory of permanent revolution in April 1917, Trotsky joined the Bolshevik faction.

Trotsky had only considered permanent revolution applicable in the Russian context. However the disaster of China led him to conclude that permanent revolution had universal applicability throughout the underdeveloped world, that is, in those countries where capitalist development had not naturally evolved but had been imposed from the outside by imperialism. The authors in this collection continue to adhere to the idea that only under proletarian socialist leadership can those countries dominated by imperialism achieve true independence and begin to break out of underdevelopment and that only by turning state power over to the working class, in alliance with the poor peasants and revolutionary intellectuals, can genuine democracy be established. The continuation of capitalist rule can only mean corrupt dictatorship and impoverishment of the masses of the population throughout the so-called "Third World."

THE DICTATORSHIP OF THE BUREAUCRACY—
THE USSR AND CHINA

By 1928 the Soviet bureaucracy's power was for all intents and purposes
consolidated. It had defeated the political representatives of the working
class', the Left Opposition, and thereafter defeated the renascent bourgeoisie, as represented by Nikolai Bukharin and the Right Opposition. Trotsky
was deported, agriculture was forcibly collectivized, and hundreds were imprisoned or killed. By the early 1930s, it was clear that there was no possibility that either the Soviet Communist Party or the Soviet government
could reform themselves and that both would be overthrown, either by the
revolutionary working class or by the restoration of capitalism.

Trotsky and his supporters worked for the former alternative. The perspective that they put forward called for a revolution which would return
political power to the working masses through their democratically elected
councils but which would maintain state ownership of large-scale industry,
state monopoly of foreign trade, and state planning of the economy—of
course, with a genuinely democratic state. Trotsky called this perspective "political revolution" as opposed to a "social revolution," which would
transfer power from one class to another. Trotsky considered the Stalinist
bureaucracy to be the leadership of the working class—albeit a parasitic and
destructive leadership—and that the Soviet state remained a *workers' state*
despite its bureaucratic degeneration. His idea was to replace the class's leadership but not to deprive the working class of the state power that it continued
to hold.

Concurrently Trotsky recognized that the Comintern (also known as the
Third International) was bankrupt as an international revolutionary force. In
1933 after the Comintern refused to confront its own errors, which had
allowed Adolf Hitler to seize power in Germany, it proposed the establishment of a new revolutionary international party, the Fourth International.
The Fourth International's founding conference was held in 1938. Among
those founding members were Chen Duxiu and Peng Shuzhi.

In 1936 Japan invaded China and put the KMT forces to rout. Their
brutality rivaled the brutality of the Nazis in Europe. The corrupt KMT,
whose leaders were more interested in lining their pockets than in their
country's welfare, were incapable of resisting the Japanese and in fact found
it profitable to collaborate with the invaders. The CCP, led by Stalinists
Mao Zedong and Zhou Enlai, was able to emerge from its mountain hide-
outs and build one of the most remarkable fighting forces in history, the
People's Liberation Army (PLA), which organized thousands of peasant guerrillas to fight for China's freedom. Similar guerrilla armies were organized in
Korea and in French Indochina (today Vietnam, Cambodia, and Laos).

By the end of the Second World War, the CCP-led forces controlled most of China's territory. Chiang Kaishek's KMT, with U.S. support, launched a civil war to destroy the CCP once and for all, but his forces were no match for the PLA. In 1949 the CCP took power, and Chiang and his associates fled to the island of Taiwan, which had been reunited with China after having been a Japanese colonial possession for nearly fifty years.

Despite the hard lessons that the CCP had learned over the years, Mao Zedong still rejected socialist revolution for China, even after the CCP had come to power. Instead he proposed "New Democracy," supposedly a transition between capitalism and socialism. Under the system of New Democracy, the means of production would remain in private hands even as the party of the proletariat held state power. There was one problem: the private owners of the means of production had no use for New Democracy nor for the Communist Party in power. Instead of investing their capital in economic growth in China, they shipped it out of the country, to Taiwan, Hong Kong, and other countries. As an added complication, the United States sent troops into Korea to prop up the capitalist dictatorship in the southern part of that country. American General Douglas MacArthur made no secret of his desire to invade China to overturn the Chinese revolution. When American troops crossed the Yalu River into North Korea, the CCP government took the threat seriously and dispatched Chinese troops to aid North Korea, where the Stalinist party had also taken power. Simply to provide the necessities of life to a people victimized by over two decades of civil war and foreign invasion, as well as to respond to a direct military threat, the CCP government had to expropriate the banks and large industries and establish a monopoly of foreign trade and a planned economy. In spite of its intentions, China had to abolish capitalist property relations within its borders.

Similar events had taken place across Eastern Europe, in countries that the Soviet army had occupied during the final stages of the Second World War, and in Albania and Yugoslavia, where CP-led guerrilla armies had defeated German, Italian, and local fascist forces. In all of these cases, the CP-dominated governments had attempted to reestablish capitalist economies and had failed because of the capitalist class's refusal to cooperate in their countries' rebuilding. The new governments, by necessity, abolished capitalist property relations and instituted economic planning along Soviet lines. Fourth Internationalists, after considerable discussion and debate, came to the conclusion that the Communist parties had established workers' states, albeit *bureaucratically deformed* from the beginning, and proposed to the working people of these countries a perspective of political revolution, as in the Soviet Union, to overthrow the working class's parasitic leadership but not the working class itself.

Trotsky, who was assassinated in 1940, had not anticipated that Stalinism would even survive the Second World War, let alone impose itself on Eastern Europe, China, North Korea, and North Vietnam. Chen Duxiu had broken with the Fourth International in 1939; he died in 1942. Peng Shuzhi, however, emerged as an important leader in the Fourth International. After World War II revolutionary leaders had to confront new and complex social and political realities, to which earlier analyses, including Trotsky's, were inadequate. Peng made important contributions to the political discussions of this and later periods until his death in 1983. A retrospective of his and his companion Chen Bilan's lives are the final two items in this volume.

REVOLUTIONARY SOCIALISM IN CONTEMPORARY CHINA

The authors in this volume are building on the political foundation left to them by the Russian Bolsheviks, by Trotsky, and by Chen Duxiu and Peng Shuzhi. Their recognition that only a process of *permanent revolution* in underdeveloped countries (and China remains an underdeveloped country) can ensure genuine national independence, democracy, and prosperity for the urban and rural working people has enabled them to understand why Deng Xiaoping's reform policies—which have made China's economy the world's fastest growing—have not benefited the Chinese people. And they show conclusively, with their detailed analysis of Chinese economic policies and their effects on the population, that Deng Xiaoping's economic reforms have lined the pockets of a small Chinese elite and foreign financiers but have left the workers and peasants behind.

The journalists of the *October Review* have proposed *political revolution* as their answer to the antiworker and antipeasant course followed by the Chinese government. Their alternative is the power of the rank-and-file workers, student youth, and poor peasants, speaking their minds freely and taking political action on their own initiative. During the massive prodemocracy upsurge of 1989, journalists of all political stripes explained to their readers and listeners what it was all about, but few let the Chinese people speak for themselves. *October Review* has taken the lead before, during, and after the 1989 events in making available to people throughout the world the Chinese workers' and students' actual thoughts and aspirations, as written in leaflets, wall posters, and demonstration speeches. Some of them are reprinted in this volume, along with accounts of the democratic movement's activities. The *October Review* has not been content merely to comment, however. The authors published here have organized and participated in activity in Hong Kong in support of the Chinese democracy movement and for workers' rights in Hong Kong itself.

Most of the selections published here were written before the momentous events of late 1991 that put an end to "Communism" as we had known it. Revolutionists today are thinking out and debating whether political revolution continues to make sense as an objective in countries where the Communist Party still holds political power. In previous decades bureaucratic regimes for their own reasons defended, sometimes militarily, state ownership and economic planning against attempts to restore capitalism. Today, however, those same bureaucrats are leading the assault on socialist property relations and are directly carrying out capitalist restoration, even as they maintain the repressive dictatorships of the Stalinist era. Clearly the bureaucrats aspire to become a native capitalist class. Whether that goal can be realized or not remains to be seen.

It is apparent that the workers' revolution in China, for which *October Review* has always argued and continues to do so, must make deep-going changes in Chinese society. It will need to overthrow an economic system well on its way to becoming the kind of export-oriented capitalism that prevails in the "Four Tigers of the Pacific" (South Korea, Taiwan, Hong Kong, and Singapore).

Nevertheless it is clear that the revolutionists whose words are published here remain undaunted, despite their realization that nowhere are the prospects for capitalist superprofits brighter and the prospects for democracy dimmer than in China. They recognize that no national economy can be isolated from the world economy and that the world capitalist economy is in deep crisis. Even the "Four Tigers" have begun to be affected by economic and political pressures. Massive strikes have rocked South Korea. The native Taiwanese people's struggle for national independence and self-determination has forced concessions from the ruling KMT, including the release of political prisoners, the legalization of the opposition Democratic Progressive Party, and turning power over to native Taiwanese politicians within the KMT. Political turmoil in Taiwan is especially significant for China, because so much of the capital investment in China's capitalist restoration is coming from Taiwan, in an ironic twist on Chiang Kaishek's dream of reconquest of the mainland.

Therefore, the *October Review* supports and builds the Fourth International, which continues the work originally begun by Leon Trotsky and his supporters in the 1930s, that is, to rebuild a world revolutionary socialist party on the ashes of the Comintern of Lenin's time. *October Review* published the greetings sent by the Revolutionary Communist Party of China to a commemoration of the Fourth International's fiftieth anniversary. The message closes with these words:

> Militants of the Fourth International must fight for the Chinese proletariat and masses who engage in the anti-bureaucratic struggle not only to

overthrow the bureaucracy but also persist in a socialist alternative, defend the system of state ownership and planned economy, realize a democratic relation of production and self-management of the community, and link this struggle with the political revolution in the Soviet Union, Poland, and other workers' states, and with the socialist revolution to overthrow capitalism in the capitalist countries.

For the solidarity of the international proletariat!

For the realization of world socialism!

It is hoped that readers of this volume will be not only informed, but inspired as well.

THOMAS BARRETT

1

The Current Situation in China and the Tasks of Revolutionaries

Adopted by the Fifth National Congress of the Revolutionary Communist Party of China

CONTENTS

1. BASIC POSITIONS

After the People's Republic of China was established, the capitalist system was overthrown, laying the foundation of property relations characteristic of a workers' state. However democratic relations of production have not been established, and socialism is not yet realized. Today's China remains a transitional society between capitalism and socialism, with a very low level of productivity. Bureaucratic monopoly by the Chinese Communist Party (CCP) obstructs the establishment of democratic socialist relations of production. As a consequence productivity cannot develop rapidly. The CCP's privileged bureaucratic caste deprives the Chinese working class of its power over production and the state. In China the state may be described as the dictatorship of the CCP bureaucracy instead of the dictatorship of the proletariat. The contradiction between the bureaucracy and the laboring masses constitutes the main contradiction in society. If China is to advance toward socialism and avoid capitalist restoration, the priority for the masses is to seize economic and political power from the bureaucracy, that is, a political revolution is necessary to overthrow bureaucratic rule. Socialist democracy then needs to be put into practice, with the state ownership of the means of production as its basis.

The above positions were written in the program, "The Development of New China and Our Tasks," adopted by the Fourth National Congress of the Revolutionary Communist Party of China in April 1977. This document uses marxist methodology to analyze the development of the Chinese revolution and the obstacles posed by CCP rule and proposes ten tasks. Today the central task of the Chinese revolution—the overthrow of bureaucratic rule and the realization of socialist democracy—remains a goal for which the people must strive. At the same time, the political and economic situation in China and the world have undergone many changes, which need to be analyzed. Propositions need to be made to meet the new situation.

2. THE INTERNATIONAL SITUATION WHEN THE DENG FACTION CAME TO POWER

The CCP faction that holds power, headed by Deng Xiaoping (hereinafter referred to as the Deng faction), carried out its reform policy under the following international situation:

Due to the confrontation between the Soviet Communist Party and the CCP in the early 1960s, the relations between the USSR and the People's Republic of China have not normalized. The two Communist Parties persist in defending the narrow interests of each bureaucracy and confront each other, but at the same time both pursue the line of "socialism in one country," seeking peaceful coexistence with the capitalist countries and supporting the dictatorial regimes and reducing and stopping their aid to revolutionary struggles in the backward capitalist countries.

The contradictions between the Stalinist bureaucracies and the masses have intensified and are expressed in the aggravation of the crisis of bureaucratic rule. Because the people are deprived of their democratic right to formulate and carry out a planned economy, their initiatives for production cannot be stimulated, and the economy develops very slowly. To activate the economy, the bureaucracies in many countries carry out a rightist economic policy.

The three crises in confidence, credibility, and conviction, which exist in the Chinese-Soviet bloc, reflect the historical decline of Stalinism. The harm done by these bureaucracies has caused misinterpretations of marxism among many people and obstructed the international workers' movement from proposing a socialist alternative to the capitalist crisis.

Another recessionary long wave of international capitalism started in the 1970s, which was expressed in the escalation of competition among capitalist countries, a slowdown in the tempo of world trade expansion, and aggravation of the capital surplus. The eruption of every economic crisis is more convulsive, and the period of recovery shorter and shorter, while the credit system swells to the brink of collapse. Protectionism rises, and austerity measures imposed on the working class are intensified. The arms race among the powers escalates, the threat of nuclear war remains, and regional wars are incessant. The social crisis in colonial and semicolonial countries exploited and oppressed by imperialism grows more acute, and struggles against imperialism and for democracy follow one after another. The capital and commodities of the capitalist world must seek new outlets; although they do not change their hostility toward the camp of the workers' states, the imperialist powers gradually change their policy on China and attempt to get a hold in the vast Chinese market.

Under this international situation, the Deng faction attempted to make use of the economic forces of capitalism to help stabilize the CCP's crisis of rule. The external policy of opening the Chinese market to the world corresponded to the domestic policy of implementing rightist economic reforms.

3. The Crisis of Rule Faced by the Deng Faction

The Deng faction faced the following crisis of rule:

Economically the CCP had long carried out a policy of high accumulation and low consumption. Under the rule of the Mao Zedong faction, the use of "political stimulation" kept the people's livelihood to the minimum standard so that funds could be concentrated in heavy industrial investment. This caused difficult lives for the workers and peasants and prevalent passivity and a slow pace of work. Bureaucratic arbitrariness in drawing up the economic plan and willful command by bureaucrats without specialized knowledge in the particular field continually caused wrong decisions to be made, incurring severe losses to the people and the state. A serious disproportion came to exist among various economic sectors: productivity stagnated, and enterprises in the cities and "people's communes" in the countryside needed urgent reforms. There was no other alternative than to reform the old economic policy.

Politically the ten years of the "Cultural Revolution," with factional struggles in the CCP, repeatedly exposed the CCP's errors, corruption, and strife, and seriously weakened its control over the people. The people rejected the autocracy of the Mao Zedong era. "Mao Zedong Thought" lost its authority; the three crisis—in confidence, credibility, and conviction—prevailed, and there was strong resentment among the people against the bureaucracy's rule and privileges.

4. Basic Policies of the Deng Faction

The Deng faction's economic policy aimed at saving bureaucratic rule. Its premise was to continue to deprive the laboring masses of their democratic power over production. The features of the Deng faction's reform policy were on the one hand, it practiced an open-door policy and hoped that with the help of foreign countries, China could introduce foreign capital, technology, and management experience; on the other hand, it relaxed the administrative stranglehold of the Mao era on the economy and decentralized power to local bureaucrats in order to cultivate a technocracy and encourage the development of commodity production and a market economy. It hoped that by this method the economy could be activated. This line, based on the technocrats and the "competent" in the countryside, fostered the development of capitalist factors in China, which was an erosion of the state ownership system, planned economy, and monopoly of foreign trade. This erosion has not yet brought about a qualitative change, but it is quantitatively increasing. The bureaucracy's present policy cannot effectively defend the socialist factors from further erosion. At present initial disintegration of part of the state ownership system is occurring; the role of state planning in production and distribution is decreasing; and the elements of the private capitalist economy are growing and are in opposition to, and contention with, the state-owned economic sector, causing the latter's weight in the national economy to diminish. The danger and harm of capitalist restoration has increased.

Politically the Deng faction did not relax the political power monopolized by the bureaucracy. Its campaigns against bureaucratism, corruption, and redundancy were carried out only against a very small number of cadres, and it was an opportunity to purge alien elements who did not support the faction in power. When the Deng faction managed to control real power and came under pressure from the masses to yield democratic concessions—in particular, when the Polish working class secured some gains in 1980 and inspired the Chinese masses, the Deng faction quickly discarded its "liberal" posture and resorted to repression. It banned the right to strike and the Four Freedoms (air views, advocate ideas, write wall posters, and debate) and deleted them from China's Constitution. It banned unofficial organizations and publications. It arrested those fighting for democracy, and it repressed writers' critical works. It carried out a campaign against "spiritual pollution." It even expelled some CCP members who advocated more daring reforms. The reaction of the faction in power to the student movements in 1986 and 1987 fully revealed its conscious effort to repress and crush the accumulated strength of the people.

Ideologically the bureaucracy attempted to blame the "Gang of Four" for government misdeeds during the final period of Mao Zedong's rule. However due to popular pressure, the Deng faction was compelled to admit some of the errors and abuses committed by Mao and the CCP Central Committee. At the same time, it tried its best to prevent the people from developing a radical assessment of Mao or the Cultural Revolution; the campaign was conducted only by the authorities within limits. Because the bureaucracy lacks a coherent ideology, it still has to continue to hold the banner of Mao Zedong thought and emasculate the content of Marxism-Leninism. The "Four Principles" on which it insisted became the central slogans for the bureaucracy's attempt to monopolize the "truth" and defend its self-interests.

The rise of the Deng faction to power has not altered the line of "socialism in one country" advocated by Stalin. On the contrary, its open-door policy and its general domestic and foreign policy is a continuation of this line. The bureaucracy still refuses to extend the socialist revolution to other countries; it simply seeks to repress the people's intervention within the boundaries of the country that it controls. It tries to carry out economic construction according to the bureaucracy's will and planning. In today's China, the CCP leadership, headed by Deng, is by nature Stalinist. The Trotskyists carry out a sustained struggle against the Stalinists, insisting on two basic propositions—socialist democracy in the country and world revolution outside the country.

5. THE DEVELOPMENT OF THE MASS STRUGGLE

The CCP has always consciously repressed the independent class mobilization and organization of the workers and peasants, strictly controlled mass organizations such as trade unions, and even persecuted or exterminated workers who thought critically and independently. This is one of the important means by which the bureaucracy safeguards its rule.

The 1976 Tiananmen mass uprising showed that the masses had developed from the previous long periods of passive resistance, slowdown, and boycott, to expressing their discontent toward the faction in power through massive spontaneous actions. It was a preview of the antibureaucratic mass political revolution. It was only by force that the CCP suppressed the rebellion.

Mao Zedong's death signified that the bureaucracy lost a central leader. It opened up a historic opportunity for the people gradually to break away from the chains of autocracy.

The masses began to exert their pressure and raised various demands in action: the end of political repression by the absolute autocracy of the Mao Zedong era; improvement of the people's material and cultural life; socialist democracy in the state and judicial system; and the reversal of false verdicts by which innocent people were victimized.

The pressure of the masses and the factional struggle inside the CCP compelled the faction in power to vindicate the Tiananmen Incident, recognizing it as a spontaneous revolutionary mass action. The partial vindication of this incident and other false verdicts (including several hundred thousand intellectuals who were branded "rightists" in 1957) further encouraged the mood of struggle among the masses, giving an impetus to the "Beijing Spring" democracy movement, with its wave of wall posters, demonstrations for democracy, protests against hunger and persecution, and the proliferation of unofficial organizations and publications.

Because the policy of the Deng faction has not altered the superstructure or the relationship between the ruling caste and the ruled people, political democratization became the central demand of the people's democratic movement.

The Beijing Spring democracy movement constituted a milestone in the Chinese democracy movement. Before its suppression in the spring of 1981, vanguard forces among the masses linked up extensively with each other. Young people, mainly workers and some former "Red Guards" who had experienced and reassessed the Cultural Revolution, gathered around unofficial publications, diagnosed social contradictions, and probed alternatives for development. Its mainstream affirmed socialism and demanded the realization of socialist democracy. In September 1980 the National Association of Unofficial Publications in China was founded, signifying a conscious joining of forces in the democracy movement to form the embryo of a revolutionary leadership. It oriented toward linking up with the working class, rooting itself in the working class, and communicating in solidarity with the international working-class movement.

The bureaucracy's repression in 1981 compelled the democracy movement to turn underground. Continual repression further exposed the Deng faction's reactionary position in suppressing the masses and further helped the vanguard elements to discard their illusions in the Deng faction.

With the unfolding of the Deng group's urban economic reform, the working class suffered new attacks: soaring price increases attacked their living standards and the contract system and the extension of wage differentials directly attacked the workers' right to work and welfare benefits. With their real living standards and working conditions under attack, workers' defensive struggles, such as strikes and slowdowns, have increased.

In the countryside the production responsibility system relieved the peasants from the bondage of the "People's Commune." However the policy of encouraging the competent elements to enrich themselves first had accelerated rural differentiation and aggravated the gap between the rich and the poor. Greater discontent developed among impoverished peasants who could not obtain effective aid from the government. The situation in the countryside deteriorated, and by mid-1987, peasant rebellions against bureaucratism took place in Shandong and Hunan provinces.

The new social contradictions and mass discontent in the cities and countryside, which the Deng faction's rightist policy aroused, began to surface in 1985. Student demonstrations and struggles were reflections of social discontent. The students took to the streets again in massive numbers in September 1985 and in December 1986. Their unequivocal demand for political democracy and their exposure of social contradictions have inspired extensive support. The masses of people are beginning to gain confidence and shed their indifference.

The Deng faction's repression of the mass upsurge will not be lenient. Repression will continue, but it will cause the masses to discard their illusions and rely on their own strength to change the present conditions.

6. THE PLANNED ECONOMY AND THE MARKET ECONOMY

The Deng faction's economic policy is to make use of material incentives and market mechanisms to activate the economy, which had been strangled by the bureaucracy. On the one hand, the regime has not up until now announced any change of its formulation of having "planned economy as predominant, market adjustment as supplement." On the other hand, it has set itself to "fully develop the commodity economy," develop the commodity market, gradually "perfect" the market system, and gradually reduce the scope of planning carried out by command. Until the end of 1986, the result of the initial reform on the planning system was the categories of products produced by command in the planning under the State Planning Commission fell from around 120 in 1984 to about 60; production of grain and other major agricultural products had changed from previous production by command to the present production by nonbinding guidance; resources centrally distributed by the state reduced from 256 kinds in 1984 to 20; and the labor market, means of production market, and capital market made their appearance. The gradual reduction of the scope of planning signified continuous decrease in the weight of the planned economy and its replacement by market mechanisms. Further development along this line might lead to the predominance of the market economy, which the CCP camouflages as "socialist commodity economy."

The market economy and the planned economy are in opposition and contradiction. The planned economy is based on the conscious analysis of society's overall demand and allocates social resources and products according to preestablished priorities. Thus what is considered is not whether individual sectors or enterprises can gain the maximum profit but how needs can be satisfied and maximum gains can be obtained by the whole of society. Under the domination of the market economy, production is geared toward satisfying those who can afford to pay but not the most basic needs of the broad masses. What decides investment is not overall consideration for the whole of society but consideration of dispersed, individual economic sectors or enterprises; hence production tends toward anarchism. This anarchic state of production is basically similar to the features of the market economy in capitalist society.

In a society in the transitional period, especially in economically backward countries, the uneven development of productivity and the insufficient supply of goods cause consumer goods to retain their characteristics as commodities, and the market and small commodity production inevitably still prevail. Administrative methods to repress or eliminate them are not effective. Only through the gradual raising of productivity and the abundance of products can their role diminish and vanish.

The CCP practiced economic planning soon after it gained power. However the plan was drawn up entirely by party cadres and was decided by those above. Those below were then compelled to carry them out. Planned economy became planned economy by bureaucratic command. Under the rule of Mao Zedong, consumer goods were scarce and low in quality, and the bureaucracy attempted to ban the market by administrative means. The result was a series of economic and social contradictions and serious demoralization of the producing workers. Faced with this hopeless situation, the Deng faction relaxed bureaucratic administrative control; at the same time, it swung to the right and permitted the market law of value to operate freely in the countryside and later in the urban economic centers. To permit market functions to operate "fully" meant more and more restoration of the anarchic state of production characteristic of the capitalist economy, together with the coexistence of underproduction in certain sectors and overproduction in others. At the same time, large amounts of social surplus products were not converted into socialist accumulation but into private capital accumulation. Because both investment and production are directed by profits, the planned economy will gradually disintegrate.

Marxist-Leninists should recognize economic laws that exist objectively and should also consciously guide and reform the economy. At the present time, it is appropriate to make use of market mechanisms; however they must be consciously restrained and subject to democratic planning.

The planned economy should play the predominant role. Based on the conditions of production, the material resources, and the state's economic strength, and considering the need of the whole people and the whole of society, the state should set priorities for production and plans for the categories, quantity, and quality of products to develop the economy harmoniously and carry out production, allocation, distribution, and sale by planning.

The economic plan should be drawn up in a truly democratic way by the whole laboring people: by collecting from below the opinions and demands of the laboring masses of all areas, conducting fully democratic discussions at various levels of workers' congresses, by permitting all different opinions to be expressed and to make reservations. The final decision on the economic plan should be made by a national congress of the laboring people, elected in a truly democratic way. In this way it can be guaranteed that the plan is drawn up according to the principle of democratic centralism. Only in this way can the opinion of the whole laboring people be reflected and a plan meeting the people's needs be drawn up. And only in this way can the people identify with the plan and carry out production enthusiastically.

7. ACCUMULATION AND CONSUMPTION

After the Deng faction came to power, there had been a slight rise in the rate of consumption in the national income. There was more development of light industry and increased production of daily consumer goods. There were also more funds for raising the state's purchase prices of some agricultural products. These were intended as incentives to stimulate production. However starting in 1983, there was a reversal of this policy; the rate of accumulation rose, and the proportion of heavy industry in industrial output value also rose. The scale of investment in fixed assets at the central, local, and nonplanned levels could not be reduced and went out of control. With the policy of priority development for heavy industry still predominant, the development of light industry slowed down, and investments in agriculture diminished every year. (Its proportion of total capital investments fell from 11.1 percent in 1979 to 3.4 percent in 1985.) Thus the proportion of consumption has shrunk and that of accumulation has risen.

Although heavy industry is the most important sector in developing the economy and in raising productivity, the planned economy should not pursue the most rapid development of a single sector but the optimal efficiency of the economy as a whole. In particular its focus should be the improvement of the people's livelihood. In fact the long periods of negligence of the development of agriculture and light industry had created serious disproportions, which in turn impeded the development of heavy industry. Hence a reduced rate of consumption did not lead to gains from the increased accumulation rate. In deciding the rate of accumulation, the consideration should not be the maximum rate but the optimal rate to bring optimal gains. This means that the state should not squeeze the maximum from the countryside to develop industry but should increase capital investments in agriculture, help agricultural modernization and raising of productivity, and meet the demands of peasants for consumer goods, so that agriculture can develop steadily and back up industrial development. At the same time, to decide on a dynamic equilibrium of industrial and agricultural development— how much should be drawn from the countryside to maintain industry, how the "scissors'" difference of unequal exchange between industrial and agricultural products can be reduced, etc.—the democratic participation and decision making of the workers and peasants is indispensable. Without this no policy can be accepted and enthusiastically implemented by the majority of the laborers; neither can there be an increase in efficiency and labor productivity.

When deciding the ratio between accumulation and consumption, the bureaucrats pose the question in the oversimplified formula of "an increase in production means a decrease in investments." This is not so in actuality. Labor productivity is an important factor. Under bureaucratic rule, in addition to the portion allocated to productive investments and consumption by producers, a considerable portion of the social product is consumed in a nonproductive way, in particular in consumption by the privileged bureaucracy and in the expenses of the redundant administrative apparatus. By abolishing the bureaucracy's economic privileges, productive investments and the producers' standard of living can both be increased. In addition the major factor detrimental to the producers' enthusiasm can also be removed. Under democratic management the massive squandering of production and circulation that exist today can also be drastically reduced.

8. THE RURAL ECONOMIC REFORM

The Deng faction's rural policy was to institute a production responsibility system and to encourage peasants to enrich themselves. The official formula proposed that a portion of people (the competent) get rich first and that their enrichment would lead to generalized wealth enjoyed by the entire population.

The contract responsibility system established the family as the unit of independent production. This meant the restoration of individual peasant production and the abolition of the collective farming of the Mao Zedong era, when the basic unit of accounting was the production brigade. Such a change meant a concession to the peasant tendency for small production, and it also signified that the CCP officially recognized that the line of the People's Commune was bankrupt. In the past the CCP compelled communalization by administrative orders, which ignored China's low productivity and poor material conditions and violated the principle of respecting the peasants' wishes. In contradicting objective and subjective conditions, the bankruptcy of the line of the People's Commune was inevitable. The Deng faction was forced to lift the bondage of the People's Commune, and the slight increase in the purchase price of agricultural subsidiary foods (which had long been maintained at a very low level) resulted in some improvements in the peasants' poor standard of living. Peasant initiative also increased. As a result in the first few years of the production responsibility system, there was a rather quick increase in agricultural and subsidiary production.

Nevertheless when the CCP changed its previous ultra-"left" policy, it swung to the other extreme: it encouraged individual peasants to enrich themselves without bounds and gave its assistance. This caused farmland to concentrate in the hands of the "competent growers." The "competent," a minority of the population, contracted subsidiary farming and enterprises. A powerful stratum has arisen in the countryside of specialized households engaged in industry, commerce, communication, construction, and services, and their capital accumulation is growing. Rich peasants, private industrial and commercial entrepreneurs, and even loan sharks have appeared, and "millionaires" have been given favorable publicity by the regime. By 1986 the fixed assets of certain private enterprises reached several million yuan. Economic consortia were also developing rapidly.

The CCP cadres in the countryside make up quite a significant portion of the rural wealthy. They make use of the power in their hands and thus have more favorable conditions in contracting land, subsidiary farming, or industrial and commercial enterprises. They are the ones benefiting most from the present rural policy. Bureaucrat capital is gradually forming.

Less productive peasants or peasants in backward, poor regions cannot compete with the strong and the rich under the competition of commodity production. They stay on the weak end, and many become hired peasants or agricultural laborers exploited by the rich peasants, private entrepreneurs, or loan sharks. Social differentiation in the countryside is developing; the gap between the backward and the developed regions (in particular between the inland mountainous regions and the coastal provinces) is widening; and social inequalities are increasing, and class contradictions are breeding.

In some state-run farms, the family responsibility system was also practiced. The state farm was divided into small farms, and the state permitted the sale of farm animals, small and medium farm tools, trucks, and staff quarters for the staff members. This means that part of the state property of the farms is disintegrating and reverting to private ownership.

In sum the Deng faction's rural policy has struck a way out of the stalemate created by the People's Commune policy, yet it breeds new contradictions. The bureaucracy's laissez-faire type of market reform, which violates socialist principles; the cadres' corruption; the privatization and concentration of wealth, means of production, and some land; the appearance of large numbers of hired laborers; the accumulation of private capital; and the expansion of capitalist production on the basis of exploitation of hired laborers and unevenness of the market economy all cause further class differentiations and constitute the motive force for capitalist restoration in China.

In the past we had opposed the People's Commune policy of the Mao Zedong era. Now we also oppose the Dengist policy of assisting the competent to enrich themselves. These two policies apparently go to two extremes, yet in essence they are the two alternatives of Stalinist bureaucratic rule. The same vacillations have appeared in the USSR and the Eastern European countries.

We suggest that agriculture should go on the road of collectivization and mechanization. Toward this end the state must assist the peasants with material resources, coupled with democratic management. Examples must be set for the peasants, and ideologic education must be conducted. After long periods of effort, the superiority of collectivization and mechanization will be clear and will attract peasants to go voluntarily on the road to collectivization, for they will see from experience that it brings them a higher standard of living. Compulsory administrative orders of the People's Commune type, the lack of mechanization and resources, the lack of democratic operation, and improvement in people's material conditions can only lead to peasant slowdown in work and low productivity. Concerning the People's Commune, in the past we proposed that the laborers' will should be respected in reorganizing the communes and production brigades; the peasants should be able to enjoy full freedom in deciding if they wanted to join or withdraw from the commune or other collectives; and all land should be proclaimed state owned and be used by the laborers following the principle of equality. Concerning the present Dengist policy, we propose that while fully respecting the peasants' will and implementing the responsibility system, the state must give massive amounts of aid to the poor peasants and restrain the rich peasants' growth. To support and aid each other and develop production more effectively, to join forces in resisting the superiority of the rich peasants and private entrepreneurs in commodity production, and to counter the exploitation of the loan sharks, it is very necessary for the peasants, particularly the poor peasants, to set up cooperatives run by the peasants on the basis of voluntarism, equality, and mutual interests, with aid such as material resources being supplied by the state, so that they can continue to advance the cooperative movement.

Because the state-run farms have received the state's long-term investment of labor and material resources, they have a higher level of mechanization, and they should have set an example to the peasants to demonstrate the superiority of mechanized collective production. Their present stagnation in production, deficit, and low staff morale are mainly due to bureaucratic policy and control. We oppose the regression of collective production to small production based on family operation. We propose that the bureaucratic control of the CCP over the state farm and the extortion of the farm workers must be abolished; all the farm workers should enjoy the right and the gains in democratic running of the farm and collective management. The council or the congress of the farm workers should decide all major questions in the farm and democratically elect deputies to participate in various levels of congresses of laboring people. At the same time, their living and working conditions must be significantly improved. On the premise that the state safeguards a minimum living standard of the farm workers, their income must be closely linked to gains in production, so that their enthusiasm for production can be stimulated, production can increase, their livelihood can improve, and an example can be set to promote extensive collectivization.

9. THE URBAN ECONOMIC REFORM

The Deng faction promoted the following structural reform in industrial enterprises: the decentralization of power to bureaucrats in local enterprises and separation of the administration from the enterprise. Enterprises now enjoy greater autonomy, bear responsibility for their own profits and deficits, and submit profits in lieu of taxes. In some enterprises the shareholding system is attempted. Some state-run and collective enterprises are contracted to individuals. The wage differentials for workers are allowed to widen. The contract system in employment is promoted.

To allow enterprises greater autonomy is a measure to reduce bureaucratic, autocratic control. Yet there are two conditions that must be met to allow autonomy of enterprises in a socialist economy: first, power must be held in the hands of the master of the enterprises, that is, all the laborers, and exercised by the congresses or councils of workers and their standing committees; second, the enterprises must participate in and comply with the economic plan drawn up democratically by society as a whole.

However, what the CCP tried to promote in the enterprises is not the autonomy of the workers or the expansion and functioning of the power of a congress of workers, but the concentration of power into the hands of the factory directors. This is intended to build up the special power of the factory directors to develop a technocracy that can support the ruling caste in the enterprises. Some of the decision-making powers enjoyed by the workers' congresses as stipulated in ordinances proclaimed by the state are now no longer mentioned. There is no longer the restraint of "party leadership" over the responsibility system of the factory directors, but neither is there the premise of "leadership by the workers' congresses."

The implementation of the planned economy still retains the abuse of the plan being drawn up by the bureaucrats. In the absence of democratic decision making and supervision by the laborers, decentralization of power and responsibility for their own profits and deficits means that the operation of the industries and enterprises is more and more placed under the law of the market, and they compete for resources and the market under the domination of the law of value. Under such competition, the pursuit of profits becomes the aim of economic operation, and for enterprises to be responsible for their own profits and deficits, various types of price increases, elimination of the weak by the strong, speculation and profiteering, etc., inevitably occur.

The state ownership system also suffers attack: some state-run enterprises practice the shareholding system, and some state-owned enterprises and rural enterprises are contracted to individuals for operation. The contract system in essence means the hiring of means of production and facilities that are state owned or collectively owned for private operation, whereby the operators employ large numbers of workers, run the enterprises with capitalist methods, increase the workers' labor intensity, and squeeze the maximum surplus value out of the workers. The relations between the contractor and the workers who are employed is in reality one of employer and employee, which is not qualitatively different from the exploitative relations in capitalism.

Today the right of ownership of some brigade-run enterprises is changing. The peasants can invest and hold some shares of the collective enterprises. This is basically similar to the bourgeoisie holding shares in capitalist society, gaining surplus value without laboring.

10. THE PRICE REFORM

A major part of the Dengist economic reform was the price reform: gradual abolition of the state's uniform setting of prices, which were allowed to float freely. The result was that the prices of the great majority of products and commodities soared, with commodities in short supply soaring the most. The commodity economy caused the price inflation to go on unrestrained. This reform had serious consequences on the people's standard of living.

A common complaint among the masses is "nine years of reform, nine years of price inflation." This reflects the continuous inflation of prices in the past nine years. In May 1988 the CCP stated that "the difficult barrier of the price reform must be crossed" and must not be "circumscribed." Thus the control over prices was further relaxed, prices soared, people's lives turned tougher, massive withdrawals from the banks occurred, and there was a rush for commodities. With this aggravation of the crisis of bureaucratic rule, the price reform was slowed down in September. In a difficult situation, the CCP's pricing policy vacillated.

The price problem is essentially the problem of insufficient products to meet the national need. If the problem is not tackled at its roots and production is not increased to meet people's needs, and instead state setting of prices is abolished, the consequence can only be soaring prices, greater disequilibrium in production, and more difficulty in meeting people's urgent needs.

The pricing policy should be a lever that the state uses in directing and allocating social resources. When a price reform is conducted, the primary task is to safeguard the actual interests of the proletariat and the laboring masses from being infringed upon. The wages and income of all laboring people must be increased to catch up with price increases. At the same time, consumers' cooperatives must be organized on a mass democratic basis to supervise the quantity, quality, and price of commodities in the market; prevent illegal and disguised price increases; and prosecute and prevent criminal acts, such as providing substandard goods or victimizing the consumers.

While there is no significant general rise in the actual income of the people, especially while there are no concrete state measures to protect the people from price increases, the state has an obligation to maintain a subsidy on the basic necessities of life.

As for the peasants, the general rise in the prices of industrial goods causes the production costs of agricultural and subsidiary products to increase substantially, so that peasant income is reduced and the "scissors" difference in industrial and agricultural prices again expands. This will cause lowered peasant incentives for growing grain and decreased grain production.

Faced with these adverse consequences, the small gains of the peasants in these few years must be defended. The state should increase its purchase of increased agricultural and subsidiary products. The purchasing price should be raised for products whose production costs have gone up due to price rises in industrial goods used in agriculture.

Besides the above price reforms concerning consumer goods, the state should also maintain its control over the prices of raw materials. A free market of the means of production will seriously affect the operation of the planned economy.

11. SAFEGUARDING WORKERS' RIGHTS

Within the economic reform, the working class' interests must be defended, and any attempt by the state or enterprise management to shift the brunt of reform onto the workers must be staunchly opposed.

The CCP has set a quota for every state-owned enterprise concerning its total amount of wages, which would only vary depending on how the enterprise accomplished the state plan and its efficacy. The CCP also allowed wage differentiations to grow within enterprises to introduce competition. The redistribution of wages within a set total amount was designed to raise labor intensity because the workers had to work harder to gain more wages at the expense of other workers. Workers unable to produce as much or those engaged in unskilled or simple labor faced reduced wages. It was a conscious attempt to sow differentiation, competition, and inequalities among workers. In addition employment on contract terms was introduced in the winter of 1986, with newly recruited workers in state-owned enterprises. These workers became essentially casual laborers, without any safeguards for their right to work or social benefits. These measures are all detrimental to the interests of the workers and should be rejected.

By the end of 1987, the number of workers in China reached 130 million; over half of them were industrial workers. The figure is more than ten times the number of workers in 1949. Moreover they are concentrated in big industrial regions, and their weight is significant.

Although the CCP had always proclaimed the workers as the masters of the country, it deprived them of power. Since 1980 due to the impact of the workers' movement in Eastern Europe, in particular, Poland, a struggle by workers for their rights has also developed in China. To prevent the eruption of a labor movement of the Polish type in China and to stimulate workers to help raise production, the CCP promulgated a "temporary ordinance on workers' councils in state-owned industrial enterprises" in July 1981. It gave workers some powers, yet the promises were limited, existing more in formality than in actuality, and the workers' councils that were set up were in general devoid of power and were basically used by the authorities to implement their policies and to raise production. Despite this the promulgation of the ordinance reflected the fact that the pressure of worker discontent had compelled the CCP to make some concessions and that the workers could also make use of this opportunity to fight for their own rights. Workers of many enterprises not only pressed the authorities to implement the ordinance but also attempted to advance it. For example it was officially provided that the workers could elect their rank-and-file leaders in the enterprise; however, workers more and more demanded election of all leaders, including the factory director. The authorities in actuality made the factory director the one responsible for the factory under the guidance of the party committee, whereas workers in quite a number of enterprises strove the make the factory director responsible for the factory under the guidance of the workers' council. This is an attempt by workers to become masters of industry, and it caused a struggle for workers' rights to unfold gradually.

Our program is this: to practice workers' democratic self-management in the enterprises, it is necessary to set up a system of democratic workers' congresses or workers' councils that hold actual power; their standing committees form the highest power organ within the enterprises and decide on all major issues in the enterprises. Workers' management of the enterprises is the basis of the proletariat's exercise of power to manage state politics, economy, and social affairs. The power organ of social self-management and economic planning should be formed by the workers electing their deputies to congresses of laboring people on the inter-enterprise, regional, and national levels. (By "laboring people" is meant manual workers, mental workers, and soldiers—the children of laborers in the army.)

Within the enterprise, a close link between the interests of the enterprises and the workers can help raise workers' enthusiasm. However because individual enterprises must comply with the overall plan, and in particular, the main industrial and transport enterprises should not be restrained by the law of the market (they are not "profitable" from the angle of the market, and yet they are the pillars of the national economy), the basic living and working conditions of the workers must be guaranteed by the whole of society and should not be mainly linked to the "profits" or "interests" of individual enterprises.

In the period of transition, the principle of remuneration according to work should be practiced rather than egalitarianism. Therefore a system of wage differentials is necessary. However as social and material conditions develop, and the cultural and technical levels of the laboring people are gradually raised, the differentials should be gradually diminished. Otherwise it would not be the basic spirit of the principle of remuneration according to work practiced in the new society but an imitation of capitalist differentiation and strengthened exploitation of workers. The various levels of congresses of the laboring people have the right to adjust the wages of all workers according to the price index; the price index is to be drawn up by the lower levels of congresses electing deputies to form local, provincial, and national congresses of laboring people, and this will serve as the basis for adjustment of wages.

The defense of workers' interests should have been the central task of the trade unions. However in China, as in other bureaucratized workers' states, the trade union does not take up this task; instead it is the tool of the party's bureaucratic rule, assisting the ruling caste in implementing its policies. The establishing of Solidarnosc in Poland indicates the high consciousness of the Polish working class, which is determined to organize its own trade union to replace the official one and to fight for workers' rights with its own trade union. In China the working class and its vanguard should also draw from the experience of the Polish trade union and fight for organizing a trade union independent of the government.

In the past two years, the workers ignored the cancellation of their right to strike and still conducted strikes. With increasing discontent about the price reform, the frequency of strikes and the number of workers participating in strikes have increased. Work slowdowns are also more generalized and acute. It shows that the working class has increasingly risen to oppose the policies of the bureaucracy that are detrimental to workers' interests.

Under the strong pressure of workers' strikes and slowdowns, the existing trade union leadership was finding it more difficult to carry out official tasks, and it was compelled to change its tone or some of its methods of work. For example it proposed that the government-run nature of the trade union should be reformed in order to realize "the mass nature of the trade union"; it also proposed the setting up of a minimum wage and a sliding scale of wages corresponding to prices. We propose that the working class should start its struggle with the fight for organizing a democratic trade union, that is, the building of a structure to fight for workers' rights, thereby consolidating its strength and combativity, from which it can proceed to the fight for establishing democratic relations of production and the control of political power.

12. INDIVIDUAL ECONOMY AND PRIVATE ECONOMY

In China in the transitional period, the state sector cannot satisfy the need of the whole nation and cannot provide job opportunities for all the people. The inadequate sectors need to be supplemented by the small producers. At the same time, when the state allows small producers to exist and play their active role, it must also channel the individual economy into coordinating with the state economy and the plan. The state, by providing funds and technology, also must encourage small producers to cooperate and form production cooperatives and supply and marketing cooperatives. On the other hand, it must suppress massive employment and exploitation of workers by private enterprises; limit the number of hired workers; draw up laws to safeguard workers' interests in private enterprises (such as minimum wage, limit on working hours, safety requirements); expand the social wage; and impose a progressive profit tax, income tax, and employment tax on private enterprise owners (for spending on workers' welfare).

In the past the CCP used administrative measures to eliminate the private economy forcibly, while the state economy and the collective economy—under bureaucratic oppression, which deprived workers of their right to decide—bogged down in stagnation, resulting in further shortages of goods. The objective situation compelled the Deng faction to change its policy. However the Dengist policy is to stimulate the commodity economy and allow private enterprises to develop in a spontaneous and unorganized way under the domination of the law of market value. The commodity economy inevitably leads to the emergence of exploiters and social polarization. A small portion become small capitalists, while the majority of people are reduced to hired laborers. The essence of this policy is for a small number of people to enrich themselves at the expense of the interests of the majority of people. (According to the estimates of Ge Lin, professor at Nanjing University, as of the end of 1987, 30 million workers were employed by private enterprises in China.)

At present the Dengist policy is to concede further to private enterprises; it extols their development and draws up legislation to defend their interests. This causes the aggravation of social contradictions.

Under this policy the development of private enterprises is very rapid. In some towns their output value comprises a large proportion of the total industrial output value. In the national economy, the weight of the state industries has fallen from 83 percent in 1978 to 67 percent in 1987 and further to 64 percent a few months later, indicating the tendency of private and other nonstate-owned enterprises to gain strength rapidly. The implication is that the advantageous position of the state enterprises will gradually be replaced, and that the gains of the 1949 revolution, the state property system occupying an economically dominant position, is continuously being eroded. This trend is very dangerous and may lead to the restoration of capitalism. Halting this tendency depends on the organization and mobilization of the proletariat to take control of the state economy, thereby maintaining its advantageous and dominant position.

13. OPEN-DOOR POLICY AND THE SPECIAL ECONOMIC ZONES

The setting up of four special economic zones, the opening of Hainan Island and fourteen coastal cities to the outside world, and the opening of many other places to varying degrees make the extensive opening of China to international capitalism.

No country can develop its economy with its doors closed. However because China's labor productivity is relatively low, it needs a monopoly of foreign trade to protect national industry from competition from capitalist economies that have higher labor productivity. Under the protection of the monopoly of trade, the state can selectively trade with imperialist countries to utilize much needed foreign technology and resources for national economic construction, as well as learning management methods. For production items that are much needed but lack state funds to develop, they can be run jointly with foreign capital but only under certain principles. The overall guiding principle should be beneficial to the overall Chinese economy, not harmful to the state property system or the planned economy, no harmful concessions to foreign capital, and no heavy political or economic price. The people must fully grasp the information, know how much and why a price is paid during the economic transactions with advanced capitalist economies, and be able to make timely revisions under their supervision and discussion.

Severe damage was done when China developed its economy autarchically under foreign economic blockade. However the need to relate economically with capitalist economies does not mean that China should fully open itself to the external world. The unprincipled opening to foreign capital by the faction in power cannot integrate the opening up of China with a state economic plan, causing unnecessary damage instead.

Under increasing pressure from foreign businesses, concessions made by China are increasingly significant: from the initial joint capital venture or joint operations to sole operation by foreign capital; from joint operation periods of several years (with the enterprise returned to China at the end) to several decades; from export only of goods produced by foreign capital to partly or even entirely domestic consumption. The state monopoly of foreign trade is also under attack. This not only provides a very favorable investment ground for foreign capitalists but also concedes part of the domestic market, hence dealing a severe blow to the national industry.

The profits that foreign capitalists make in China can be converted to foreign currency and freely remitted out of China. This means the wealth produced by Chinese workers and national resources can be appropriated legally and without restraint.

The CCP makes big concessions, but the actual gains are small. The balance is unfavorable. In these years the investment of foreign capital is small and mostly concentrated in the nonproductive sectors, such as tourism and real estate; China even has to provide loans or invest jointly. The importation of industrial technology and equipment is far from what is expected.

The activities of foreign capital in China and the interests of the economic system that they represent are in acute struggle with China's state economy. The more foreign capital invests in China and coordinates its activities with the growing individual economy and private industry and commerce in China, the greater its strength and role becomes and the more it threatens to erode the state economy. Because the labor productivity of foreign capitalist countries is much higher than that of China, when China spontaneously adapts to and integrates with the world capitalist market, surplus value will flow out of China in massive amounts, and China's national economy will find it difficult to develop independently. It will also be affected by the periodic crises of world capitalism. The experiences of some Eastern European countries have illustrated this.

When the CCP argues for opening up to foreign capital, it misleads the people into believing that capitalism is superior to state ownership and the planned economy and fosters illusions in capitalism and a loss of faith in true socialism, state ownership, and planned economy.

Under the coordination of foreign capital, exploitation is being revived in different areas in China. More working people are exploited, social differentiations increase, inequalities expand, the privatization mentality strengthens, the concept of "money as top priority" becomes more widespread, and the social mood worsens.

Of particular concern is the inclination of some bureaucrats to be converted from parasites in the state ownership system to parasites in the market economy. Instead of seeking private interests with the power in their hands, they turn to becoming property owners making private investments. When large amounts of foreign capital enter China, comprador capital may form. If capitalist forces develop in China more rapidly and extensively and the powerful intervention of the people is absent, then at a certain moment of crisis the CCP will have to choose between these two alternatives. Either it changes its present rightist policies and restrains the activities of foreign capital and Chinese capitalist forces, or it continues to be swept away by the capitalist forces and undergoes transformations until the private ownership system assumes predominance and capitalism is reinstated. A final showdown is inevitable.

14. NUCLEAR POWER PLANS AND ENVIRONMENTAL POLLUTION

The earnest construction of the Qinshan Nuclear Power Plant in Shanghai and the Daya Bay Nuclear Power Plant in Guangdong Province indicates that the CCP bureaucrats refuse to accept the experience and lessons of foreign nuclear power plants, disregard the safety and health of the densely populated people of China and its neighboring regions, and refuse to consider grave issues such as the potential economic burden. This is very irresponsible. Neither the Three Mile Island nuclear plant accident, the Chernobyl nuclear accident in the USSR, nor the hundreds of big and small nuclear power plant accidents all over the world has led the CCP bureaucrats to reassess the danger and grave cost of nuclear power; they continue to be bent on this.

The two nuclear power plants are situated near densely populated regions and directly threaten the safety and health of over 10 million people. The potential pollution of the grain-producing regions of the whole of East and South China will affect hundreds of millions of people. Even in the fortunate eventuality that no accidents occur, the daily operation will still cause radiation pollution to the natural environment, affecting water sources, soil, and the ocean. The nuclear power plants will also be a heavy and inestimable economic burden on China. Besides the immense costs in construction, the operation and maintenance funds will also increase, and there is also the question of disposal of nuclear waste and maintenance after the stoppage of production about ten years later. This does not include the immense economic and social costs when accidents happen. These are the primary reasons for the general decline of the nuclear power industry in the world economic, apart from the massive opposition of the people.

The flaws in the CCP bureaucratic management system, the neglect of safety and human lives, the lack of effective supervision, the irresponsibility, and the consistent covering up of facts and dangers cause the nuclear power plan in China to be a very dangerous time bomb. If the nuclear power plan cannot be stopped, a catastrophe will sooner or later erupt and endanger the lives and property of extensive regions. We are strongly opposed to the CCP's continuation of the construction of nuclear power plants, and we demand the use of the funds to develop thermal, hydroelectric, and solar power. Nuclear power and nuclear technology are important items in modern science and technology. From the position of scientific research, experiments should be conducted. However up to now, the consequences of nuclear reactions cannot be controlled, and so it should not be applied to the generation of power. As a matter of principle, workers' states should oppose any form of application of nuclear technology to weaponry. We propose that the worldwide elimination of all nuclear weapons be pursued.

The CCP has always shown its neglect of environmental protection and ecological pollution. Massive and unplanned lumbering, regardless of consequences, has caused serious water loss and soil erosion. The pollution by rural waste and industrial waste gas and material has serious consequences to the natural environment and people's health. It has been reported that the CCP, disregarding the question of pollution and the potential danger of radiation, stores nuclear waste in Xinjiang for Western Europe. We denounce the CCP's environmental policies that disregard safety and call on the people to rise up and change them.

15. FOREIGN POLICY AND WORLD REVOLUTION

The different social and class basis of the capitalist countries and the workers' states are the basic differences between the two camps. Capitalism's structural need for expansion and its determination to overthrow the state ownership system of the workers' states is the basic threat that all workers' states face in common. It is impossible to defend the gains of the socialist revolution and conduct socialist construction by the strength of one country, in particular the strength of a poor and backward country. It requires the economic, political, and military cooperation among the workers' states; irreconcilable struggle against capitalist and imperialist countries; and support for revolutionary movements in the backward countries. Only when victory is won by the proletarian revolution in the whole world (including social revolution in the capitalist countries and political revolution in the bureaucratized workers' states) can the construction of a socialist society advance on a world scale. The promotion of the world revolution must be the main content of the foreign policy of China and other workers' states.

China's foreign policy takes the opposite road. It does not promote world revolution to eliminate the capitalist system but pursues peaceful coexistence with the capitalist system.

Toward the bourgeois regimes in the developing countries, the CCP has long maintained the Five Principles of Peaceful Coexistence and has given them economic aid and political support. The CCP improves its relations with some ruthless regimes that bloodily repress the mass movements (such as Zaïre and Indonesia) and helps them stabilize their rule. Toward the revolutionary movements in these countries, other than some support in the early years of the People's Republic of China, it has now stopped its material aid on the pretext of nonintervention in the internal politics of other countries. Thailand, Malaysia, and the Philippines are obvious examples.

Toward the imperialist regimes, the CCP has beautified them (except the United States) as the "Second World," attempted to rope them in, and hoped for their solidarity and strengthening. In recent years the CCP no longer mentions the concept of the "three worlds," but its policy of approaching the bourgeois regimes remains. This betrayal of the interests of the proletariat deals a blow to the revolutionary movement of the international proletariat and in turn weakens the system of state ownership on which the CCP bureaucracy has attached itself as a parasite.

Since the establishment of Sino–U.S. diplomatic relations in the early 1970s, the CCP has gradually given up its propaganda of "the USA being one of the two hegemonies." Under the Dengist open-door policy, it tries to ingratiate U.S. imperialism and seeks to strengthen economic cooperation with it. The CCP has the illusion that the United States would cooperate with it against the USSR, that the United States would help China, which has a different social system and class basis, to develop its economy and strength rapidly. This can only be an illusion.

The imperialists have their own position and would not be used by China nor would they form an alliance with China against the Soviet Union. They only use China against the Soviet Union and strengthen their pressure to force the Soviet Union to concede to the West. At the same time, they pull China to the right onto the track of capitalism.

Their cool response to Beijing's proposal and the Reagan administration's stubborn support for the Taiwan regime has caused Beijing to turn to improving its relations with Eastern Europe and the Soviet Union.

Such a turn does not indicate that the CCP has returned to the class position that it should have. Its foreign policy is still opportunistic.

We certainly do not oppose the establishment of diplomatic relations and development of economic contact between China and the United States and other capitalist countries. However it must be clearly understood at the same time that these imperialist and capitalist regimes are irreconcilable enemies of the workers' states, and the latter should not help them stabilize their rule and attack the proletariat in their countries. Furthermore there should not be the spread of illusions. On the contrary they should be constantly exposed, and the mass revolutionary movements in different countries should be given political, economic, and material support. However the CCP pursues a very wrong foreign policy toward capitalist countries.

16. CHINA'S RELATIONS WITH THE USSR AND OTHER WORKERS' STATES

The conflict of narrow interests of "socialism in one country" is the main reason for the breakdown in relations between China and the USSR. However this cannot justify the increasingly rightward policy of the CCP. In fact the bureaucracy of each workers' state, standing on narrow nationalism and defending its own ruling interests, is hostile to each other, attacks each other, and even starts wars. These are extremely wrong.

The invasion of Vietnam by the Chinese army in January 1979 was a chauvinistic bureaucratic crime against the interests of the toiling masses of China and Vietnam, causing the class brothers of Vietnam and China to kill each other, and weakened each country to the benefit of imperialism. This kind of armed conflict between workers' states must be opposed. Disputes between different communist parties and workers' states, especially policy differences, should be solved through open debates, discussions at meetings, and so on; the contents of all differences and disputes should be publicized so that the toiling masses can participate in the debates and solve them together.

The differences and disputes between ruling communist parties should not affect the relations between workers' states and should not be used as a criterion to judge the nature of the other state.

Both China and the USSR are bureaucratized workers' states, and neither of them is as yet a socialist society. Before the relations between the CCP and the Communist Party of the Soviet Union (CPSU) turned hostile, the CCP denied the presence of a privileged bureaucracy in the USSR, denied that it had long ago bureaucratically degenerated, and maintained that it was a "socialist state." After the breakup of relations between the two parties, the CCP gradually acknowledged the presence of a privileged bureaucracy in the USSR. It later declared that the USSR had not only restored capitalism but had also become a "social imperialist" state, the most dangerous source of war and the main enemy of China. These declarations are totally wrong.

In recent years these arguments are no longer heard; the USSR's name as a "socialist state" has been restored, although this description is completely unscientific. However to this day, state relations between China and the USSR have not yet been normalized. The CCP insisted on three preconditions from the USSR, one of which is the withdrawal of Soviet troops from the Chinese northern border. That should not be difficult to do. The other two conditions are the Soviet army's withdrawal from Afghanistan and the Vietnamese army's withdrawal from Kampuchea. These withdrawals are necessary in principle, but the CCP also bears important responsibility: the CCP strongly supports the murderous Khmer Rouge and bourgeois reactionary forces in attacking the Hang Semrin regime, thereby forcing the Vietnamese army to remain in Kampuchea. The CCP also supports, through Pakistan, Afghan antigovernment guerrillas fighting the Soviet army. China insists that the USSR correct its wrongdoings and wrong diplomatic policies before normalizing relations between states. However when it established diplomatic relations with the United States, China did not raise such conditions, and the United States in fact still supported the Taiwan Guomindang regime, sold arms to it, violated the CCP's sovereignty over Taiwan, stationed U.S. troops in some Far Eastern countries and posed threats to Chinese security. It can therefore be seen that the CCP holds no constant principle but instead double standards on the question of restoring relations between China and the USSR and establishing relations between China and the United States.

Because of the breakup of relations between the CCP and CPSU, the state relations between China and the USSR cannot be "normalized." This is harmful to the people's interests in both countries. Both the CCP and CPSU should take the initiative to restore normal relations between their two states, support and cooperate with each other on an equal basis, exchange scientific and technological knowledge, and expand trade and interchange. This kind of cooperation and interchange should be practiced among all workers' states.

Because the bureaucracies in all workers' states are facing a ruling crisis, in trying to solve the crisis and practice rightward policies, they learn from and support each other. They also have a common interest in repressing the rise of the workers and the masses. This explains why, after the Polish bureaucracy repressed Solidarity in 1981, the CCP provided material aid to the Polish Communist Party, and helped it stabilize its rule and strike blows against the people's antibureaucracy political revolution.

Thus in defending its own narrow interest, the bureaucracy in each state hostilely attacks each other and also joins hands in repressing the rise of the people's revolution.

The effort to reach a truly equal and cooperative relation between workers' states that is beneficial to the development of socialism cannot be done under the rule of the bureaucracy. It is necessary for the people of each workers' state to carry out a political revolution and overthrow the bureaucracy to reach that goal.

17. THE QUESTION OF HONG KONG AND MACAO

The sovereignty of Hong Kong and Macao must be recovered from imperialism. This is what we always advocated, in as early as the "Program of the Revolutionary Chinese Communist Party" adopted in August 1948. After the establishment of New China, because of its conciliation policy toward imperialism, the CCP in fact still submits to the unequal treaties signed between the Qing government and Britain and Portugal. The Deng faction continues this policy and only after the expiration of the lease treaty on June 30, 1997, will it "recover" the sovereignty over Hong Kong. Nevertheless the act of taking back the sovereignty of Hong Kong and Macao should still be supported.

British imperialism initially tried to retain its rule over Hong Kong. Failing that it hypocritically posed as fighting for the rights of Hong Kong's people, when in fact it exploited their fear and discontent toward the CCP to defend bourgeois interests—both local and foreign—in Hong Kong.

During the negotiations on Hong Kong, the Chinese and British governments kept the content of their negotiations absolutely secret, thus depriving the Chinese people—and in particular the people of Hong Kong, who are the most affected—of their right to know, to speak out, to intervene, and to decide. It shows the effect of the initial extension of the CCP's bureaucratic rule over the people of Hong Kong.

At the moment the Chinese and British governments are investigating models of joint rule over Hong Kong by the Beijing bureaucrats and the rich. The Chinese–British Joint Declaration states clearly that the people of Hong Kong enjoy a "high degree of right to self-rule," administrative control, and legislation after 1997. But it states that the Hong Kong Basic Law must be defined by Beijing in accordance with the contents of the Joint Agreement. The Basic Law Drafting Committee that the CCP appointed and the Consultative Committee that is appointed indirectly enable it to control totally the drawing up of the Basic Law.

The sovereignty over Hong Kong belongs to China, meaning it belongs to all the people of China, *including* the people of Hong Kong. Because historically and economically Hong Kong has been separated from the Chinese mainland, before the people of the two places achieve unity through democratic means, Hong Kong should be ruled democratically by its own people. It must be noted that this proposition is raised within a definite historical period and does not mean that Hong Kong will permanently hold a special position.

The fight for the return to China of sovereignty over Hong Kong within the framework of democratic self-rule of Hong Kong means to resist the bureaucratic rule of Hong Kong by the CCP and the implementation of the people of Hong Kong's right to decide the social and economic system in Hong Kong. The CCP's policy of "one country-two systems" stipulates that after recovering the sovereignty over Hong Kong the capitalist system will be maintained unchanged for fifty years. This policy not only deprives the people of Hong Kong of any power to decide, but it also denies the possibility of the proletariat's rising up and overthrowing the capitalist system in struggle. In "theory" it advocates that within a "socialist state," two social, economic, and political systems with totally different natures can coexist for a long time. This contradicts the marxist principle of socialism and the theory of class struggle, which consider that the written history of humankind is the history of class struggle; the bourgeoisie and the proletariat, the capitalist system and the socialist system, are hostile to each other, in struggle, and cannot be reconciled. The capitalist system must be replaced by the socialist system. The "theory" of "one country-two systems" is a fundamental betrayal of related theories of marxism.

If Hong Kong continues to practice capitalism, has the integration and support of international capitalist forces, has a higher productivity and productive efficiency than mainland China, then it will become the beachhead of world capitalism in its expansion into China; the contradiction between the capitalist economy in Hong Kong and the state economy in mainland China will sharpen day by day, and the corrupting effect on the latter will increase daily. This kind of "two systems" will become a forceful element in the restoration of capitalism in China. If there is no intervention from the masses, the "two systems" will conflict and struggle against each other because of contradictions. The final outcome will either be a change in CCP policy to strike at the bourgeois forces and overthrow the capitalist system in Hong Kong or that the social and economic system in China will go through capitalist restoration.

In our opinion to realize the unification of China, for Hong Kong to integrate into China and to overthrow the capitalist system in Hong Kong, bureaucratic rule in mainland China must be overthrown and socialist democracy must be practiced in conjunction with a single system of state property. To achieve this the mobilization of the masses of mainland China and Hong Kong is a must.

In Hong Kong the mobilization of the people will start with struggles for day-to-day economic interests and democratic rights. The central slogan at the moment is the demand for a Hong Kong People's Congress with full power and constituted by general elections to replace the colonial regime and that the Hong Kong People's Congress should draw up the Basic Law. In advancing this struggle, the Hong Kong working class must become the main social force in struggle and lead the other toiling layers. As working-class struggles in mainland China and Hong Kong rise, revolutionaries should raise the slogan of convening a Congress of Toiling Masses to replace the slogan of a Hong Kong People's Congress, so as to meet the new objective requirements at that time and push the struggles to a higher plane.

The more generalized the struggle of the people of Hong Kong becomes, the more possible it will be to encourage the people in mainland China and, in return, help the people of Hong Kong to gain more rights. The democratic future of the people of Hong Kong is tightly linked to the democratic future of their fellow Chinese on the mainland.

The question of Macao is basically the same as that of Hong Kong. The Chinese and Portuguese governments have agreed to return Macao to China and end Portuguese rule in Macao on December 20, 1999. In similar fashion to their handling of the Hong Kong question, the Chinese government appointed its officials and supporters to draw up the Basic Law for Macao to ensure strict control.

The aspirations of the struggling people of Macao are the same as those of the people of Hong Kong: democratic self-rule, that is, the democratic self-rule of Macao by the people of Macao. The concrete means is through universal suffrage to constitute the Macao People's Congress as the highest power organ of Macao and the election of a drafting committee to draft the Basic Law for the Macao Special Zone, which, after adoption by the Macao People's Congress, will be presented as a record to the National People's Congress, thus guaranteeing that the people of Macao can fully exercise all democratic rights. From today on the residents of Macao must unite and organize together and fight for the right to take initiative, to participate, and to decide. The struggles of the people of Macao must also link up with the struggles of Hong Kong and mainland China in mutual solidarity.

18. THE TAIWAN QUESTION

The people of Taiwan have lived for nearly forty years under the military dictatorial rule of the Guomindang (GMD) and the repressive terror of its martial law.

The victory of the 1949 revolution finally brought down the Jiang Jieshi (Chiang Kai-shek) GMD regime in the mainland. However because the revolution was limited only to military struggle, without the outbreak of workers' uprisings in the cities to conquer power, the GMD had time to withdraw, taking to Taiwan the massive capital that the bureaucrats robbed, along with some weapons and military personnel. This bureaucrat capital, together with the massive economic aid from the United States to the GMD regime and continuous investment and loans by the United States, Japan, and others, provided the favorable conditions for industrial development in Taiwan.

The Taiwan government helps the capitalists by imposing a long-term, low-wage policy to exploit the Taiwanese workers savagely; it uses martial law to deprive the workers of the right to strike and organize, enabling foreign capital to obtain huge superprofits. On this basis Taiwanese industry has developed relatively rapidly, so that the per capita national income is over ten times higher than that of mainland China.

Industrial development brings changes in the production structure. The weight of agriculture has decreased significantly, while the weight of industry has increased. In addition because Taiwan has maintained a low staple price policy, it is difficult for the peasants to depend on agriculture as a livelihood, and the number of people leaving the farms for industrial work has increased. Low wages and low staple prices maintain a low cost for industrial products, but the interests of the worker and peasant masses are sacrificed, aggravating the social contradictions.

Taiwan's resources are limited. Major raw material, capital, advanced technology and equipment, the sale of products and so on are dependent on foreign trade; thus the Taiwanese economy is deeply affected by other countries. In particular when an international economic recession occurs, Taiwan suffers a blow.

The GMD regime had maintained martial law for a long time, reflecting its extreme fear of the people. Politically it maintained a one-party dictatorship. Other opposition forces outside the party, especially the political forces of the native Taiwanese people, suffered repression by the regime for a long time, with no freedom of speech, the banning of publications, the frequent arrest of activists, and long incarceration of political prisoners.

But high-handed repression cannot stop the Taiwanese people's struggle for democracy and freedom from the rule of the GMD. Their struggle has finally forced the regime to rescind the curfew order and ban on parties and to recognize the actual existence of the first opposition party (the Democratic Progressive Party) after thirty-seven years. All these events mark a major breakthrough in the Taiwanese political situation, favorable to changes in the relationship of class forces. But the regime has replaced the curfew order with the "State Security Act" and continues to repress the people's democratic rights. This will certainly be met by continued opposition by the masses and demands for the abolition of the State Security Act and all repressive, undemocratic laws.

Although the CCP has called for the liberation of Taiwan for a long time, the dismal results of its rule on the mainland has kept the workers and peasants of Taiwan away, damaged the attractiveness of the Chinese revolution, and objectively helped the GMD in continuing its reactionary rule.

Many years ago the CCP suggested the opening of shipping, mail, and trade to the Taiwan government. Although the latter refused, the people of Taiwan have in fact gradually broken through the ban and increasingly visited, by way of Hong Kong, relatives on the mainland, and they have struggled for civilian exchanges across the strait. This is an irreversible trend.

Later the CCP again proposed "cooperation between the GMD and the CCP for the third time," the "peaceful unification" of Taiwan and the mainland, retaining the ruling status and the army of the GMD in Taiwan, maintaining the socioeconomic system and the status quo of Taiwan, and practicing "one country, two systems" also in Taiwan. These proposals were rejected by the GMD government on a firm bourgeois class position.

The Taiwan government relies closely on the strong backing of U.S. imperialism, which sees Taiwan as the unsinkable aircraft carrier in the Far East and a trusted aide, an important fellow fighter in the future possible offensive against the Chinese, Soviet, and other workers' states.

Therefore the United States never stops its practical support of the Taiwan government, especially its economic and military aid. Even after the establishment of diplomatic relations between China and the United States, the United States did not reduce the sale of weapons to the Taiwan regime, despite the CCP's protest. If the Chinese People's Liberation Army were to invade Taiwan in the future, U.S. imperialism would certainly try its best to protect the latter. Whether through peaceful negotiation or through military attack, it is very difficult for the CCP to force Taiwan to unite with mainland China.

Only with the upsurge of the Taiwanese workers and peasants can the GMD regime be overthrown. Only when the CCP regime on the mainland is replaced by a truly democratic workers' regime, with the people on the mainland enjoying democracy, freedom, and a marked improvement in their standard of living, will the people of Taiwan be willing to unite with mainland China in one family. Otherwise the demand for "the people of Taiwan to determine their own future" will be further strengthened. Such a demand has been raised semilegally in Taiwan over the last few years and is gaining support among the people. We think that the rights and desires of the residents of Taiwan should be fully respected, regardless of whether such a desire is against the wish of any of the ruling layers.

The rule by the Jiang family ended with the death of Jiang Jingguo. The conservative forces of the GMD elders who came from China are waning. The political representatives, with Li Denghui at their head have taken over the main positions and have been forced to institute a more open and liberal policy, mainly to safeguard the interests of the Taiwanese bourgeois class. This is because the social contradictions that have been accumulating and have been suppressed for a long time have surfaced. All forms of street demonstrations, rallies, and protests by the lower and middle layers of the masses and strikes by workers have been occurring almost every day for years. Various opposition parties, including a Labor Party, have appeared and are in action. The development of the political situation in Taiwan is more favorable to the masses than before. The aim of the struggle of the Taiwanese people is to overthrow the bourgeois regime and establish a socialist democratic political system. Around this aim, the struggle in the current phase is

- For the people to enjoy all democratic rights, including complete freedom of speech, publication, meeting, association, demonstration, rallies, formation of unions, strikes, boycotts of classes, and so on, without any restrictions;

- For the complete removal of the ban on parties and for the right of all political parties to exist legally and conduct their activities on an equal basis;
- For the release of all political prisoners and innocent detainees and restoration of their full rights;
- Against the GMD regime's policy of "no compromise, no negotiation, no contact," and for the opening up of the border to allow people to visit, correspond, trade, and travel;
- For the disbanding of the "People's Assembly," "Legislative Council," and "Monitor Council," as well as for the convening, on a fully democratic basis, of a universally elected Taiwan People's Congress to be the highest power organ in Taiwan, empowered to solve all major questions within Taiwan.

19. THE QUESTION OF NATIONAL MINORITIES

The reality of the "right to self-rule" that the CCP gives to the national minorities provides valuable experience for what it says today of the "right to a high degree of self-rule" that Hong Kong, Macao, and Taiwan will have after unification.

Since the establishment of the new state, the CCP has not followed Lenin's policy on the national question and does not allow the national minorities the right to self-determination. The "right to self-rule" exists in name only, while in fact a Great Han policy has been pursued, control by the Great Han bureaucracy has been imposed on the national minorities, and national oppression is carried out, leading to long-term conflict between different nationalities. There is a wide gap in the standard of living of the national minorities from other regions of the country. Many years ago the government expressed "determination" to try within five to six years to make Tibet "surpass the highest standard of living in its history." This indeed acknowledges that their living standard is not better than before but much worse.

This has, in fact, led national minorities to demand "independence" in word and in action.

In the autumn of 1985, students belonging to national minorities held demonstrations in Urumuqi of Xinjiang, Beijing, Shanghai, and other places, raising many demands, such as stopping the nuclear tests in Xinjiang, letting local national minorities elect their own leaders to replace the Han officials appointed from Beijing, economic self-determination, political self-rule, ending forced birth control plans in the regions inhabited by national minorities, stopping the sending of "labor reformees" to Xinjiang, increasing the educational assistance to national minorities, and so on. They reveal once again the national oppression suffered by the national minorities and their extreme discontent as a result. This mood has reappeared in the action of the people of many towns in Xinjiang in opposition to bureaucratic rule.

Especially violent are the riots in Tibet around September and October 1987. These riots explain once again the seriousness of the national question in China. The suppression by force of the Tibet rebellion by the bureaucracy twenty-six years ago has far from solved the sharp contradiction between the bureaucracy's rule and the national minorities.

In recent years the CCP has been forced to relax somewhat its policy in some national minority areas, withholding acquisition until 1990, cancelling negotiated buying under the plan of food staples and others, allowing various forms of trade, and promoting the production responsibility system in agriculture and animal husbandry.

However it is totally insufficient simply to relax the economic exploitation of the national minorities. Their localities are usually poor, backward, mountainous, or remote. Transportation and communication to and within their districts are in urgent need of improvement. The state's responsibility in these areas cannot be shirked. The state must provide the material means to aid them substantially, to allow their economy to develop, and their standard of living to be improved.

More important is their liberation from political discrimination and oppression, letting them enjoy the right to self-determination, including the right to separation. This is the recognition, by the actual actions of the state, of the basic rights of national minorities, and is also the basic Marxist-Leninist principle on the national question.

We insist on the freedom of separation of the national minorities as advocated by Lenin: "Not at all because we advocate their separation, but because we advocate a free and voluntary affinity and merging." Historical experience proves that only free and voluntary integration is effective, while forced integration is the evil root of national contradictions and conflicts.

20. POLICY ON EDUCATION AND INTELLECTUALS

To raise productivity quickly and develop the economy of the whole country, it is necessary to strongly develop educational, scientific, and technological work, raise the country's cultural, scientific, and technological level, and breed a large and fine team of scientific and technological personnel.

The longstanding policy of the CCP has been the opposite. The CCP very much neglects the development of educational, scientific, and technological work; the financial expenditure in these areas is particularly low (in percentage terms it is much lower than that of many other underdeveloped countries). It does not emphasize developing scientific and technological personnel; it also discriminates and penalizes intellectuals (especially during the period of the Cultural Revolution), whose wages are very low and whose living is very difficult.

At present, China still has 220 million illiterates, comprising 20 percent of the population. Especially shocking is the fact that in recent years over 2 million illiterates are added each year. This is the result of the long negligence of education by the ruling faction.

The Deng faction's economic reform needs technological bureaucrats, and for several years there has been talk about the need to respect knowledge and qualified personnel. Still the expenditure on education has not increased much.

The present educational reform that the CCP is promoting still suffers from the excuse that "it is limited by the level of economic development," saying that the low education expenditure and low income for teachers "can only be reformed gradually." Although it decides to practice "step by step" nine years of free education to change the sad situation of charging school fees, even for primary education, for more than thirty years and because the state is still not willing to increase educational expenditure substantially, students and parents are still forced to shoulder school fees, which take the form of all kinds of items of payment.

High prices, as a result of the price reform and other factors, together with sharp increases in school fees and miscellaneous charges, cause a big increase in students' and teachers' cost of living. Although teachers' wages have increased slightly in recent years, they still have not kept up with increases in the cost of living in recent years.

In actual fact whether from the angle of developing production or undertaking the construction of socialism, education expenditure is a necessary investment. The percentage of education expenditure to gross national product is about 9 percent in the Northern European states, about 7 percent in the Soviet Union and in Cuba. Therefore China must reverse the previous serious mistakes and massively increase education expenditure. The immediate task is to eliminate illiteracy, prioritize education, gradually reaching the investment level of the countries named above; the exact figure should be decided by a National Laboring People's Congress. At the moment the education expenditure should not be less than 15 percent of the total budgetary expenditure.

To raise the educational, scientific, and technological level of the entire country rapidly, it is necessary to carry out free education fully, oppose schools' charging fees and making profit, and enable all children of school age to go to school; it is also necessary to reduce greatly the administrative charges, state defense charges, and basic foundation investment amounts and use them to increase funds for education and scientific research. Such funds must be used in the right place and guarded against embezzlement, appropriation, or waste. The income of educational, scientific, and technological personnel must be substantially increased, so that their economic difficulties can be relieved and so that they can work with their minds at ease.

Although the Deng faction raised the slogan of respect for the intellectuals, the state has not allocated large funds to improving their living and working conditions. Moreover with the development of the commodity economy and serious increases in the rate of inflation, the fixed wage income of intellectuals has been seriously eroded.

Besides their economic problems, intellectuals are still under the control of party bureaucrats in the process of their professional research, and they cannot develop in a free environment. As long as political restraints remain in place, intellectuals cannot fully realize their potential.

As one layer of the working masses, intellectuals have basically the same interests as the workers and peasants. The bureaucracy's rule hinders the establishment of democratic relations of production and hinders the intellectuals in actively assisting the development of productivity. In the previous period, the bureaucracy especially targeted the intellectuals and divided the intellectuals from the workers and peasants. Under the Deng faction, there is still no provision for the intellectuals to integrate with the workers and peasants to increase productivity rapidly.

Under the bureaucracy's rule, starting from opposing the CCP's policy on education and on intellectuals, the intellectuals will advance to criticize the main contradictions of society, from fighting for freedom of speech and publication to fighting for democracy and for power. Some intellectuals stand at the forefront of the antibureaucratic struggle, as especially shown by the upsurge of the student movement and in the outspokenness of the intellectuals in the arts.

21. POLICY ON LITERATURE AND ART

Under the excuse of "literature and art for the service of workers, peasants, and soldiers," literature and art have been transformed into tools for the regime and propaganda for its policies. Bureaucratic rule suffocates literature and art, denying writers and artists creative freedom.

After 1978 when those framed as "rightist elements" were rehabilitated, many writers recovered considerable freedom in creative work, and many fine works appeared, revealing and criticizing the reality. Many artists struggle against bureaucratic restraints and fight for freedom of speech, thought, and publication. Although constantly hit by the bureaucracy, with many forced to use more obscure methods to counter it, many writers still fought bravely while under siege from the officials. Some artists even linked up with or echoed democracy movement activists and challenged the CCP's ruling ideology. After the massive arrests of samizdat editors in April 1981, although also under repression, the artistic community still managed to resist the pressure and continued in its dissident role. The government initiated a "clean spiritual pollution" campaign in late 1983, partly pointing at some avant-garde art works, but failed because of the writers' resistance.

In recent years the ruling factions policy regarding the arts has vacillated, with different degrees of control, not because the ruling faction favors an open policy, but because it faces such strong pressure for literary freedom that it can no longer control the situation as tightly as it could under Mao Zedong, and it can hardly maintain a dominant ideology. The expulsion from the party of writers such as Liu Binyan, Wang Ruowang, and others only expresses the government's shaming into anger.

All writers must enjoy complete freedom of thought, subject matter selection, and artistic expression to give free rein to their talents and produce works that the people will love. At the same time, they must enjoy freedom of publication, as freedom of speech, for writing and publication cannot be separated. Their need is the same as the need of the people for food for the mind. This is their source of strength in the antibureaucracy struggle. Their struggle will break through the bureaucracy's control. Good, independently written literary works, when welcomed by the masses, can only arouse greater opposition if the bureaucrats try to suppress them. And with each victory, the struggle rises to a higher level.

22. THE PRESENT SITUATION OF WOMEN

After the liberation of mainland China, more women have become integrated into productive work; therefore, their social position and freedom have improved considerably. However in the economy, education, society, and other fields, the unequal status of women and discrimination against them still exist. For example opportunity in employment and education is unequal; women are still concentrated in jobs with lower pay and lower social status. Pay and promotion opportunities remain unequal even for women doing the same work as men. Women also do not enjoy the same benefits; for example, in many places, the right to an apartment is denied. In the relation between the two sexes within a family, especially after the ruling faction's policy of severely restricting birth, instances of women receiving unfair treatment or even battering have become more common and more serious. After the economic reforms, the burden of birth and work on women has become even heavier. Although there are some public services, such as child care centers, kindergartens, clinics, centers for the care of the elderly, and so on, the fees have generally been increased, reversing the trend of socialization of housework, pushing the responsibility back to individual families, especially onto women. This is a blow against women's rights and the possibility of their full participation in social production, the raising of the cultural and educational level, and the development of individuality. On the other hand, with the popularity of "all eyes on money," it is becoming widespread for female youth to be treated as commodities in marriage. Prostitution is reappearing. The promotion of the commodity economy has caused many ugly social phenomena to reappear and the oppression of women to deepen.

Therefore the struggle for equality between men and women; the breaking of all chains of discrimination, oppression, and battering of women; the opposition to all unequal and unfair ideas; and crimes against women become urgent tasks. At the same time, it is necessary to socialize housework, for society to undertake child care and care for the elderly, to provide the conditions for women to enjoy the same opportunity as men to participate in productive labor. Without the above social conditions, the liberation of women becomes impossible.

On the road to liberation, Chinese women need to join with male workers in overthrowing the bureaucracy's rule and in establishing democratic productive relations and social self-management.

23. POPULATION AND BIRTH CONTROL

The government has blamed the slow growth of the Chinese economy partly on the large population and high birth rate. This is indirectly using the Malthusian population theory to explain away its errors. It does not dare point out that the laboring people create immeasurable wealth for society, far exceeding their consumption!

To limit birth a few years ago the CCP brutally set a quota for lowering the national birthrate for the following years, strictly limiting each couple to only one child. Local cadres have vigorously carried out the orders from above, forcing women to undergo abortion and sterilization, using fines and deductions from wages to penalize couples with two or more children.

This frenzied bureaucratism is doing severe damage to many families. The saddest incidents are the killing of newborn babies, especially baby girls and even small girls, and the ill-treatment of mothers who give birth to girls. Such tragedies become increasingly common, causing much discontent among the people. The population has generally resisted the CCP measures, as seen by the fact that the quota has failed for many years.

We always advocate that the people have the right to decide freely on love, marriage, birth, birth control, abortion, and other matters; no person, party, or state apparatus has the right to intervene. The act of the CCP in recent years in brutally limiting birth, forcing abortion and sterilization, and direct and indirect killing of babies must be condemned and opposed.

24. SOCIAL MOOD AND SOCIAL ORDER

The long-term stagnation in the economy, incessant factional struggles leading to political turmoil, special privileges, corruption and degeneration, abuse of power for private gains, hoarding and speculation by the bureaucrats, little improvement in the people's living standards, and widespread deprivation of education and unemployment among the youth all lead to the long-term worsening of the social mood and social order.

The open-door reforms lead to the attraction and invasion of bourgeois ideology and living habits. Social inequality and division have aggravated the contradictions, causing a worse social mood.

For years the authorities have stepped up their repression of criminal offenders. Many prisoners who deserved several years of imprisonment under the law were in fact executed casually, implying that the CCP is not trying to eradicate the basic causes of crime but attempting to use heavy sentences and indiscriminate killings to maintain order.

Even under its current criminal law, this is an open violation of the rules of trial and punishment. It once again shows that the CCP habitually ignores the rule of law and holds the people's lives in contempt.

Such behavior shows that the rulers knowingly break the law and kill indiscriminately. They intentionally sacrifice the lives of tens of thousands of people as scapegoats to their false policies. This must be strongly opposed.

25. THE CRISIS OF THE PRIVILEGED BUREAUCRACY

The bureaucratization of the CCP has become more ossified since it came to power. It practices the nomenclatura system: job and remuneration for life and high salary favoritism. CCP cadres also act as state officials, enjoying political and economic privileges. The higher their position is, the greater the privileges. This totally contravenes the following principles that Marx drew from the experiences of the Paris Commune: all state officials must be popularly elected and can be removed at any time and can only receive the wages of skilled workers.

Special privileges make the CCP more bureaucratized, forming a more consolidated bureaucracy, totally out of the control of the people; bureaucrats, big and small, go after personal privileges and comfort in life, become increasingly corrupt and degenerate. With the reform and economic opening to the imperialist world market, the situation has worsened.

To moderate the people's discontent and to maintain political power, the CCP, starting in 1951, has carried out many campaigns against corruption, degeneration, waste, and bureaucratism. But as long as the root cause of the privileged bureaucracy and its system is not eradicated, these evils cannot be eliminated and can only become more serious. The CCP leadership acknowledges that it is a matter of life and death for the party. The crisis in confidence, belief, and faith in the CCP is a concrete reflection. Although the ruling faction has time and again initiated campaigns against corruption over the past ten years, claiming that it will overcome the crisis, this cannot be achieved.

The crisis of the CCP is also reflected in the composition of its members. Youth, women, and national minority members constitute a very small proportion of the party. First-line production worker members are even fewer. In recent years after the reform, many new party members came from the rich peasantry, specialized households, and newly emerging private entrepreneurs. They used the political status associated with party membership to guarantee their acquired economic interests.

According to the marxist theory of the state in the transition period from capitalism to socialism, the dictatorship of the proletariat must be established to guarantee that the majority of the people enjoy full democracy and freedom and that repression is carried out only on the exploiters and oppressors. The imposing, repressive character of the state will gradually diminish, until it withers away, rather than becoming increasingly strengthened. But the state regime under the rule of the CCP goes against that theory.

The facts over a long time reveal that the CCP is not in fact the dictatorship of the proletariat as advocated by Marx but the dictatorship of the bureaucracy over the proletariat.

The privileged layer that constitutes this dictatorship of the bureaucracy terribly seizes and wastes social wealth, the extent is in direct proportion to the overstaffed state organs. Besides the yearly jump in visible administrative expenses, other private seizures and bureaucratic waste are even more shocking. Most importantly to maintain its rule it practices the policy of deceiving the people and sabotaging the production and work incentive of the people, thus causing incalculable loss to the economy and society.

This privileged bureaucracy is a parasite on the state property system. Just like a tumor in the body, it does not constitute a necessary organic part of the state property system; rather it is a factor that is suffocating and strangling it. Today its rightist policy is causing even greater danger to the state property system, increasing the probability of the latter's eventual disintegration. Its cadres take advantage of the policy of restoring private ownership, owning means of production, accumulating massive wealth, enjoying the protection of law. They not only become rich peasants but new bourgeois class elements as well. These cadres potentially will be the vanguard of capitalist restoration in China in the future.

26. THE CCP's "PROPOSAL" FOR POLITICAL STRUCTURAL REFORM

To overcome the crisis of the bureaucracy, Deng Xiaoping proposed to carry out political structural reform. He acknowledged that the CCP and

the present government often do their work badly, "hindering, even seriously, the full development of the advantages of socialism." For the leadership and the cadre system, the main problems are bureaucratism, too great a
concentration of power, patriarchy, lifetime posts, and all forms of special
privileges. These problems increasingly conflict with the economic reform
that Deng is promoting and seriously hinder its development. Therefore he
and his supporters are forced to say that it is necessary to carry out political
structural reforms. This reflects that the objective necessity and urgency of
the reform of the political system are so great that even the leaders of the
bureaucracy are forced to acknowledge them.

But the "political structural reforms" of the Deng faction so far only
propose the separation of party and state, decentralization of power, younger
cadres, and so on; the real meaning of these measures is to remove cadres
who are not firm supporters of the Deng faction's policies and to replace
them with economic technocrats. This means a redistribution of power within
the bureaucracy. Although the system of functioning for life for some old
cadres is nominally ended, in reality their lifetime privileges are still maintained. Even in situations in which old cadres have become "consultants,"
their political privileges are still maintained, and when necessary, they still
play the role of central committee members or central political bureau members—for example, in the enlarged political bureau meeting in which Hu
Yaobang was deposed as general secretary.

It is therefore clear that the bureaucrats will not give up their political
and economic privileges voluntarily. Even limited changes in some cadres'
privileges are met with full resistance. The wider the scope of change, the
greater the resistance, hence the inability to make bigger "reforms." From
the time Deng Xiaoping talked about the need for political structural reforms years ago, the many difficulties in their actual implementation show
the enormity of the resistance.

In the Thirteenth Congress held in 1987, the leaders of the CCP proposed political structural reform, but they did not touch on the power position of the entire bureaucracy, nor on eliminating the political and economic
privileges of CCP members, nor on abolishing the existing bureaucracy system.

27. THE CCP's REVISION OF MARXISM

The CCP has always proclaimed its belief in Marxism-Leninism, advertising
socialism and communism. Under this coat it makes anti–Marxist-Leninist
deals, producing all kinds of "distorted and damaging" phenomena, and is
the antithesis of socialism.

During the 1925–27 revolutionary period, the CCP followed the wrong
line of the Third International under the control of Stalinist bureaucrats.

That was the start of its departure from Marxism-Leninism. In the soviet regions and during the War of Resistance, the bureaucratic party system of the CCP and its control of the masses were reinforced. After the CCP took power, it carried out a series of measures to strengthen the privileged rule of the bureaucracy, dominating and oppressing the worker and peasant masses. As the ruler, its concerns are to guard its rule and maintain privileges.

The CCP's words and deeds obviously are against the principles of marxism and socialism, and it faces widespread criticism both inside and outside the country. Finally the CCP faction in power has discarded the fig leaf and openly declares: "We cannot ask the writings of Marx and Lenin to solve our current problems" (later "revised" to "all of our current problems").

The theory of scientific socialism, the principle of proletarian dictatorship during the transition period, the organizational principle of democratic centralism in a workers' party, and other principles advocated by Marxism-Leninism have decisive significance in solving the current basic problems. The ideas that the CCP is openly advocating today are attempts to spread doubts about marxism in order to facilitate the justification of its revisions of marxism.

Deng and others reportedly advised an African state leader not to construct socialism, not to develop state economy as China did, indicating that Chinese leaders not only are openly sick of socialism and the state economy, not only revising in words and in theory, but also politically rejecting the important positions of marxism.

From borrowing marxism as cover to negating the value of Marx's and Lenin's works, the CCP's revisionist words and deeds are becoming apparent. This can help those who are cheated politically by the CCP to see its true countenance and distinguish the line between it and marxism.

28. THE TASKS OF REVOLUTIONARIES

The foregoing discussion confirms once again that the CCP bureaucracy cannot reform itself and will not voluntarily relinquish its ruling position. This judgment has also been proved by the valuable historical experience of Polish Solidarity and the bureaucratic counterrevolution. Only by the Chinese working class leading the toiling masses in carrying out a political revolution, overthrowing the bureaucracy, practicing socialist democracy and correct policies, promoting and aiding revolutions in other countries, and, finally, together with the working class of all countries, realizing a worldwide socialist federation can humanity progress to a scientific, democratic, socialist society.

The central task of Chinese revolutionaries is to carry out that political revolution. Facing the current situation, revolutionaries' overall tasks are using marxist analysis to insist on socialism as the way forward; to defend the state property system against capitalist restoration; and to defend the interests of the worker and peasant masses against privileges, exploitation, and repression. To accomplish these tasks, we must pinpoint the existing problems, raise our views and perspectives, especially pointing out the dangers of strengthening capitalist power as a result of the economic reforms and open-door policies and pointing out all measures that can lead to capitalist restoration in China and all policies hurting the interests of the broad masses; before it is too late, we must explain them in time to the masses, especially their advanced layers, in order to fight forcefully with them.

Based on the "tasks and perspectives" in our program on China adopted in 1977 and summarizing the analysis of the new situation and problems, we again state our principal perspectives as follows:

1. practice proletarian internationalism, help the revolutionary struggles of the masses in other countries, promote world revolution;
2. overthrow the bureaucratic dictatorship of the CCP, practice socialist democracy, let the democratically elected National Laboring People's Congress exercise the highest state power and local laboring people's congresses at all levels function as local governmental powers;
3. practice true and full socialist democracy; working people should enjoy all democratic and liberal rights (including the freedom to form parties and conduct activities fairly and legally), the freedom and good name of dissidents should be restored, and the CCP's use of any excuse to limit or deprive them of their rights must be opposed;
4. form independent worker unions and student, youth, women's, and other mass organizations to represent and safeguard the masses' rights and oppose the control and manipulation of the CCP;
5. consolidate and develop the nationalization of the means of production; oppose their privatization;
6. define economic plans democratically by all working people and put the planned economy in a dominant position; the market mechanism may be allowed to exist, but it must be restrained consciously and subject to planning; oppose the domination of China by market forces;
7. maintain the state monopoly of foreign trade and oppose opening China up for free competition among various regions and enterprises;
8. production should aim at fulfilling the people's and society's needs; change the longstanding low consumption/high accumulation ratio, and strive at changing the high investment/low efficiency situation; the ratio between consumption and accumulation must be determined democratically by the working people;
9. on the basis of peasant free will, advance toward agricultural cooperation, collectivization, and mechanization; the state should help with material aid and at the same time help the poor peasants and restrict the growth of the rich peasants;
10. realize workers' democratic self-management in the enterprises, establish a workers' council or workers' congress system to become the highest

body of an enterprise, to make the major decisions within the enterprise and practice collective leadership; oppose the personal dictatorship of the factory director or manager;

11. allow individual businesses to exist but restrain the tendency of proliferation of private industrial and commercial enterprises and the exploitation of employees;

12. massively reduce the investments in fixed assets, administrative expenses (including "social group consumption"), defense and armament expenses, to improve concretely the people's standard of living and to increase massively expenditures on education and scientific research;

13. ensure that the working people's living standards are not hurt by rising prices; wages are to be adjusted in accordance with the cost of living; the state must provide subsidies to the people and subsidize or raise the purchase price for agricultural and subsidiary food products;

14. protect the Chinese economy; oppose the CCP's current special economic zone policy, especially its allowing the products from these zones to be sold in the domestic market; protect the working class' rights in those regions from being attacked;

15. protect the lives and health of the people and the environment; oppose the construction of nuclear power plants and the pollution and dangers from industrial wastes;

16. fully restore as soon as possible the normal relationship between China and various workers' states; carry out economic, cultural, scientific, and technological cooperation and interchange; strengthen the solidarity between the working people of the workers' states;

17. recover Chinese sovereignty over Hong Kong and Macao by the Chinese people; convene a popularly elected and sovereign Hong Kong (and Macao) People's Congress; practice political democracy; oppose the CCP's policy of "one country, two systems;"

18. end the Guomindang's dictatorial rule and allow Taiwan to be ruled by the residents on the basis of democracy (including freedom of political party activities); the future of Taiwan to be decided by all the residents of Taiwan; we call on the Taiwanese working class and other toiling masses to rise up and overthrow the capitalist system and achieve unification of Taiwan with mainland China on the basis of true socialism;

19. all national minorities must enjoy the right to self-determination (including the right to separate); the oppression of national minorities by Great Han chauvinism and bureaucratic rule must be opposed;

20. the people must have complete freedom on marriage, birth, abortion, etc.; the official compulsory policies and administrative means must be opposed.

To overcome this crisis and to accomplish the task of political revolution in China, it is necessary to build a proletarian revolutionary party that is strong and correct in line. The Fourth International and its Chinese section, inheriting Marxism–Leninism, the correct tradition in the struggles of the

First, Second, and Third Internationals, and the organizational principles of democratic centralism have persisted for over half a century in difficult struggles, and their program has been tried and tested constantly in historical events.

The organizational task facing the Chinese section of the Fourth International is to go among the masses, especially among the worker masses, and together with them fight for democracy, defend their rights, extend and consolidate a revolutionary nucleus, to develop gradually into a mass revolutionary party. Victory can be won only when the masses are won over.

2

The Economic Situation under Deng Xiaoping

LIN FENG AND WEI WEN

[The following is a summary of the article published in *October Review*, April–August 1987, on China's economic situation.]

AGRICULTURE

In June 1985, fifty-six thousand rural communes, which had been the basic units of state government, were dismantled. Because of the decollectivization, 98 percent of peasant households farm under the contract system. Liberation from the bondage of the people's commune and incentives for production, coupled with higher prices for agricultural products and provision of light industrial goods, have encouraged growth in agriculture. Between 1978 and 1986, the total agricultural output rose 2.5-fold in absolute terms, from 156.7 billion yuan to 394.7 billion yuan; grain output rose by 28 percent, and cotton output rose by 63 percent.

However the increase has essentially been obtained by a laissez-faire policy, which is not supported by a greater state investment in agriculture. In fact investment in agriculture as a proportion of investment in capital construction dropped steadily from 10.6 percent in 1978 to 3.4 percent in 1985. The absolute figure also dropped from 5.3 billion yuan to 3.7 billion yuan. Apart from this a sample survey shows that peasants have also reduced their investment in agriculture: in Hebei, Shandong, and Henan provinces, investment in agriculture dropped by over 30 percent in 1985 as compared to 1983.[1] Another survey shows that the productive investment in fixed assets as a percentage of total peasant expenditure was highest in 1983 (5.7 percent), but began to drop after 1983 to 4.7 percent in 1984, 3.8 percent in 1985, and 3.43 percent in the third quarter of 1986.[2]

61

This reduced investment in agriculture is a major factor in the fluctuation of grain production—an annual increase of 9 percent for 1982 and 1983 but an abrupt drop of 7 percent in 1985. It is also manifested in the steady drop in the area plowed by tractors—34.92 million hectares in 1984 as compared with 40.97 million hectares in 1978. This has to do with the drop in production of large- and medium-sized tractors (113,500 in 1978 to 33,600 in 1986, compared with the increase in production of walking tractors from 324,200 in 1978 to 822,500 in 1985) and the privatization of the means of production (for example, private ownership of tractors rose significantly: 38,000 in 1980, 380,000 in 1981, 1 million in 1982, 2 million in 1983, 3.11 million in 1984). Mechanization may be employed on big areas contracted by specialized farming households. For example, *China Daily* in its issue of September 9, 1983, reported that in Fenglian Township, Yangxin County, Hebei Province, a farmer contracted five to six hectares of land that "nobody else wanted," and "thanks to mechanized cultivation he harvested 30,000 kilograms of grain and sold 23,500 to the state—equal to the total quota of the production brigade." Yet this might not always be the case. W. H. Hinton reported that "in Taiyuan, agricultural officials told me about one peasant who contracted 750 mu of land. When I said his mechanization must be impressive and that I would like to see it, they said he had no machinery at all. He farmed 750 mu with hired labor."[3]

Apart from the difficulties in agricultural mechanization, other developments are also slow. The growth in fertilizer production after 1980 has been slow, with negative growth in 1985 (8.69 million tons in 1978, 12.32 million tons in 1980, 14.6 million tons in 1984, 13.22 million tons in 1985). The production of insecticide steadily dropped from 1980 to 1985, from 537,000 tons to 211,000 tons. With the slight increase in 1986 (223,000 tons), it is still only 40 percent of the 1978 figure (533,000 tons).

In this situation the state intervened to maintain grain output. In 1986 measures were taken to encourage farmers to grow grain—the contract quota was reduced so that peasants could sell more grain in the free market, and the selling price was increased. Fertilizer, insecticide, and seeds were provided to peasants at a special price. This led to a 3.2 percent increase in grain output in 1986, though this came from increased acreage rather than increased productivity. (Grain output rose from 2.53 tons per hectare in 1978 to 3.61 tons per hectare in 1984. It then dropped to 3.48 tons per hectare in 1985.) In addition to the aforementioned measures, in 1987 the state granted interest-free loans to peasants equivalent to 20 percent of the contract quota.

However peasants' actual gains were still limited. According to the *People's Daily* (November 1986) only 52 percent of the increase in peasant income in that year came from the price increase in agricultural products, as compared with 92 percent in 1979.

PEASANT INCOME AND STANDARD OF LIVING

The structure of peasant income has undergone much change. Income from household economic activities has become the main source of income, replacing income from collective economic activities. In 1985 the former comprised 81.1 percent of peasant income (26.8 percent in 1978), whereas the latter comprised only 8.4 percent (66.3 percent in 1978).

Between 1978 and 1986, the absolute increase (before deducting for inflation) in national income was 135 percent; worker income, 117 percent; and peasant income, 216 percent. (The average worker's wage increased from 614 yuan to 1,332 yuan; income for living expenses per person in a working-class family increased from 316 yuan to 828 yuan, and net income per peasant from 134 yuan to 424 yuan.) In the same period, industrial and agricultural output increased by 174 percent and 152 percent, respectively. This set of figures, if compared with the 1957–78 figures, demonstrates a significant improvement in people's standard of living—in 1957–78 industrial output increased by a factor of 4.78, and workers' wages rose by only 1 percent; agricultural output rose by a factor of 1.92, and average peasant income rose by only 84 percent.

After 1978 the retail amount of social commodities rose by a factor of 1.8. The proportion sold in the countryside rose from 49.7 percent in 1957 to 52 percent in 1978 and to 58.5 percent in 1985. Peasants' expenditures on food dropped from 67.7 percent in 1978 to 57.8 percent in 1985; expenditures on daily necessities rose from 6.6 percent to 11.4 percent and that on housing from 3.2 percent to 12.4 percent. In addition from 1978 to 1985, durable consumer goods owned by every one hundred peasant households rose significantly: bicycle ownership by a factor of 1.6, sewing machine ownership by a factor of 1.2, radio ownership by a factor of 2.1, and watch ownership by a factor of 3.7. Television sets owned by every one hundred peasant households rose from 0.39 in 1980 to 11.74 in 1985, that is, by a factor of 29. Still the figure is low compared to that of worker households—93.33 television sets per one hundred worker families in 1985. Besides, no official statistics are given on the number of washing machines and refrigerators owned by peasant households, which indicates that the figure may be very low.

The improvement in peasant income and living standard has been the major pride of the Deng "reform." However one must take into account several factors when assessing the actual rise in peasant income. One factor is inflation. Inflation after 1978 has been unprecedented. Official statistics say that the nominal wage increase of workers between 1978 and 1985 was 88 percent, and the real increase was 44 percent. One can remember the important price reform of 1985 when restrictions on subsidiary food prices were unfrozen. In fact the prices of most industrial consumer goods were by then fixed by the enterprises, and prices fluctuated widely. One of the slogans raised by the September 1985 student demonstration was against the price increases. Still the 1985 official statistics for retail price inflation was 8.8 percent, and for cost of living, 9.3 percent.

Another factor is the inaccuracy of official statistics. The *People's Daily*, in the issue dated August 17, 1985, carried a rural survey report that said that there are inaccuracies in the calculation of peasant income; for example, grain, firewood, and foods produced by peasants for their own use have been calculated at current market prices, and this income accounts for 30 to 50 percent of the peasants' annual income. Output value is equated with income. Some calculations are based on memory or estimates, and cadres cheat and falsify. The same report also pointed out that the peasants face various sorts of tariffs and dues, and "the reasonable and unreasonable social burden comprises ten to twenty percent of the peasants' income." The official statistics, which say that the "net" income of peasants in 1986 is 424 yuan, must be considered in this light.

WORKERS' STANDARD OF LIVING

Workers' real wages in state-owned enterprises were kept at a low level since 1957, with a reduction in 1970–77, and a 6 percent to 8 percent annual increase in 1978–80. The 1980 figure reached only the 1957 level. At the end of 1985, the figure was a mere 66 percent increase over 1952.

The pattern of consumption in worker households in 1981–84 had not changed much. In 1985 there was a slight drop in the proportion of food expenditure (−4.6 percent) but a slight increase in the expenditure on daily necessities (+2 percent). The possession of durable consumer goods increased. In 1980, 30 percent of households possessed a television set; in 1985, 90 percent had one. In 1981, 6 percent of households had a washing machine; in 1985, 50 percent had one. In 1981, only 0.2 percent of households had a refrigerator; in 1985, the figure was 10 percent.

The greater supply of consumer durables has to do with the rather rapid development of light industry in 1980–85 and the adjustment in the rate of consumption. From 1979 to 1982, the increase on the consumption fund is greater than that of the accumulation fund. After 1982, a reverse trend set in. The rate of consumption fell from the peak of 71.7 percent reached in 1981 to 66.3 percent in 1985. As reflected in the output of light industry, its proportion in total industrial output rose from 43 percent in 1978 to 51.5 percent in 1981, but fell after this year.

SOCIAL DIFFERENTIATION

A conscious measure of the Deng economic reform is the expansion of workers' wage differentials to provide incentives for production and increase labor productivity. In June 1985 a reform of the wage system was introduced in the state apparatus and in state-owned enterprises. The reform affected 10 million workers.

The proportion of basic wages within total wages of workers' in state-owned enterprises decreased from 85 percent in 1978 to 58.5 percent in 1984, whereas the proportion of piece-rate wages rose from 0.8 percent to 9.5 percent and that of bonuses and subsidies from 8.8 percent to 28.9 percent.

According to a survey conducted in 1980 on urban income, the poorest 40 percent of the population had 30 percent of the total income; the richest 20 percent had 28 percent of the total income; and the richest 10 percent of the population had 16 percent of the total income. The Gini coefficient was 0.16.[4] This indicates that the inequality in urban income in China was much lower than in developing countries in general, whose Gini coefficient was 0.43.

However with the practice of the contract system, the piece-rate system and the expansion of wage differentials during these years, the gap between the rich and poor has widened. In 1983, 23.9 percent of urban households had an income 20 percent below the average, and in 1985, the percentage had risen to 27.47 percent.

The authorities acknowledge that the gap between the rich and poor in rural areas has widened. The World Bank Report of 1981 pointed out that the Gini coefficient of China's rural income distribution was 0.31 in 1979, which was not much better than that of the four poorest developing countries (Bangladesh, India, Pakistan, and Sri Lanka). The poorest 40 percent of the population had 20 percent of the rural income; the richest 20 percent had 39 percent of the total income; and the richest 10 percent of the population had 23 percent of the total income.

The situation has aggravated since the institution of Deng's reforms. Michel Chossudovsky, in his book *Towards Capitalist Restoration?—Chinese Socialism after Mao*, provided data obtained in his field research in rural China in 1980–83. They showed that rural inequality was more serious in the richer regions. For instance in Guangdong Province, Dali Township, with a population of approximately 23,000 households, the average household income (1983) was around 2,500 to 3,000 yuan; 1,300 households (6 percent of the total) had incomes in excess of 5,000 yuan, and 120 households (0.5 percent) had incomes in excess of 10,000 yuan. The richest household has earnings of 150,000 yuan, more than 50 times the average income. In Ninguan village, Yuongqu County, Liaoning Province, the average households income was around 3,000 yuan. Twenty percent of the households had average incomes of 12,000 yuan, 6 times that of the poorest household (2,000 yuan). In Daqing Township in the same county, 10 percent of households had incomes of 1,700 yuan; average households income was 2,400 yuan, and 20 percent of the households had incomes over 6,400 yuan. The richest household specializing in transportation had an income of 20,000 yuan.

The New Spring Commune in Nangang County, Heilongjiang Province, belonged to the affluent category, yet the poorer households had incomes of only 600 yuan. According to Chossudovsky, the disparity between the rich and poor in affluent regions was on the average of 1 to 7, though often in excess of 1 to 10. The absolute income gap between the rich peasant in a rich region and the poor peasant in a poor region was on the order of 1 to 100.[5]

On August 17, 1985, the *People's Daily* reported a survey on eleven counties and townships in Heilongjiang Province and pointed out that the per capita income of the Province in 1984 was 416 yuan, 61 yuan above the national average. The survey conducted in March and April 1985 showed that only 18 percent of peasant households belonged to the affluent group, that is, with per capita income of over 500 yuan, and 10,000-yuan households made up only 0.18 percent. The Statistics Department calculated that the basic annual expenditure of a peasant was 239 yuan. Peasants with per capita incomes of less than 200 yuan were considered poor, and they constituted 21 percent of the households in the eleven counties. Peasants with per capita incomes of less than 150 yuan constituted 8.5 percent in the more affluent Keshan County but 29 percent and 43 percent, respectively, in the poorer Baiquan and Hingshui Counties. The survey also showed that only 40 percent of peasant income could be used in daily expenses; social duties constituted 10 percent to 20 percent of their income. In 1984 in Heilongjiang Province, over 100 million yuan of agricultural loans could not be recovered that year, and 500,000 peasant households owed over 100 million yuan in taxes. The statistics of the Agricultural Department of Fujin County showed that 5 percent of peasant households had per capita income of less than 150 yuan, whereas the Civil Administration Bureau recorded that 14 percent of peasant households belonged to this category, and 19,300 peasant households (36 percent) did not have enough food.

REGIONAL DISPARITIES

On the national level, Heilongjiang Province had greater industrial and agricultural output. One can imagine the difficulty of peasants' lives in the poorer provinces.

In general, provinces with high per capita industrial output also have high per capita agricultural output, with the exception of Shandong, Fujian, and Xinjiang Provinces, whose industrial output was higher than their agricultural output. (If the national average is 100, the former in 1985 were respectively 88.5, 63.4, 67.5, and the latter were respectively 152.8, 96, and 107.8. Tibet's, by comparison, were 8.2 and 61.1.)[6]

Let us first look at the per capita industrial output value. In 1979 the figure for Shanghai was 11 times higher than the national average; Beijing's and Tianjin's were 5 times higher. Nine provinces (excluding Tibet) were 40 percent (40 points) lower than the national average. Provinces with per capita industrial output higher than the national average rose from 4 in 1979 to 7 in 1985, and those with significant improvement were Zhejiang (up 48 points), Jiangsu (up 28 points), Hubei (up 22 points), Guangdong (up 14 points), and Xinjiang (up 13 points). However, 9 provinces (including Tibet) were still 40 points lower than the national average, with Inner Mongolia and Guangxi dropping further by 6 and 18 points, respectively. Guizhou, Henan, and Anhui did not show much improvement.

Despite the disparities in per capita industrial output, the average wage of the workers of different provinces did not differ much, thanks to the implementation of a national scale of workers' wages. With the exception of Tibet and Qinghai, where wages were particularly high (115.1 and 134.4, respectively, for state-owned enterprises in 1981), the difference between other provinces was less than 27 points for state-owned enterprises and 36 points for collective enterprises in 1981, and less than 33 points in 1985. It is interesting to note that the workers did not necessarily have higher wages in regions with higher per capita industrial output; in 1985, of the 7 provinces with higher per capita industrial output than the national average, 6 had workers' wages lower than the national average.

The changes in workers' income in 1984 and 1985, however, indicated a new trend. Of the 29 provinces and major cities, a rise in the wage index (the national average being 100) occurred in only Shanghai, Beijing, Zhejiang, Hebei, Guangdong, Fujian, Yunnan, and Tibet (most of the above being coastal areas), and all the other provinces experienced a deterioration.

Let us now look at the per capita agricultural output. Of the 15 provinces and major cities above the national average in 1979, 3 experienced a sudden drop to below the national average (Hebei dropped by 24 points, Hunan by 27 points, and Tibet by 66 points). Those that had an increase included Beijing, Liaoning, Jilin, Shanxi, Shandong, Zhejiang, and Fujian. The 5 provinces that were more than 20 points below the national average in 1979 (Guizhou, Gansu, Yunnan, Guanxi, Sichuan) without exception worsened (the decreases were respectively 14, 24, 14, 15, and 17 points). Eight more provinces joined the category of provinces with 20 points below the national average. Thus 13 provinces had per capita agricultural output value 20 points lower than the national average, and 11 of them were 30 points lower than the national average.

The situation reflects a serious problem, that is, the disparity between the provinces was intensifying under the Deng policy, which has been one of supporting the rich and the able.

The income of the peasants, who enjoy less social security than the urban workers, corresponded to the per capita agricultural output of the region. The income disparity was 202 points in 1979 and 138 points in 1985, showing a narrowing of the gap. In 1979 and 1984, there were 4 provinces with per capita peasant income 20 points below average. In 1985 there were 5 provinces. There were 16 provinces and major cities with per capita peasant income above the national average in 1979, 12 in 1984, and 10 in 1985.

Peasant income was closely related to agricultural output. Agricultural output figures for Guizhou and Gansu were 65.1 and 67.9, respectively, in 1979, and peasant income figures were 55.6 and 67.9, respectively. In 1985 Guizhou and Gansu were the poorest provinces, with per capita agricultural output of 61.1 and 44.2 and per capita peasant income of 72.3 and 64.6.

Ten provinces and major cities had an increase in per capita peasant income from 1979 to 1985; six were coastal provinces and major cities.

Before 1985 agricultural output included the value produced by village-run industries. Even if this figure is deducted, Gansu and Guizhou still remained the lowest, with the indices being 56.5 and 67.2 in 1984. The difference between the highest and lowest provinces or major cities was 135 points, that is, 2.5 times.

To narrow the regional disparities and overcome the imbalances in regional development, the state must consciously allocate resources on a national basis according to a general state plan. Backward regions need particular support, and their development based on increased investments will facilitate a more balanced accumulation and development of productivity. This is necessary for the overall and long-term development of the national economy. However the Deng policy of maximization of existing advantages and the open-door policy combine to cause resources to flow from the hinterland provinces to the coastal and more developed regions. Thus the disparities between the better developed and the less developed regions have been growing.

INDUSTRY

Due to the CCP's long-term policy of developing heavy industry at the expense of the people's standard of living, the masses' living standards had been kept at very low levels. This caused their initiative in production to be diminished and production to stagnate. After Deng Xiaoping came to power, the situation improved for a short period of time.

In 1978 investments in industry comprised 54.5 percent of total investments, and those in heavy industry were 8.4 times greater than those in light industry. In 1980 the proportion dropped to 4.4 times, and in 1981 to 3.98 times.

However after 1982, the trend began to reverse, and the proportion rose from 4.58 times in 1982 to 6.3 times in 1983 to 7.1 times in 1984. A slight readjustment occurred in 1985, with the proportion dropping to 6.05 times.

Still despite the decline in the proportion of investments in light industry after 1982, the light industry's growth rate continued to rise, reaching 18.1 percent in 1985. Though there was negative growth in the production of yarn and cloth in 1983 and 1984, the proportion of bicycles, electric appliances, and watches increased rather significantly.

In heavy industry, the production of steel was 30 million tons in 1978 and 50 million tons in 1985. However it still could not meet China's domestic demand. In 1985 steel production increased by 3.1 percent, the lowest growth rate since 1982. In that year China had to import 19 million tons of steel, which accounted for one-third of domestic consumption. This cost a large amount of foreign currency.

The production of coal was 0.6 billion tons in 1978. Growth was slow in 1978–81 but more rapid in 1982–85. Total output increased only by 40 percent from 1978 to 1986, whereas the increase from 1965 to 1978 was 160 percent. The same situation can be found with the output of electricity and oil. Electricity output increased by 280 percent from 1965 to 1978 but only by 70 percent from 1978 to 1986. Oil output increased by 800 percent from 1965 to 1978 but only by 25 percent from 1978 to 1986.

THE TRANSPORT SYSTEM

Railroads remain the central means of land transportation. The series of reforms aimed at alleviating the burdens on the railways were not very successful. The proportion of freight transportation carried by rail rose from 44.2 percent in 1978 to 48.3 percent in 1985, whereas that carried by truck fell from 34.2 percent in 1978 to 28.2 percent in 1985.

Private enterprise has been encouraged by the reforms in road transportation. In 1985 transport vehicles owned by individuals reached 280,000. The turnover of freight carried by vehicles managed by the state transport department increased from 26.8 billion tons/kilometer in 1979 to 35.4 billion tons/kilometer in 1985, an increase of 30 percent. On the other hand, the turnover of freight carried by nonstate managed vehicles (including private vehicles) increased from 47.7 billion tons/kilometer in 1979 to 141.6 billion tons/kilometer in 1985.

It should be noted that the role of the private transportation sector has been increasing significantly in the 1980s.

The same situation can be found in water transportation. By the end of 1985, private boats for water transport reached 200,000, comprising half of the national tonnage.

Air transport remained rather underdeveloped. Its freight volume was only 64,000 tons in 1978, and increased to 195,000 tons in 1985. Despite a two-fold growth, its proportion of total freight volume was less than 0.01 percent.

Undermining State-Owned Enterprises

The impact of the Dengist policy on state-owned enterprises is manifested in the relative number of state-owned enterprises and their proportion of total output.

In 1978 state-owned enterprises comprised 24 percent of all enterprises, but in 1984 their proportion fell to 19.2 percent and rose to only 20.2 percent in 1985. Since 1979 the proportion of output value of the state-owned enterprises has fallen steadily, from 81 percent in 1979 to 70.4 percent in 1985, whereas that of collective enterprises rose from 19 percent to 27 percent and that of foreign-invested enterprises from 0.6 percent to 1.9 percent. Though the output value of state-owned enterprises still comprised the greatest proportion of gross output, its drop is significant and notable since 1983, for it dropped from 77 percent in 1983 to 70.4 percent in 1985. The trend appears to be continuing at the present time.

The Distribution of Capital

In past years the state's investment has been decreasing and scattered. The proportion of financial investment by the central government in total social investment dropped from 53 percent in 1978 to 20 percent in 1985. Private investment, on the other hand, rose to 21 percent (53.5 billion yuan).

More capital is now scattered in society. The proportion of urban and rural savings in state capital rose from 18.8 percent in 1979 to 25.8 percent in 1985. Cash in peasants' possession had increased significantly as a result of rural reforms. In 1985 peasants held 60 percent of the total amount of cash in the market; 65.3 percent of peasant income was in cash. Little productive investment flowed to agriculture. Neither peasants nor local governments showed an interest in agricultural investment. In the Shanxi Province, for example, capital investment in agriculture comprised only 1.6 percent of total capital construction of the province in 1985. Peasants tended to spend more on nonproductive consumption. In Fengyang County, Anhui Province, peasant expenditure on wedding and funeral matters increased 5 to 10 times from 1980 to 1985. Retail sale of commodities to the countryside took up 60 percent of the total amount in 1986. Capital also flowed to developing individually run industrial and commercial enterprises. In 1985 urban and rural private investment was 62.5 billion yuan.

DEVELOPMENT OF INDIVIDUAL ENTERPRISES

Urban and rural laborers employed in individual enterprises increased rapidly from 0.04 percent of the total laboring population to 0.9 percent in 1985. Registered individual enterprises increased from 2.6 million in 1982 to 11.71 billion in 1985, employing 17.66 million people. Over three-quarters of enterprises and laborers were in rural areas. Over half of the enterprises in 1984 were engaged in commerce; 80 percent of all retail shops, restaurants, and services were run by individual enterprises.

The Chinese authorities use the term "individually run enterprises" to designate enterprises not run by the state or the collective, and they avoid using the term "private enterprises." However it is rather difficult to draw a line between "individual" and "collective" enterprises, because the latter may also belong to the category of "private" enterprises. The majority of rural enterprises that flourished in recent years were run by private capital. This type of enterprise formed 72.8 percent of rural enterprises in 1984 and 84.5 percent in 1985. They evidently outnumbered enterprises run by local government authorities. In addition, information shows that some civilian-run enterprises invited local authorities to take some shares. Thus they could obtain the status of "state-run local enterprises" to safeguard their existence.

RURAL ENTERPRISES

A survey on two counties in Fujian Province shows the different trends in the development of rural enterprises. In Jinjiang County, enterprises of collective capital increased rapidly from 2,100 in 1984 to 3,997 in 1985, with a total output value of 187 million yuan in 1984 and 475 million yuan in 1985. In Anqi County, enterprises of individual capital developed more rapidly and increased from 2,489 in 1984 to 4,286 in 1985, with a total output value of 12 million yuan in 1984 and 16 million yuan in 1985. In terms of productivity, the former was higher than the latter by a factor of 1.6.

Rural enterprises have assumed a more important weight in the national economy. By the end of 1985, rural enterprises reached 10.94 million, employing 64.16 million people; the labor force comprised 18 percent of the total rural labor force and 34 percent of the nonagricultural labor force in society. Their total output was 15.3 percent of gross national product and 40 percent of gross rural product.

Rural enterprises depend much on primitive accumulation of capital for expanded reproduction. In 1980–83 of the new capital of 33.2 billion yuan in all rural enterprises, 56.6 percent came from accumulation from within the enterprises, 12.6 percent from funds raised by the enterprises, and 30.8 percent from loans from banks or credit unions.

A significant structural feature of rural enterprises is their small scale. In 1979 nonagricultural rural enterprises employed an average of 22.93 persons per enterprise. The figure was 29 in 1985. If household enterprises and joint-household enterprises are also counted, then the average was 10.61 persons in 1984 and 12.74 persons in 1985. The number of workers varies with different types of enterprises—in 1985 the average was 75.6 persons for construction enterprises and 32.56 persons for industrial enterprises.

WAGE LABOR

From 1979 to 1985, 45.77 million people had shifted from agricultural to nonagricultural activities. Every year 6 million people left their villages to work as temporary workers. About 1 million new employees every year were recruited from the peasantry. In general terms, since 1979, 20 percent of rural laborers had changed their place of employment or residence or their actual social status. The shift of labor is more remarkable in more developed regions. For example in Jiangsu Province, the agricultural labor force dropped from 71 percent in 1979 to 45 percent in 1986; in the suburban regions of Shanghai, only 35.4 percent of labor was still devoted to agriculture.

Rural enterprises absorbed much of the rural surplus labor. According to statistics from 1970 to 1978, the average increase of new rural labor was 2 million per year; from 1978 to 1983, the figure was 6 million. In regions where rural enterprises were particularly flourishing, surplus labor began to run out. For example in cities or counties like Changshu, Wushi, and Shazhou in Jiangsu and Henan Provinces, about 75 percent of the rural workers had entered industry, and surplus labor began to run out. Tens of thousands of laborers had to be recruited from other provinces every year.

Large numbers of wage laborers came to be employed by privately run enterprises. A survey of specialized households in the whole country engaged in the second and third industries in 1985 found that for households employing over eight workers or apprentices, the average number of workers employed was 10.97 persons. Their total assets were estimated to be 1 billion yuan. Another survey shows that in Wenzhou City, household industries grew rapidly in the recent years. Some households had capital of over 1 million yuan. In the rural regions of Wenzhou City, 13,125 households employed laborers totaling 42,163 persons; 120 households employed over 30 workers, and 1 enterprise employed 110 workers.

Another nationally known example is the case of Guan Guangmei of Benqi City, Liaoning Province. Guan was formerly a saleswoman. In 1985 she leased a subsidiary food store and later bid on seven more food stores. The chain employed over one thousand workers. Its total sales were one-third of the city's total retail sales of subsidiary food, and its profit was half of the city's total profit from retail sales.

INCOME DISCREPANCY

Social differentiation has increased. As an example Guan Guangmei's personal income was twenty times that of her employees, and it reached an accumulated legal income of 44,000 yuan. The former CCP secretary Hu Yaobang said to foreign journalists in November 1986 that some entrepreneurs in China earned an annual income equaling that of Ronald Reagan—U.S. $200,000.

"Ten Thousand Yuan Households" have also been increasing, though official propaganda is now downplaying them. A survey of households engaged in individual economic activities in Changchun City shows that their minimum monthly average income was 250 to 300 yuan, which was above the maximum average monthly income of staff in state-owned or collective units. Ninety percent of households engaged in individual commercial or industrial activities for over two years in the city's Guangfu Road Market had become Ten Thousand Yuan Households; some even became Hundred Thousand Yuan Households.

According to the *Shanghai Industrial Economic Journal* of July 1987, taxpaying households in individual trade in Shanghai had an average monthly income of 307 yuan, which was 1.3 times higher than the average income of staff in state-owned enterprises and 1.7 times higher than staff in collective enterprises.

Another survey also finds a serious discrepancy in income. The Nanjing Commercial and Industrial Management Bureau conducted a survey of almost one-half million households in individual trade and found that the average annual income was around 4,000 yuan; 1,387 households had an income of 5,000 to 10,000 yuan, and 52 households had an income of 20,000 to 50,000 yuan.

It should also be noted that loansharking is being revived in the countryside. The *Northeast Collective Economic Journal* reported that the authorities had conducted a survey of the rural villages and found that in some villages over 70 percent of the households were in debt, and private loan interest rates rose from the former 1 to 2 percent to 9 to 10 percent, which was nine to fifteen times higher than the state regulated rate of 0.66 percent.

CHANGES IN OWNERSHIP

In the countryside collective property forms have undergone fundamental changes: (1) Collectively owned fixed assets (almost all farmland and a considerable part of pastures and forests) have been contracted to peasant households;

after 1984 the lease period was extended to over fifteen years. In 1985 total
farmland was estimated to be worth 2 trillion yuan, and every peasant household
on the average had land worth 10,500 yuan. (2) Collectively owned farm
animals and large and medium farm tools have gradually been sold to individual peasants. It is estimated that by the end of 1985 over 20 billion yuan
worth of collective property had been transferred to individual peasant households. (3) Fixed assets originally belonging to commune-run enterprises have
partly been contracted to the collectives or the managers and partly to production brigades or peasants in the form of shares or cash.

By the end of 1985, property relations in rural China had been transformed in the following ways: total property in the countryside was valued
at about 3 trillion yuan. Land valued at 2 trillion yuan belonged to the
collective and was contracted to peasant households. Of the productive fixed
assets valued at 270 billion yuan, 42.43 percent belonged to the former
collective, and the rest was owned in different private forms. Of the nonproductive resident houses, valued at 500 billion yuan, 90.6 percent belonged to peasant households. Peasants held over 60 percent of the 200
billion yuan in savings in cash or in kind.

The property rights of peasants have been consciously promoted by the
authorities. At present 62.42 percent of peasant property is in the form of
nonproductive estate; productive fixed assets only account for 20.79 percent. Of private productive fixed assets, 57.4 percent are farm animals and
large tools and pieces of farm machinery. Total peasant assets amounted to
700 billion yuan in 1985, 1.68 times higher than in 1981.

THE RISE OF THE SHAREHOLDING SYSTEM

What is notable in the countryside is the expanded reproduction of capital
by means of combination of capital or of shares. Around 1980 the shareholding
system began to be introduced in some production brigades in Gansu, Shaanxi,
and Jiangsu Provinces. By the end of 1984, the practice of shareholding in
enterprises was already quite prevalent in such provinces as Henan, Shanxi,
Shaanxi, Gansu, Anhui, and Shandong. In the southern provinces, the system of dividends had become a prevalent form of capital accumulation.

In one form of capital combination, the rich households emerge as big
shareholders and mobilize other peasants to join with smaller holdings. In
Cizao Township, Jinjiang County, about 90 percent of the households
were shareholders.

This new trend of stockholder-owned enterprises is spreading very quickly
and surpassing the development of industrial and commercial enterprises run
by individuals. Comparing September 1985 with June 1984, enterprises formed
by combining capital increased from 3,374 to 5,524, with an increase of

from 50,000 to 90,000 people employed. There are different forms of shareholding—with provision of capital, technology, factory, or labor. There is no limit on the number of shares. Most adopt the form of receiving dividends.

According to statistics, even with enterprises that distribute dividends based on labor, the dividends from capital are much higher in both absolute amount and in proportion. The Chuiping Food Canning Factory in Mashengqiao Brigade, Ji County, Tianjin City, is one example. In 1983 four peasants set up the factory with an investment of 500 yuan from each. Villagers were employed in production with an average monthly wage and bonus of 55 yuan. At the end of the year, the profits were divided in the following proportion: 30 percent accumulation, 30 percent dividend for capital shareholders, and 40 percent for labor shareholders. In 1984 the profit was 72,000 yuan. Each worker obtained a labor dividend of 230 yuan; each capital shareholder received 5,000 yuan, which was over twenty times higher than the workers' dividend. In addition the accumulation fund in fact belonged to the investors.

The State Council issued documents providing that dividends should be based mainly on labor contribution, that dividends on capital should not exceed 15 percent of the share capital, and that the remaining profit should be divided into a central provident fund, a welfare fund, and dividends on labor contribution, with the proportion negotiated by all members of the enterprise. Yet the practice is not so. In the above case, the dividends on capital contribution was 1,000 percent, not 15 percent, of the capital invested.

Spurred on by the law of the market, many consortia run by joint stock or joint capital have developed across regions and across sectors. There are even chains of consortia combining state-owned enterprises and private enterprises. For example the "Er Qi" Motor Group consisted of 148 factories and cooperated with a further thousand or so rural enterprises, the latter producing a certain spare part for the Motor Group with their characteristic small scale, wide distribution, and cheap labor. The same form of operation existed with the "Standard" Sewing Machine Group of Shaanxi Province and the "White Orchid" Washing Machine Group of Beijing.

The newly developed chains of consortia in Suzhou, Changzhou, and Wushi include horizontally different sectors such as science and technology, education, finance, circulation, foreign trade, and transportation, and vertically different levels ranging from national companies to enterprises on the provincial, county, township, and village levels, and even up to specialized households. They have their own agricultural food base; they have their own links with the foreign market, and some groups (such as the "Gold Lion" Group in Changzhou) even planned to set up their own banks to manage financial matters within the consortium.

These types of consortia—which are rather similar to trusts—are developing from the former combination of strong and weak enterprises to the new combination of strong enterprises, and they are even developing toward monopoly. The chains sell shares, and even state-owned enterprises have their assets estimated and then sell shares to facilitate the allocation of dividends. In Wushi City the "Plum Blossom" Group had each share worth 100,000 yuan. In the first phase, the major member factories invested a total of 4 million yuan. Those holding two shares were directors; those with over five shares could be chief or deputy chief directors. The "Great Wall" Group of Suzhou City had a capital investment of eight million yuan. The "Gold Lion" Group of Changzhou had in the first phase a total capitalization of 5 million yuan, and the shares could be sold or transferred. It should be noted that the "Gold Lion" Group was not only related to markets, harbors, and train stations through joint investments but also joined capital with foreign investors.

Figure 1 shows the magnitude of such groups.

	Number of Consortia	Number of Member Enterprises	Total Output Value in 1985 (Billion Yuan)	Percentage of the Region's Output Value*
Changzhou	56	443	3.38	32.86
Wushi	14	217	3.68	25
Suzhou	31	218	3.42	17.7

*Not including output value of village enterprises
Source: Economic Research 5 (1987): 54.

In these consortia chains, the key enterprises are in general state-owned enterprises. State ownership is constantly being undermined. Some state-owned enterprises practice a lease system and are in transition to the system of enterprise ownership. For example the Shenyang Motor Industry Factory has leased twenty-one subsidiary factories, one of which had over one thousand workers. The system of assigning the responsibility to the factory directors also hands over the right of operation and management to factory directors or managers through the system of lease. According to People's Daily, June 3, 1987, incomplete statistics by the CCP Central Propaganda Department show that about three thousand state-owned enterprises have practiced contracting or leasing. The share system is also being introduced into state-owned enterprises. In July 1984 the "Tian Giao" Shopping Arcade in Beijing announced that it would raise capital from the general public in share form. It was the precedent of state-owned enterprises raising capital from the public. Soon afterward state enterprises in Guangdong, Shandong, Liaoning, Shanghai, and Zhejiang followed the example and issued shares or bonds to their own staff and to the public. In 1986 some enterprises obtained the permission of their superiors to issue bonds or shares through the bank, without a limit on the number of shares, so a shareholder could hold shares of several thousand or several tens of thousands of yuan. Both bonds and shares could be sold or transferred on the open market at a price higher or lower than the surface value.

Xue Muqiao, a prominent CCP economist, took pains to argue that the form is still a socialist one:

> Since the shareholders are not laborers of the enterprise, there is no limit on the number of shares held by each person, and the shareholders receive dividends according to their capital; hence, these share companies are apparently similar to share companies in capitalist society, and they have certain capitalist nature in them. However, in China, the initiators of such companies are often the state institutions or state-owned enterprises or may be state banks, and not big capitalists or consortia of capitalists, thus the right of operation and management is still in the hands of the initiators, and the socialist nature is still predominant.

He added, "issuance of shares within a state-owned enterprise can be experimented, but it should not develop to the sage of changing the nature of public ownership." Xue stated that he was opposed to proposals to assign ownership of the enterprise to the enterprise or the individual staff members of the enterprise.

In the past two years, controversies have arisen among CCP economists as to the definition of the new forms of ownership—for example whether the new economic consortia are cooperative companies or share companies. There are different views as to whether the development of the individual economy toward capitalism should be restrained or encouraged. Some economists even propose that the abstract form of worker ownership should be concretized by dividing the greater part of the assets of state-owned enterprises into worker ownership coupons and allocated to the staff according to their rank and years of service, and the rest would be regarded as state investment to be repaid by the enterprise. Once the amount is repaid, enterprise ownership can be established.

Such daring proposals for changing the form of ownership of state enterprises are still under discussion and not actually practiced on a wide scale. Still their appearance in the CCP journal of economic theory, *Economic Research*, shows that the authorities have such changes under consideration.

THE IMPACT OF THE MARKET ECONOMY ON AGRICULTURE

When market mechanisms are introduced, the flow of capital inevitably gets beyond the control of the planned economy. The disparity in the profit rates in different regions or sectors causes capital to concentrate in certain areas. Because the rate of profit from investment in agriculture is low and unstable, capital flows away from this sector. This is the major reason for a continual reduction in capital investment in agriculture.

One consequence is the instability caused to the national economy. Grain output dropped a sudden 7 percent in 1985 after an increase of 5.1 percent in 1984. Such vacillation is abnormal. The development of the commodity economy replaces unpaid labor by paid labor, and collective irrigation work is reduced due to the lack of money to hire labor. In 1981–84 irrigated land decreased by 7.3 million mu. The reduction of the capacity to resist natural disasters brings serious economic losses. The Liao River flood in 1985 could have been prevented if 20 million yuan in repair work had been done, but the authorities concerned refused to allocate this sum. Just the cost of repairing engineering works that were washed away amounted to 200 million yuan.

Now expanded reproduction relies on accumulation by the peasants. It is estimated that for fulfillment of the Seventh Five-Year Plan, 100 billion yuan in agricultural investment is required. If average peasant net income can reach 560 yuan as projected by the plan (the 1986 figure was 424 yuan), the maximum investment from within the agricultural sector can be 50 billion yuan; 10 billion yuan is expected from rural industries, 10 billion yuan from local authorities, and 14.68 billion only from the state. Still the necessary amount will not be raised. Moreover part of the 50 billion yuan in agricultural investment expected from peasants will be invested in nonagricultural production.

Another consequence of the market economy on agricultural development is in land use. Large areas of land have been withdrawn from cultivation. Since 1978 the cultivated area has been decreasing. If 1952 is established as index 100, the 1978 figure was 106.3, and the 1983 figure was 101.9.

Another worrying phenomenon is the use of land by industries. Since 1979 land taken up by rural enterprises was about 100 million mu, which was 25 million mu more than the total area of land the state had taken over in three decades.

THE IMPACT OF THE MARKET ECONOMY ON INDUSTRY

Due to the limited capital of individual households, most rural industries are small in size with much lower efficiency than big enterprises. This causes a waste of resources and an increase in production costs. According to the *1986 Statistical Yearbook of China*, rural industries' productivity in 1985 was only 34.5 percent of that of state-owned industries. In the case of bicycle production, small enterprises' production costs were double those of large enterprises. The Department of Light Industry estimated that eight efficient factories, each producing 3 million bicycles a year, can meet the national demand, yet China now has 140 factories manufacturing bicycles.

In order to lower production costs, many small enterprises produce sub-standard goods. The situation is particularly serious in the sector producing capital goods. In Yongjia County the pass rate for various kinds of valves was lower than 20 percent. The quality of electrical goods produced in Liu Township in Leqing County is worse. None of the twenty-two samples of eight types of electrical on-off switches produced by the Township's ten factories managed to pass the state test.

The arbitrary development of industries also creates ecological problems. Pollution by millions of sewer pipes and chimneys is critical. Labor-intensive industries retard the advancement of technology. Small industries compete for energy and raw materials.

Small enterprises survive partly because they fill the gaps left by big- and medium-sized enterprises and partly because they have the protection of local governments that illegally set up internal barriers to prevent resources such as raw materials from flowing to other regions and to prevent goods from flowing in. Regionalism is serious. For example in Shanxi Province, the price of imported coal in the free market is three times higher than that of locally produced coal. The bureaucrats, in control of the transport system, often refuse transport of goods that compete with their "own" factories. Herein is reflected the contradiction between local interests and state interests.

In recent years there has been a decrease in the number of enterprises. An article in *Economic Research*, no. 4 of 1987, said that under fierce competition, relatively backward rural enterprises are being eliminated. In the early 1980s, their output value on the average doubled every two years. Recently their rate of profit has gone below that of state-owned enterprises; in 1985 the former was around 9 percent, and the latter was around 15 percent.

OPENING UP TO FOREIGN CAPITAL

The introduction of foreign capital and the opening of China to the West are important elements of the Dengist economic reform.

From 1979 to June 1986, aggregate inflow of international capital amounted to U.S. $24.88 billion, of which $6.69 billion was direct investment and $18.19 billion was foreign loans.

However in China's international balance, capital outflow from China in the three years from 1982 to 1984 was U.S. $9.8 billion, which was 96.8 percent of capital inflow. In 1984 the outflow was greater. If both long-term and short-term capital were counted, the total capital inflow for the three years was U.S. $10.7 billion, and the outflow was U.S. $11.6 billion. Together with the item "errors and miscalculations," which showed a capital outflow of U.S. $1.019 billion, the total net capital outflow was U.S. $1.919 billion.[7]

The quantity of foreign capital is not satisfactory; neither is the quality. Most foreign capital is concentrated in nonproductive sectors like tourism and estates and in general industries like textile and household electrical appliances. Little capital is invested in priority industries. From the technological point of view, most foreign capital is invested in labor-intensive industries and the products intended for domestic consumption. Thus it cannot meet the expectation of introducing advanced technology and aiding China in earning foreign currency from exports.

To open up to the West, four Special Economic Zones (SEZ) were set up in 1980 in Guangdong and Fujian Provinces. In 1984, fourteen coastal cities were opened. Under the law of market value, major resources in the whole country (capital, technology, and specialists) flow to this coastal zone, causing this zone of 200 million inhabitants to reproduce over half of the nation's total agricultural and industrial output. Its disparity with the hinterland is widening. The speedy economic development of the coastal regions is partly due to the inflow of foreign capital but largely due to their existing economic base and domestic forces. For example, the Shenzhen SEZ was set up to attract foreign capital, but foreign capital only accounted for 30 percent of Shenzhen's construction capital.

It is also necessary to point out that though foreign capital provides jobs for Chinese workers, surplus value is being drained out. In Guangdong Province, about nine thousand enterprises work on processing and assembling for Hong Kong and Macao factories. Almost 1 million workers are thus employed. It is estimated that China's labor cost is thirty times lower than the average wage in comparable industries in advanced capitalist countries and several times lower than in Southeast Asia.[8]

FOREIGN TRADE

From 1978 to 1986, China had a trade surplus only in the years 1981, 1982, and 1983. The trade deficits for the next three years were, respectively, U.S. $0.94 billion, $8.416 billion, and $12 billion. The official explanation was that China had increased her imports of production equipment and market goods.

In 1985 the government tightened its control over the currency, foreign currency, and trade to resume control.

China's exports are basically manufactured goods (textiles), minerals, fuels (petroleum), food, and livestock. Textiles accounted for 15.1 percent of total export in 1984, and petroleum accounted for 18.9 percent. Imports are basically machinery and chemicals. Steel constituted 16 percent and chemicals 11.7 percent.

In reviewing China's major problems in foreign trade in 1985, the authorities pointed out that there was blind introduction of automobiles and high-class consumer goods and repetitive introduction of assembly lines for TV sets, refrigerators, and washing machines, etc.

In general the pattern of China's foreign trade resembles the unequal exchange between backward countries and advanced countries.

Concerning China's trading partners, from 1978 to 1985, her major trading partners were the industrially advanced countries. The proportion of her trade with countries with central planning fell from 14.1 percent to 8.3 percent. Imports from Hong Kong and Macao rose significantly, from 0.7 percent to 15.2 percent. This indicates that Hong Kong and Macao have become convenient entrances into china for foreign goods.

The above are official figures. The authorities admit that much illegal trade has been going on. The extent of the losses suffered by the state on illegal trade is unknown.

SUMMARY

This chapter has attempted to collect data on China's economic development from 1978 to 1986 to provide readers with a preliminary understanding of the Dengist economic reform. It is necessary to point out that it is not a comprehensive review; it only focuses on certain new phenomena in China and points out some unresolved or newly evolved problems.

Many important questions have not been addressed in the chapter, notably the following: due to the lack of democratic workers' control, serious economic losses caused by bureaucratic command (such as the construction of the Shanghai Baoshan Steel Factory or the sinking of the Bohai No. 2 oil driller); serious wastage caused by bureaucratism (for example effective utilization of state-owned industries is only about two-thirds; 15 percent of the 28.5 million tons of steel stored in warehouses at the end of 1986 was substandard); large expenses of the redundant bureaucratic administration; and notorious corruption.

We have also not discussed the question of the motive force behind Deng's reform—not socialist democracy nor workers' self-management but the replacement of the bureaucracy by the technocracy. In the cities the reform relies on the technical management strata and the so-called "entrepreneurs"; in the countryside the reform relies on the able, the rich. This question must be scrutinized when one compares and contrasts the Dengist line with the Maoist line.

In comparing the two different economic lines divided by the year 1978, it can be seen that while the Dengist line frees production from certain restraints of the Maoist line, new contradictions have been fostered behind the apparently active economic scene:

- The contract responsibility system alleviates the stranglehold on peasant incentive in production, yet grain output only increased by 28 percent from 1978 to 1986. The cultivated area has decreased, and the tractor-plowed area has decreased. In 1986 total horsepower of agricultural machinery doubled from that of 1978, yet most of the increase was in transportation and rural industries.
- The peasants enjoy more freedom in cultivating cash crops and in subsidiary production; hence supply and peasant income have increased. However the law of market value affects prices, and supply is at one time in surplus and at another in shortage. Urban residents are discontented with rising prices, and the peasants also suffer losses.
- Rural industries flourish and provide jobs that absorb much rural labor. It can no longer be claimed that China has 800 million peasants. In 1985 the urban population was 380 million, and rural population was 660 million, of which 20 percent was engaged in nonagricultural production. The rural industries also increase the supply of commodities to the countryside. Yet from the point of view of rational national planning and allocation of resources, the existence of many rural industries is unjustified.
- The regime negates its previous line of "poor communism" under the slogan of "getting rich"; some people indeed prosper, and private economy has been developing quickly. The process of primitive capital accumulation has started, but it seems the government's expectation that those who get rich first will help the poorer ones to get rich has not materialized. Instead of everyone getting rich, large numbers of wage laborers have emerged, and class differentiation is intensifying. Capital is also concentrating under the law of competition and elimination.
- The reform in state-owned enterprises hands power to the managers and the technical strata. The right of ownership is first separated from the right of management, and then the shareholding system is introduced. On the part of the workers, the contract system is introduced (in 1986 there were 5.18 million contract workers in state-owned enterprises, an increase of 56 percent over 1985). Wage disparities are widened, and piecework is introduced. This reform is in the initial stages, but it has already met with worker resistance.

Under old and new contradictions, the following imbalances need urgent resolution:

- Supply of goods and consumer demand;
- Total amount of goods and total money income of the people;
- Total investment and total production;
- Quantitative increase of goods and qualitative improvement;
- Improvement of productivity;
- Amount and types of export and amount and types of import;
- Average income of peasants and average income of workers;
- Wealth of owners of capital and property and wealth of wage laborers;

• Development of poor hinterland provinces and development of coastal provinces.

By reducing the role of planning and increasing the role of market mechanisms, greater imbalances are inevitable. This is reflected in periodic soaring of prices, budget deficits, decreases in foreign currency reserves, unemployment, and intensification of social inequalities. The bureaucracy in power can simply adjust and readjust from time to time, but it cannot propose a radical solution. The socialist principle of planning and the capitalist principle of market mechanisms are not, as the CCP theorists claim, complementary; in fact they are hostile opposites. To borrow the capitalist "panacea" to cure the stifling "planning" under the bureaucratic dictatorship, as the Deng faction has attempted over the past eight years, can only give temporary symptomatic relief while in fact aggravating the severe illness.

Notes

1. "China's Rural Economy," no. 2 (1986).
2. "Economic Research," no. 1 (1987): 11.
3. Michel Chossudovsky, "Towards Capitalist Restoration?—Chinese Socialism after Mao," 59.
4. The Gini coefficient is a measure of the degree of inequality: its value can range from zero, indicating complete equality, to one, indicating that all income is accruing to a single recipient.
5. Chossudovsky, "Towards Capitalist Restoration?" 63–64.
6. Due to the lack of space, the table showing the regional disparities cannot be reproduced here. Readers can refer to the table in *October Review* (May/June 1987): 25. The five columns are, respectively, Provinces/Major Cities; per capita industrial output; per capita agricultural output; per capita income of peasant families; average workers' wages (the first two subcolumns are 1981 state-owned enterprises; 1981 collective enterprises); per capita income of worker families. The thirty rows are, respectively, Provinces/Major cities; Shanghai; Beijing; Tianjin; Liaoning; Heilongjiang, Jiangsu; Jilin; Gansu; Shanxi; Shandong; Hubei; Zhejiang; Hebei; Ningxia; Shaanxi; Guangdong; Ginghai; Hunan; Inner Mongolia; Fujian; Guangxi; Xinjiang; Sichuan; Jiangxi; Anhui; Henan; Yunnan; Guizhou; Tibet. The national average is 100.
7. See *Economic Daily* (September 2, 1985), quoting figures of the State Foreign Currency Management Bureau.
8. Chossudovsky, "Towards Capitalist Restoration?" 149, 178.

3

A Critique of the Rural Reform after 1978

XIAO DIAN

Since the launching of the rural reform at the end of 1978, major changes have taken place in China's countryside. Official figures show an extraordinary 9.48 percent average annual increase in total agricultural output from 1979 to 1984, and 17.1 percent in 1984. Nonagricultural enterprises began to develop in the countryside after 1979, reaching a climax in 1984 and 1985. The average annual increase of the output value of rural enterprises was 40 percent to 50 percent. In 1985 reform on the unified purchase of subsidiary products spurred the production of meat, seafood, and vegetables, along with a high rate of price increases.

However after 1985 the rate of growth in the rural economy gradually slowed, marking the end of the previous period of rapid growth. The rate of growth was 1.6 percent for 1985, 3.5 percent for 1986, and 4.7 percent for 1987. Yet the strong impact of the rural economy on the national economy as a whole has not weakened; the CCP is forced to carry out more radical reforms in industry and prices, which triggers off an acute social crisis.

It is therefore necessary to analyze the changes in the rural economy since 1978.

BACKGROUND TO THE 1978 RURAL REFORM

In 1978 after two decades of harm caused by the fickle rural policies of the Mao Zedong period, the rural economy was in a state of stagnation. Per capita net income of peasants was 134 yuan (RMB) a year, that is, $0.40 a day. Compared with the 73 yuan a year in 1957, the average annual increase was only 2.9 percent. The peasant household had on average 32 yuan of savings, 30 catties of reserved grain, and less than 500 yuan in the value of its house. About 200 million peasants lived below the poverty line.

84

There are several reasons for this phenomenon, but the basic problem is the very low initiative for production among the peasants. The fact that peasant productivity on collective land was only one-fifth to one-seventh that of productivity on their own pieces of land is eloquent testimony.

Peasant initiative was low mainly because of the egalitarianism of the People's Commune Policy. The collectivism imposed on peasants went beyond the subjective cognition of peasants and objective agricultural levels of productivity. In addition party bureaucrats were arbitrary and repressive, causing peasants to feel divorced from the land, the means of production, and the end product.

Another reason is the CCP's Stalinist policy of stressing heavy industry and ignoring light industry and agriculture. This contrasts with the Leninist and Trotskyist policy of even development of industry and agriculture. The CCP, by the scissors difference between industrial and agricultural prices, maintained low wages and low costs of raw materials for big industries, thus obtaining funds for the building of heavy industry. For long periods agriculture has lacked the funds for reinvestment.

To maintain this policy, the CCP carried out a series of measures in production. It made land collectively owned, forbade land transactions, and bound peasants to the land by household registration. In distribution it maintained low purchase prices and supplied low-cost agricultural equipment. In circulation it imposed a state monopoly and closed down free markets, restricted interregional trade, and controlled prices.

The result of these measures was the bondage of 800 million peasants to the land, with per capita farmland being one-half hectare only. It was a waste of labor resources and an obstacle to mechanization and effective management of farmland. Peasants did not have the right to leave the land or to decide what they grew. When the rural economy was stifled, the potential of machines and transport produced by industry could not be put to use.

DENG'S RURAL REFORM POLICY

At the end of 1978, the CCP faction in power, headed by Deng, promoted a rural reform. With the household as the basic unit, collectively owned land was contracted to peasant households; collectively owned animals and machinery were either sold or allocated to peasant households; and commune-run enterprises were either contracted to the enterprise collective or manager or distributed to peasants in the form of shares. Almost all peasants responded in favor of changing the people's commune system.

The state recognized the right of peasants to own property and accumulate private wealth. The state also allowed peasants the right to engage in

different economic activities; thus peasants had the freedom to change their
social status. The status of brigade-run and privately run enterprises was
confirmed. The right to use land could be transferred, peasants could go to
the city, the market was reopened, and the monopoly of trade by state-
owned enterprises was ended. These measures laid the basis for the restoration and expansion of market mechanisms.

In 1979 and 1980 the CCP also increased purchase prices of agricultural
products, and peasants had better income to conduct primitive accumulation and expand their consumption. This helped stimulate peasant initiative
for production.

Under the rubric of giving aid to specialized households so that those
getting rich first could aid the rest, the state provided loans, technical help,
and priority in purchasing their products to the specialized and able households. Regions originally better off, such as the coastal provinces, benefited
from this policy and produced quite a number of 10,000-yuan households.

The CCP also encouraged, especially through loans, the growth of rural
industries in the form of cooperative or private enterprises. This led to a
rapid growth in rural industry, commerce, and services.

INITIAL ACHIEVEMENTS OF THE REFORM

Extensive changes in the countryside resulted from the reform. From 1979
to 1984 the average annual increase in agricultural output was 9.48 percent,
higher than the 8.96 percent of total social output. Grain output increased
by an annual 4.95 percent, though grain farming area decreased by a total of
6.4 percent. From 1978 to 1986 per capita peasant income increased from
134 yuan to 424 yuan, a 320 percent increase. Although this was still only
half of the income of workers, the difference had diminished. It was estimated that in 1985, peasant households on average owned fixed assets, cash,
savings, and reserved grain totaling over 3,800 yuan. However, due to discrepancies in peasant income, the gap between the income of the 10 percent to 15 percent of peasants who had the lowest income (about 100 million)
and the rest had widened.

A major achievement of the reform was the transformation of a larger
sector of the rural economy from a small peasant economy to a commodity
economy, creating a social division of labor and thus laying the basis for
raising agricultural productivity. From 1978 to 1985 the total amount of
subsidiary foods purchased doubled. The commodity rate of rural products
was 64 percent, and peasant cash income on average constituted 65 percent
of peasant income. Peasants had over 50 percent of total purchasing power
in society, and 60 percent retail amount of commodities was sold in rural
areas (compared with 52 percent in 1978).

Major changes also occurred in the rural labor force. Between 1979 and 1985, 45.77 million rural workers changed to nonagricultural activities. The urban population increased by a net 127 million persons, and, in addition, over 1 million migrant workers stayed in the cities to find a living. Every year 6 million people left the countryside for temporary work. In sum about one-fifth of the rural labor force had changed their work, residence, or social status.

The CCP's unequivocal support of rural enterprises in 1984 spurred their rapid development. The output value of rural enterprises constituted 44 percent of total rural output value and 17 percent of total national output value. They provided 64.16 million jobs and helped free 17.3 percent of the rural workers from the land.

ANALYSIS OF THE ACHIEVEMENTS

How have the reform's achievements been brought about? Are they the positive results of the Deng policy? Are they a negation of the policy of the Mao Zedong period? It must not be forgotten that the present leadership also supported and implemented the Mao Zedong line and cannot shirk its responsibility for the state of affairs caused by the past policy. To look at the question more profoundly, has the political system that facilitated the implementation of the past (and present) policies changed because of the Dengist reform?

The Deng faction discarded the people's commune system and directly connected the peasants to the fruit of their labor through the household responsibility system. This helped raise the peasants' initiative for production and caused labor intensity to rise. This is the primary reason for the growth in agricultural production. This confirms in the negative that compulsion of and forced appropriation from the peasants can only lead to passive resistance, stagnation in rural productivity, and a heavy cost paid by the whole of society. The forced collectivization in the Soviet Union in the 1920s and the communalization in China in the 1950s brought about extremely serious consequences. CCP theorists only recognize the truth today that the transformation of the peasants cannot be forced.

The increase in agricultural products' purchasing prices allows capital accumulation by the peasants and a development toward industry, commerce, and subsidiary farming. With some peasants freed from the land, concentration of land has started, and mechanization has been possible. Productivity per hectare has been increased.

Another factor for the active rural economy is the growth of individual and family enterprises and rural enterprises. The previous policy neglected the consumption needs of the rural and urban population, and so there was a strong potential demand for agricultural and subsidiary products, consumer goods, and various services. The shortage of consumer goods and services had caused society to accumulate a great deal of purchasing power. When the administrative constraints were lifted, the demand and purchasing power propelled a rapid development of economic activity.

Some household industries took off from a very primitive basis, making use of waste materials from the productive process; despite low quality they could meet the low standard demand in the countryside. Later they improved technology and mechanization, raising their productivity. Thus potential or wasted social material and technological conditions were used to help rural industries develop quickly from a very low level. Improvements in agriculture were partly the result of stressing and employing agricultural technology, knowledge, and new species.

The three decades of industrial and technological development in China has provided the necessary material conditions for the development of rural industries (such as medium and small tractors, raw materials for industrial production, insecticide, chemical fertilizers, etc.). Without these objective conditions, the rural economy could never have developed at such a speed.

To sum up the Dengist rural reform rectified the extremely irrational pre-1978 rural policy and to a certain extent removed past constraints on peasant initiative. Propelled by a massive social demand and unused purchasing power, relying on a free market and coordinated by existing but not yet rationally used social material conditions, technology, and potential for production, compensatory rapid development of the rural economy was spurred. This is the secret behind the initial successes of the Dengist reform. The rapid rural development cannot be credited to the Dengist policy.

ADVERSE DEVELOPMENTS IN RURAL REFORM

Since the rise in agricultural production in 1979–84 was basically not due to the increase in productivity and was, on the other hand, a make-up for the big gap left by the wrong policy of the past, thus in 1984, when the peasants' labor intensity reached a peak, when grain production reached the highest level in history and a temporary overproduction of grain appeared, when overproduction caused grain prices to drop drastically, peasants felt difficulty in selling grain, and some were attracted to other subsidiary farming and nonagricultural activities. Peasants reduced the farming area and also reduced their labor in agriculture. This led to a reversal in grain production after 1984.

From 1978 to 1984, grain production per hectare increased every year, offsetting the reduction in farming area. In 1985 grain production per hectare decreased, and with a rapid reduction in farming area, total output decreased by 7 percent. Total grain output in the next two years did not rise to the 1984 level. The instability in grain production cannot be settled easily.

The good 1984 grain harvest caused the price to drop by 12.5 percent in the free market, lower than the state purchasing price. The state's unified purchase became a serious subsidy and a heavy burden for the state. It also caused a crisis in storage. Under such circumstances, the CCP announced in 1985 that unified purchase by the state would be canceled and would be replaced by the contract system.

This policy soon met with difficulties. Due to reduced grain production, the grain price in the free market rose higher than the contract price, and peasants were unwilling to sign contracts. Faced with this crisis, the CCP resorted to administrative measures and announced that contract purchase was under the category of command planning, and peasants had to fulfill the submission despite their reluctance. At the same time, in some regions the free market was restricted, and interregional trade of grain was forbidden. This led to peasant grievances. This shows CCP arbitrariness in policy changes and also the fragility of the policy.

The rural reform has caused the rural economy to produce anarchically for the market. Often a whole village turns to production of a certain crop or product, and production suffers from market fluctuations. The bureaucrats cannot provide guidance; on the contrary they encourage peasants and enterprises in anarchic production. As a result there is serious overproduction of certain products and serious underproduction of other products. The peasants become the main victims. This is just the opposite of the CCP's original intention of having the peasants respond in a timely way to society's needs through market mechanisms.

Another aim of the reform was to promote specialization in the countryside, so that the able could help raise productivity. However rural specialization reached the highest level of 2 percent in 1984 (the number of specialized households among peasant households) but fell to 1.7 percent in 1985, showing a reverse trend. This might be due to too much risk in market vacillations, hence peasants felt it safer to spread the risk out.

Another phenomenon that ran contrary to Dengist expectations has been the failure of the price of subsidiary foods and consumer goods to drop, even though their amount has increased. One reason is that circulation and transport facilities are insufficient; hence monopolistic superprofits can be earned in the transport and retail sectors. Quite a number of products are still in shortage, so there is hoarding and speculation. Another important reason is that various levels of bureaucrats arbitrarily demand fees and taxes, obstructing the links between production and circulation by various pretexts, to increase government revenue and personal income. Regionalism flourishes, and the direct and indirect losses caused by customs duties and retention of goods lead to a big difference between the market prices of goods and the selling prices obtained by peasants. Both peasants and consumers are victims.

NEGATIVE EFFECTS OF THE RURAL REFORM

The reform cannot fulfil the initial expectations, and some negative effects and underlying crises have developed.

On the national level, though the number of tractors had increased substantially, they were basically medium and small tractors; tractor-plowed areas had decreased, reflecting the decrease in the use of large tractors. There were also the visible and invisible social costs—machinery depreciation, fuel, insecticide, and air pollution. Thus the overall efficiency of mechanized farming was reduced. When the peasants were still enthusiastic in production, this deficiency could be offset. But when the peasants' enthusiasm was affected due to the development of market production and other nonagricultural activities, the consequences and long-term effects of this regression would be more pronounced.

Irrigation work had not developed because the state had reduced investments and the peasants were unwilling to provide uncompensated labor. Long-term negligence and desertion would seriously affect China's capacity to resist natural disasters and incur inestimable losses. This is a question that merits much concern, because the climate on this planet is changing drastically, and droughts, floods, and storms are much more frequent. Lately the droughts and floods that the Chinese authorities stressed were not unrelated to the drop in the efficiency of irrigation works.

Another underlying long-term crisis is the question of protecting the fertility of land and the water, soil, and forest resources. Peasants who contract land and forests tried to obtain the maximum profits during the period of contract. This would in the long run gravely affect the productivity of land and forest resources. For this reason the CCP gradually extended the contract period to over fifteen years and hoped that the peasants could consciously protect the land and forest resources, but this is by no means a positive solution. The peasants were wary of the fickleness of CCP policies and would still try to squeeze the maximum amount of profit in the short term.

A more direct consequence of the rural reform was that caused by rural industries. Initially rural industries provided consumer goods to fill previously unsatisfied demand and so developed rapidly. However they were mostly low in productivity and substandard in quality. Their massive development quickly seized the raw material, transport capacity, and energy required by big industries of high efficiency; this caused soaring prices and extensive speculation. In addition regionalism was flaring, and barriers were erected by local governments. This affected the normal production of big industries in developed regions. The overall efficacy of production was seriously affected, and confusion was on the order of the day.

Another consequence of the reform was the prevalence in society of the notion that studying was useless. In the countryside, there were many withdrawals from schools. Though individual specialized households turned to pursue more specialized knowledge, this could not compensate for the general neglect of education. Faced with soaring prices, teachers were compelled to take part-time jobs, negatively affecting the quality of teaching. The crisis of the education system was aggravated.

Besides the cooperative sectors of production in the countryside, such as forest preservation departments, veterinary stations, irrigation works departments, and supply and sale cooperatives, were in a state of paralysis or disintegration due to the rapid development of the responsibility system, whereby members of staff were drained away, capital was deficient, and management was in disarray. Before new cooperative organizations could be set up extensively, a serious blow had been struck.

There was in addition an underlying crisis in overall agricultural investments. One aim of the Dengist reform was to reduce state investments in agriculture and rely more on spontaneous investments by peasants. The proportion of state investment within total capital investment had been dropping—from 11.1 percent in 1979 to 3.4 percent in 1985. As for the peasants, while their income had risen, their productive investment had declined; in 1983 the proportion of productive investment in total peasant expenditure reached a zenith of 5.7 percent and then dropped to 3.8 percent in 1985. It was particularly significant in the cultivation sector. This was especially worrisome because this sector depended a great deal on peasant investments.

Because the CCP gave active support to the "competent" and the specialized households, much land, resources, and production equipment were accumulated in the hands of a small number of people through contracting. In only a few years, they earned an income of tens of thousands of yuan. Quite a number of individual businesses and small enterprises exploited the immense unevenness in circulation and sale and gained considerable incomes. There was a much larger income gap between peasants who did not make use of opportunities to enrich themselves and the rich peasants, and the standard of living for some even deteriorated due to price inflation. Some peasants became wage laborers. Generally speaking social differentiation and class differentiation among the peasants had intensified.

On the other hand, coastal regions and provinces obtained advantages from the reform, and with the effect of the market law on investment, these coastal regions obtained more capital and could develop at a quicker pace. The development for the backward regions and provinces was relatively slower, and with the additional reason of an impeded flow of resources, the gap between rich and poor regions widened. Another phenomenon was that within rich regions the difference between the rich and the poor was much bigger than that in poor regions. In the former the rich households and poor households had a difference of income up to 100-fold. In sum the social differentiation was not what the Dengist propaganda described as those getting rich first would aid those getting rich later but enlarged differences. The income and riches of a small number of persons increased at an astounding rate, including bureaucrats and cadres who got rich by the use of power, corruption, and speculation.

Quite a number of bureaucrats, besides corruption, made use of the shortage in raw materials and consumer goods to engage in hoarding and speculation. They interrupted the normal supply of resources, caused many man-made shortages, and accumulated wealth in this way.

The CCP had not taken active measures to restrain such activities. It proposed a 35 percent flat profit tax for enterprises and a 40 percent flat income tax for enterprise investors. It did not apply a sliding tax structure on persons or enterprises who secured huge profits. More important still, serious loopholes existed in the tax system, and the practice of the tax system was arbitrary and irregular. It provided one more channel for bureaucratic corruption. This again demonstrated that under a dictatorial bureaucratic system where social control is absent, even the best system can be employed by bureaucrats as a means of securing power, wealth, and privileges.

THE SOCIAL CRISIS IN THE COUNTRYSIDE

The intensification of income gaps and social differentiations and the instability of income due to market competition aggravated contradictions in the countryside. The peasants' discontent and envy was frequently expressed in attacks and acts of sabotage, such as poisoning other peasants' fishponds. In July 1988, twenty thousand peasants in Henan Province seized tons of watermelons worth 2 million yuan from two hundred households, and dozens of peasants were wounded in the scramble.

Peasant grievances against bureaucratic corruption and incompetence and market confusion developed in some cases into peasant riots. In May 1987 the peasants in Shandong Province participated in a mass riot involving thirty to forty thousand peasants. The government had encouraged peasants to grow garlic, but when the harvest was very good, the government stopped purchasing garlic from the peasants, and they rioted and attacked county government offices. This unprecedented resistance against the CCP regime was a concrete manifestation of peasant discontent and a change of attitude toward the ruling regime. It was also an indication of the grave consequences caused by the combination of bureaucratism and blind production in the commodity market.

The regime's credibility was quickly declining. Whereas the market economy increased social differentiations, the CCP itself took the lead in corruption, privileges, and speculation. Because the reform relaxed the regime's control over peasant residence and grain allocation, the peasants were no longer bound or afraid, and there were incidences of mass robbery, riot, and even beating of tax collectors and security men. Under the influence of the ideology of "getting rich" and "money as priority," the original social ideologies and moral standards were disintegrating. The CCP's own decay intensified its crisis in the countryside. The Dengist intention of basing itself on the rich peasants eventually caused it to lose further support of the poor and middle peasants.

More serious than the ruling crisis of the CCP is the threat of capitalist restoration and the reversal of the gains of the Chinese revolution. The Dengist reform promoted the concentration of wealth and resources in the hands of a small minority and strengthened the objective conditions for capitalist restoration. The capital accumulated by the specialized households or the bureaucrats could be used in the now more generalized commodity production to conduct expanded capitalist production by employing more laborers and making use of the unevenness in the economic structure. The privatization of land (though it was only the right of use) and other means of production and their flow into the hands of capitalists would force more people to sell their labor. The massive appearance of wage laborers is a danger signal. Another danger signal is the rise of loansharks in the countryside who charged interest rates of 100 percent. All these indicate a dangerous trend in capitalist development in China's rural areas. The antisocialist market reform and the corruption of the cadres are the impetus of capitalist restoration in China.

URBAN REFORM AND WORKER RESISTANCE

The question China now urgently faces is: When the Dengist faction had changed the previous wrong rural policy, how would it conduct reforms in the cities and big industries, stimulate workers' enthusiasm for production, and raise or at least maintain the workers' living standards?

In the past the persistent policy of stressing industry at the expense of agriculture gave rise to a rigid price structure that covered the unequal exchange between industry and agriculture and underpinned the low efficacy, redundancy of the bureaucratic structure, and irrationality of the industrial structure under bureaucratic command.

The rural reform partially changed the artificially low prices of agricultural products and raw materials, and in addition, due to impediments by the bureaucratic structure and large expenses in the field of circulation, the market prices became much higher (though the producers did not benefit from this). With raw materials already in shortage, the problem became more acute when rural enterprises competed for them and bureaucrats engaged in their speculation. The prices of raw materials rose to an irrational level. Coupled with the problems of transport and energy, urban enterprises were severely affected, and production either dropped or stopped. Thus, when the crisis in the rural reform was developing, the crisis in the cities also intensified. It was estimated that 80 percent of the urban population was seriously hit by soaring price inflation.

The problem that agriculture faced in the past was the millstone of irrational bureaucratic policy around the neck of peasant initiative and conditions of production. When this millstone was by and large removed, agricultural production could carry on in a more normal way, and a compensatory leap took place in 1979–84 until the market and the bureaucracy slowed down agricultural development. However the problem that industry faced could not be temporarily solved by correcting a few wrong policies.

The major problem that industry faced was low initiative for production among the workers. Industrial production is essentially different from agricultural production, and the system of responsibility cannot be applied here. Nor can initiative for production be raised by widening the income gaps among workers. To have the workers increase their production efficiency, they must either be forced to produce for their living as in the capitalist mode or exercise their enthusiasm as real masters of society under genuine socialism. The former can be implemented only with a counterrevolution in which the present state ownership system is privatized, that is, a general restoration of capitalism, but its prerequisite is a victory of the workers' defense of the state ownership system. At present this counterrevolution has not appeared, though with the wrong Dengist policy, capitalist development in the countryside has expanded. The prerequisite for the latter is the overthrow of bureaucratic rule so that genuine workers' control can be realized. Of course this path will not be charted by the bureaucracy, and only with the workers leading the peasants can the political revolution be carried out and genuine socialist democracy be established.

The Dengist reform at present tries to shift the cost of the reform onto the workers and at the same time compel the workers to work harder: power was decentralized to factory directors and the technocrats, wage differentials were expanded and a piecework system was imposed, and contract employment replaced long-term hiring and dismissals were used as a threat to workers. Social securities and subsidies, such as on water, electricity, housing, medical care, pensions, food, and necessities, were gradually canceled. There are now signs that the workers are passively or actively resisting these measures; strikes have increased, and general social discontent is surfacing. The official trade unions obviously are feeling this pressure and are forced to respond. Student movements have erupted in different forms. Of course, for the working class to develop from discontent to organized resistance and even to the level of the Polish Solidarity workers' movement, there is still a distance. However more Dengist reforms in the cities would undoubtedly incur a strengthened resistance by the working class.

THE REAL ALTERNATIVE

In order to advance the development of China's countryside and cities in a truly persistent way, neither the Maoist People's Commune and priority in heavy industry nor the Dengist arbitrary market economy and policy incurring differentiations can work.

To promote economic development in the countryside truly, the policy toward the peasants must first be correct. The mode of production must comply with the general productivity level and the voluntary will of the peasants. Forced collectivization and even communalization can only incur passive resistance of the peasants. The consequences are obvious. The workers' state must not let peasants remain at their present productivity level. It should provide cheap and high-quality industrial goods, sufficient insecticide, fertilizer, tractors, agricultural technology, irrigation, and electricity to aid peasants in raising their productivity and mechanization. It should expand the exchange of social products between the peasantry and the working class, strengthen social division of labor among the peasants, gradually attract peasants to engage in social production, absorb the surplus labor released from higher rural productivity into the industries, and help peasants set up supply cooperations to avoid exploitation in the process of the sale of products. On the other hand, the state should adopt unequivocal laws to impose appropriate restrictions, including a sliding tax structure, prohibition of loan sharking, encouragement of cooperatives, heavy taxes on rich peasants who employ agricultural workers, a minimum wage, and all these measures should aim at preventing capitalist accumulation, concentration of land, and capitalist exploitation. The state should provide production assistance and coordination and set up a certain amount of goods storage to offset the consequences of big fluctuations in production.

The development of rural commodity production definitely carries with it a capitalist inclination. To develop China's countryside, the Maoist attempt to leap over the state of rural commodity economic development is not feasible; this is conditioned by the peasants' petit bourgeois nature. Yet when tolerating or even encouraging the development of commodity economy in the countryside, the working class cannot allow it to develop arbitrarily as the Dengist policy does and must not actively promote social and class differentiations as the Dengist policy does. A correct rural policy is to repress consciously the capitalist inclination of the commodity economy and aid the poor peasants and recruit the support of the middle peasants. Loans should be given to the peasants according to class criteria, their taxes reduced, and cooperatives formed on a voluntary basis. Poor and middle peasants should also enjoy a privileged allocation of land and supply of tractors, fertilizers, insecticides, and seeds of new species. The strength of the regime in the countryside should be based on the poor and middle peasants to counter the influence of the rich peasants. In the final analysis, the development of rich peasants is based on repressing other peasant layers and impeding their development of productivity, and as a result, on the general social level, a greater and greater sector of agricultural productivity is repressed. Hence in the interest of the development of the rural and the overall economy, the working-class regime should help the poor and middle peasants instead of the Dengist policy of aiding the rich and the competent.

More fundamental is the selfless aid to the peasants bestowed by the working class in workers' states, and peasants are not rejected or exploited because they are individual producers not integrated in the state ownership system and economic planning. Here lies the real difference in attitude toward peasants between genuine workers' states and the so-called "socialist" Stalinist bureaucracy. The working class regards peasants as their allies, helps them raise productivity, collectivize, and gradually integrate into the socialist family. The Stalinist bureaucracy strives to control and manipulate the peasants and squeeze the maximum interests from the peasants in order to support heavy industries controlled by the bureaucracy. The bureaucracy also does not give importance to the development of light industries because they are mostly for consumption by the "people" whereas the products of heavy industries are controlled by the bureaucracy and can facilitate its consolidation of power.

Although the Dengist faction proclaimed that it would give the peasants freedom in the production of commodities, in reality the bureaucracy's interruption and control was still there. The market economy opened a path for bureaucrats to seek privileges in consumption and also supplied the means and the goal of accumulating capital by use of their privileges. This not only aggravates the corruption and decay of the bureaucracy but also strengthens the objective forces for capitalist restoration.

In order that China can develop, the state ownership system be defended, the gains of the 1949 revolution be safeguarded, and capitalist restoration be prevented, the Chinese working class needs urgently to be organized and to ally with and lead the poor and middle peasants to overthrow the CCP's bureaucratic rule, advance the world revolution, and realize genuine socialism in China and the whole world.

4

On China's Reform of the Labor System—The Practice of the Contract System

ZHANG KAI

In the wave of general economic reform, reform of the Chinese labor system is also unfolding.

The basic feature of the existing labor system is: the state has full power to control and allocate jobs to the entire urban and rural labor force; all workers are allocated to enterprises in the status of regular workers; a regular relationship is established between the workers and the enterprises, and the right to a job is guaranteed.

Since 1949 under the policy of the Communist Party, the Chinese proletariat has enjoyed a more privileged status than the peasants mainly because their support is necessary in countering the influence of the bourgeoisie, the landlords, the remnant forces of the Nationalists, and the military threat and economic blockade of American imperialism. More recently their support has been needed to counter the strong pressure of the Soviet bureaucracy.

At least the CCP still considers the system of regular jobs to have played an active role in China's economic construction.

However in the past few years, the authorities have been attacking the "abuses" of the system: "big pot of rice" (same remuneration for all, disregarding differences in individual contribution); "iron rice bowl," nurturing lazy people, "too much control, too strict allocation, one cannot get out once being put in an enterprise, and one's whole life is determined by one allocation."

The present reform is carried out first on new recruits of state-run enterprises. The system of regular jobs is replaced by the system of contract jobs. The new system is also applied to new recruits in state institutions, enterprises,

97

and societies. In fact such a system has already been practiced in nonstate-run industrial and commercial enterprises.

The contract system has been tried in state-run enterprises for a few years. According to the statistics, 3.5 million workers now work on a contract basis and make up 4 percent of all workers in state-run enterprises.

On October 1, four Temporary Stipulations relating to the contract system in state-run enterprises promulgated by the State Council began to take effect. Let us look at how the reform affects contract workers in light of the Stipulations.

STIPULATIONS UNFAVORABLE TO WORKERS

First the term of the contract is short; hence contract workers have no guarantee to their right to work. The enterprises determine the contract term according to the needs of production and work and recruit workers on a short-term (one to five years), on a long-term (over five years), and on a temporary basis (less than one year). When the term expires, the contract can be renewed by mutual agreement; otherwise the workers will be unemployed.

Second the workers are liable to dismissal at any time. The Stipulations provide that the contract can be annulled under the following conditions:

1. During the probation period, the worker is found not to be up to the requirements of recruitment.
2. The worker cannot resume his or her work after convalescing from an illness or injury not caused by his or her work.
3. According to the "Temporary Stipulation on the dismissal of workers in state-run enteprises who breach discipline" promulgated by the State Council, the following circumstances justify dismissal: serious violation of labor discipline; violation of operation procedures, thus inducing economic loss; bad attitude of service; disobedience to normal work transfer; fighting; or "committing other serious errors."

Thus the enterprises have the power and the excuse to dismiss workers at will. An example of the application of the first condition occurred in Wuhan, the Jiangxia Motor Repair Center, which is run as a joint venture (it is not a state-run enterprise), recruited sixty-four workers from four hundred applicants, but forty-four workers (70 percent of all recruits) were dismissed during the probation period (*People's Daily*, October 5, 2).

Third psychological pressure is strong and labor intensity is increased. The contract stipulates the quantity and quality quota of production, labor discipline, and liability on breach of contract.

Fourth the contract stipulates compensation to be made for damage caused by violation of the contract. Apparently both parties are responsible, but in fact the worker is the one liable, because the worker has no right to resign before the term expires and resignation can be considered violation of the contract. The Temporary Stipulations do not provide for the right of the worker to resign except on the following conditions: adverse sanitary or safety conditions, nonpayment of wages, noncompliance with the contract, and workers' pursuit of study on the agreement of the enterprises.

Fifth contract workers enjoy fewer benefits than regular workers. According to the Stipulations, wages, insurance benefits, bonuses, and subsidies of contract workers should be the same as those of regular workers in the same enterprises. However the following are different:

1. When the contract expires, the worker can receive unemployment compensation for a short period. Workers who have worked for less than five years can receive unemployment compensation for no more than twelve months at a rate of 60 to 70 percent of their basic wages. Regular workers need not face the problem of expiration of the term of service nor unemployment.
2. When a contract worker is dismissed after a stipulated period to convalesce from an illness or an injury not caused by his or her work, the enterprise pays a medical subsidy of three to six months of basic wages and unemployment compensation for not more than twelve months. For a regular worker under the same circumstances, when he or she leaves the job after six months of medical treatment, he or she enjoys a relief fund paid every month equal to 20 to 30 percent of his or her basic wages, until resumption of work or until death.
3. The contract worker has to contribute to a pension fund. The amount is no more than 3 percent of the monthly basic wages (the enterprise contributes 15 percent of the wages). The pension the worker receives is the total amount paid. A regular worker, on the other hand, need not contribute to the retirement fund and after retirement receives 50 percent to 75 percent of his or her wages every month until death.

Welfare items such as residential quarters, child care service, etc., are not mentioned in the Stipulations, reflecting the fact that contract workers have no right to them.

Besides the above unfavorable items reflected by the Stipulations, contract workers suffer a lower social and political status. Their work is temporary and unstable; their relationship to the enterprises is one of casual wage labor.

WORKERS AGAINST THE CONTRACT SYSTEM

The workers' opinion of the contract system has been revealed in the newspapers since the contract system was first tried a few years ago. On January 29, 1983, the China News Agency referred to a commentator's article in the *Workers' Daily*: "At present, the cadres and workers of many enterprises still harbor doubts and anxiety over the system of contract labor. Some workers worry that once the relationship between the enterprise and the workers under the contract system becomes one of wage labor, will the political status and political treatment of workers be changed and their livelihood not safeguarded? Such worry is understandable."

The same opinion is reflected in the *People's Daily* today. On September 20, the *People's Daily* quoted questions put forward by readers: Are workers on contract the masters of the enterprises? Will all regular workers become contract workers? The September 23 Editor's Note said, "Quite a number of readers ask: What is the difference between China's system of contract labor and the capitalist system of wage labor?" On October 5, the *People's Daily* carried an article entitled, "Does the system of contract labor harm the interests of the workers?" It said that after the practice of the system of contract labor, "some people worry that the interests of the workers will be harmed." It then quoted Minister of Labor Personnel Zhao Dongyuan's answer to these questions.

To the question of whether there exist any differences between the system of contract labor and the capitalist system of wage labor, Zhao explained that the two are qualitatively different because (1) the system of property ownership is different; (2) the aim is different—the capitalists go after surplus value, whereas the system of contract labor aims at creating social wealth, satisfying the needs of society and the needs of the laborers; and (3) the relationship and status of the two parties are different—it is a relationship of exploiting and exploited in the capitalist system of wage labor, whereas the status of the two parties signing the contract is equal.

However from the workers' viewpoint, will they not think that the enterprises use the means of extortion to seek profits, even if such means are not termed exploitation to seek surplus value? Will they not think that the phrase "workers are masters" is simply empty words? The factory directors wield much power and can dismiss workers, but workers have no right to resign. When workers are unemployed, they are obliged to accept official "referral" to a job, because if they refuse the referral twice without a proper reason, their unemployment compensation will be cancelled.

WORKERS ARE NOT MASTERS

Does the Chinese proletariat have the status or spirit of the master of the country?

Jiang Yiwei, the former deputy head and now the adviser of the Institute of Industrial Economic Study under the Academy of Social Sciences, said, "It is still a central link in ideological and political work to establish the spirit of master among the worker masses." He said, "If workers have no right to intervene in the major decisions of the enterprises, it is difficult to assert that workers have the status of master in the enterprises. . . . If the workers cannot feel that they are master in real life, it is empty talk to educate them to have such a spirit."

If the general workers are in such a situation, how can contract workers, whose jobs are not even secure, be the masters of the enterprises?

All along, the proletariat has been "master" in name only. The real ruler is the CCP. The workers are only required to work "hard, fast, well, and frugally." In addition with China poor and backward, the living standard of the workers and the people as a whole is very low. On the other hand, the party cadres enjoy material privileges and lead a corrupt, luxurious life, which contrasts with the people's hardship. These factors frustrate the enthusiasm and creativity of the workers and peasants for production.

THE STRUGGLE BETWEEN THE WORKERS AND THE BUREAUCRACY

In the three decades since 1949, the Chinese proletariat has increased from 16 million in 1952 to the present 120 million. The workers' general cultural level has also risen significantly. They resist attacks on their gains. The CCP's attempt to replace the system of wages calculated on an hourly basis with a system of piecework wages or floating wages was carried out at a very slow pace due to the workers' strong resistance. The authorities then promoted a system of bonuses in an attempt to create differentiations among the workers and stimulate them to compete in production. But the workers divide the bonuses among themselves, and as a consequence the bonuses cannot play the role for which they were intended. Model workers that the authorities attempted to nurture are generally rejected and isolated by other workers.

Now with the promotion of the contract labor system, the authorities quickly clarify that the rumor that regular workers will also be converted to contract workers is "a rumor without any basis in policy." Zhao Dongyuan admitted that the present reform of the labor system "concerns the interest of workers in general and will bring about some changes in traditional concepts; the reform inevitably will encounter various difficulties."

The workers not only oppose the system of contract labor, they also disagree with the reforms of prices, wages, encouragement of a minority to get rich first, and the development of the commodity economy. The mood is reflected in the speech of Luo Gan, deputy chairman of the General Federation of Trade Unions, at the working conference on ideological work among workers convened in early August. He said that old concepts and habits have quite a considerable influence on the worker masses. For example some workers view the thaw on prices as "socialist superiority"; have doubts about the reform of the price system; view the wage reform with the selfish and egalitarian mentality of a small producer; fail to understand the extension of wage differentiations; reject the encouragement of a minority to get rich first; consider the "iron rice bowl" labor system as the sign of the proletariat being master; have the opinion that the application of the contract labor system will create a system of wage labor; fail to understand the development of the socialist commodity economy, etc. "All these illustrate that old concepts and old habits are indeed the invisible force obstructing the smooth development of the reform. If these old concepts and old habits are not eliminated, it will be difficult for the workers to devote themselves to the reform with enthusiasm and initiative." Luo Gan appealed to "the broad mass of workers to actively eliminate old concepts which do not correspond to the reform" (*People's Daily*, August 4, 1986).

At the same time, the General Federation of Trade Unions published a "random sampling survey" on six hundred forty thousand workers, which simply said that "94.78% staunchly support or basically support the reform, and 92.95% staunchly support or basically support the open door policy" (*Wen Hui Bao*, October 14, 1986).

It is quite generally accepted that China needs reform and needs to open to the West. Yet serious differences exist concerning what should be reformed and how the reform should be conducted, not only between the rulers and the people but also within the ruling strata. The report did not state the concrete questions put to those interviewed, so it is difficult to deduce much from the above statistics. Nevertheless the report also said that the workers who were interviewed "strongly demand the right of decision, of electing the factory director, of assessing and recalling cadres, and also of democratic management in the sphere of economic distribution."

Thus the results of this random sampling survey, conducted from March to May this year [1986], does not overturn the appeal made to the "broad workers" by the deputy chairman of the General Federation of Trade Unions.

The rejection of certain concrete reform measures and the "strong demand" for democratic rights in the functioning of the economy indicate a rejection of the growth of capitalist forces. It signifies a new awakening of the Chinese proletariat.

5

The Special Economic Zones and Potential Transformations

Y. F. LIN

In March 1982 I wrote an article for the *October Review* entitled "On Special Economic Zones in China" (the article appeared in English in the same issue). I pointed out the basic characteristics manifested by the Special Economic Zones (SEZs), the social contradictions that their development would generate, and the potential change from a quantitative to a qualitative one in political and economic areas. I also pointed out that the rapid deterioration of the CCP's ruling position had compelled it to change its ruling policy by resorting to the aid of capitalism. At that time I did not go further to an analysis of the CCP's ruling policy, nor did I discuss the question of the Special Administrative Zones (SAZs).

Fourteen months have gone by. Although the amount of foreign capital or advanced technology introduced into the SEZs has been small,[1] the CCP's stress and effort on the SEZs have increased. In this period much manpower and material resources have been allocated to the SEZs. At the same time, there have been pains to seek a theoretical basis (and legal principles) for the development of the SEZs. Also the concept of SAZ is being concretized.

The SEZ question has shown its significance in relation to the direction China's political and economic developments will take.

In this article I shall analyze China's potential transformations in light of the SEZs.

WHAT IS SPECIAL ABOUT THE "SPECIAL ZONE" POLICY?

Why did China set up SEZs and promote SAZs? Should such special zones be set up in China, where property is state-owned?

These questions must be seen in their implications.

First of all the SEZs were set up to attract foreign capital.

We agree with Lenin's idea on principled exploitation of foreign capital. The transfer of advanced technology, production equipment, and management experience from capitalist countries to China through foreign capital activities is a concrete manifestation of the objective trend of history overcoming its uneven development while still under interruption or control by capitalism. That is, under the situation when backward countries lack sufficient capital or material resources and when proletarian revolution has not succeeded in advanced countries, the objectively necessary transfer has to be realized through the activities of imperialist capital. Imperialist capital, whose introduction is made possible under severe conditions and with toxicity, must be restricted within specified scope so that the national economy of the workers' state will not deviate from its track. In other words a workers' state, in exploiting foreign capital, must follow the principle: she must assure the functioning of the state ownership system and secure a principled break in imperialism's restriction or control on the transfer of world resources by paying only a limited cost—temporarily tolerating imperialism's toxicity in individual items in economic construction. And because the ability of workers' states to bring their subjective factors into play depends in the final analysis on the consciousness of the laboring masses and their active participation in state affairs, the placing of government policies and foreign capital activities under the people's supervision are indispensable. The foregoing is the basic position of revolutionary marxists on the question of how to exploit foreign capital.

Let us now look at how the CCP exploits capital by way of the SEZs.

Hong Fu, the former chief editor of *Red Flag* and one of the most prominent CCP theorists, elaborated on the reasons for the SEZs:

> One main reason for our attempt at SEZs is the exploitation of international resources and exploration of international markets in order to expedite our country's socialist modernization. . . . From this SEZ "window" and channel, we can learn advanced technology and management skills, develop and train our personnel, accumulate experience for our domestic institutional changes, and heighten our ability to develop on our own. This is the real purpose of our attempt at SEZs.[2]

Concerning how the state can attract foreign capital to the special zones and how foreign capital operates there, Hong Fu said,

> here, the forms of absorbing foreign capital, such as processing on imported material, compensation trade, cooperation ventures and joint investment ventures, are similar to many areas in the mainland. . . . Only, here we also have independent investment ventures by foreign capital. . . . Since foreign capital here enjoys more favorable conditions, it has a larger share in the profits than foreign capital on the mainland.

Moreover,

> since the production and sale of products are mainly for the international
> market, they generally do not have direct links with the domestic market.

Hong Fu concluded that "what is 'special' about the Shenzhen SEZ is only
in these aspects."[3]

Yet during the CCP-convened "academic conference on the Guangdong
Province SEZs," some scholars considered that

> from the point of view of the economic infrastructure, superstructure,
> and economic law, the special zones have a dual nature—both socialist
> and capitalist. Their capitalist factors are under the supervision and con-
> trol of the socialist state. Thus, the nature of the special zones is state
> capitalism under socialist conditions.[4]

This shows that some participants in the conference considered that the
SEZs have a "state capitalist nature."

Because the absorption of foreign capital in the SEZs has failed to come
up to expectation, there have been reproaches on insufficient policy liberalization and flexibility. During the conference,

> on the question of "what is the legal principle of SEZs," one viewpoint
> was that the specialty of the SEZ policies should be reflected in more
> liberalism, more favorable conditions and more convenience, and all these
> must be reflected in legal form in order that the clients can dispel their
> worries and more investors can be attracted.[5]

This means that a capitalist order must be reinstalled through legislation
before large amounts of foreign capital can be expected to come in.

If the CCP strives to integrate established interests from outside, whatever
economic interests China can obtain from the special zones are precondi-
tioned by the reinstallation of capitalist order in these regions. The crucial
point in the SEZ policy is to channel the international bourgeoisie and the
Chinese bureaucracy to reinstall capitalist order in some regions in China. A
marxist standpoint opposes this CCP policy.

Second, the SEZ question brings up the question of style of management
of enterprises and the degree of autonomy of enterprises vis-à-vis the central
authority. In the SEZs the style of management in government enterprises
or joint venture enterprises is capitalist. Whereas the "state capitalist" factor
in similar enterprises in the mainland is still conditioned by the socialist
planned economy, in the SEZs there is a swift turn toward market economy
and conditioning by the international capitalist market. On the other hand,
the leadership institutions and local officials in the SEZs hold much greater
power than their counterparts on the mainland, for the reason that they can
more flexibly answer to the pressure of foreign capital and the international

market. The assertion that "the capitalist factors are under the supervision and control of the socialist state" has merely the theoretical supposition that socialist countries should supervise and control capitalist factors, whereas the actual fact is that the Chinese central government has not done so. It is wrong to think that "state capitalism" in a whole region can be practiced "under socialist conditions," for state capitalism is ultimately capitalism. When capitalist factors are still isolated, individual economic items, they will be conditioned by the planned economy, but when they spread to a whole sector, they will demand breaking away from the state's supervision and control. If the state encourages the development of capitalism in a whole region, the internal logical trend is to have all "socialist conditions" transformed to "capitalist conditions" by gradually abandoning the planned economy and gradually reinstating private possession of the means of production.

IMPORTANT REVELATIONS BY THE SEZs

Let us examine the actual developments in the SEZs for other revelations besides their conditioning by capitalist forces.

The *People's Daily*, May 6, 1983, reported "immense changes" in the Shenzhen SEZ. The town area has increased tenfold; the output value last year was 360 million yuan, five times more than that of 1979. The report credited the outcome to "a series of reforms in the institution and system." They include certain decentralization of power, reallocation of capital through competition (such as through bidding), reduction of the cycle for expanding reproduction, changes in the employment and wage system, and even "secret ballot to elect cadres above the manager level in a democratic way and without any candidate standing for election."

The above reforms have to a certain extent changed the original bureaucratic structure in Shenzhen, and different levels of cadres have to consolidate their power and position by new ways.

The *People's Daily* admitted that "constructions in Shenzhen do not depend on large amounts of investments by the state; they are mostly joint investments with or loans from foreign merchants." The development of Shenzhen "does not depend solely on foreign capital"; "the crucial question is to arm ourselves" and "grasp the initiative in our own hands."

It may be argued that the laboring masses in the Shenzhen SEZ double their labor input due to high wages, and labor effectiveness is heightened because of material incentives.

This is partly true. But in a workers' state, the positive function of "material incentives" should refer to a reasonable distribution of the means of living and not a simple application of reward according to the input of labor. If a large amount of "surplus value" is first extracted from the products (as the capitalists do) or a large amount of accumulation put aside (as the Gang of Four did or today's power-holders do in mainland China), the wages are inevitably calculated on an unreasonably low criterion and cannot basically improve the livelihood of the workers or heighten their enthusiasm for production. But in today's Shenzhen, some special situation has evolved. The bureaucrats have to depend mainly on the workers in economic construction, because for the time being they can depend on no other force. Thus workers' basic wages are much higher than those on the mainland.

At the same time, the functioning of the managerial layer cannot be separated from a minimum supervision and trust by the laboring people. The *People's Daily* admitted that "it is of the greatest importance that the masses supervise the cadres and have the right to elect and recall cadres." For the cadres, they have to rely more on the masses, because they are now judged by their performance.

Third, the CCP has recently embarked on the setting up of SEZs. It can now clearly be seen that the crux of the Special Zone policy is not to restrain capitalist factors in China but to guide capitalism into China to delimit boundaries of rule with the state ownership system. It is a step further than the CCP's former practice of "peaceful coexistence"—now it is "peaceful coexistence" with capitalism *inside* China. That is why the CCP stresses that "two economic systems can be practiced in one country." To preserve its own privileges, the CCP strives for an alliance between rulers through the mutual recognition of their differently based privileges. In the name of "realizing the unification of China" and "contributing to China's Four Modernizations," the CCP appeals to the capitalists of Taiwan and Hong Kong to invest boldly in China. The recognition of capitalism as a system to be installed in China inevitably gives a direct push to the rapid institutionalization of capitalist factors in the special zones and inevitably gives strong stimulus to the demand of capitalist factors in the mainland for institutionalization. China is under the dual disruption of the bureaucracy and the capitalist forces.

To sum up the CCP Special Zone policy has an internal and external aim. Internally it sets up testing points in specified areas to practice "state capitalism" to see if the central authority of the bureaucracy still maintains effective control over enterprises and cadres that operate according to capitalism, to measure what extent of the use of market mechanisms can be attained for the state ownership economy still to maintain dominance over the entire society, and to examine the necessity for the bureaucracy itself to break away gradually from its original parasitic base—the state ownership system—and become a capitalist class. Externally it demonstrates to the international bourgeoisie that, besides maintaining its present rule, it will not do anything harmful to the bourgeoisie, and it is expecting unprecedented integration with them.

Deep-Going Changes Are Taking Place in China

As a backward country, China does not have the economic basis for practicing socialism, that is, for satisfying the living needs of modern society by relying on a system of public ownership. Therefore after setting up the state-ownership system and collective ownership, China in its social nature is still a specific transitional society that can revert to capitalism under internal contradictions and external pressure.

The situation in today's China reflects that changes are taking place that can lead to a reversion to capitalism.

During the later period of Mao Zedong's rule, he apparently attempted to prevent China from reverting to capitalism. Yet while strictly repressing capitalist factors, he also rejected any intervention into state power by the people, and even repressed the people by iron-fist policies. The result is that all production activities did not get encouragement from the inherent merits of the state ownership system or from material well-being. The people have a very low standard of living, and the bureaucrats fully bring into play their characteristics as social parasites. Society goes from stagnation to degeneration, which is first manifested in the absolute incompetence and general decadence of the bureaucrats. Mao Zedong's rule, rather than preventing society from reverting to capitalism, prepared much greater "motive forces" for society to revert to capitalism, because he had totally blocked the road to socialism, could not satisfy the people's increasing daily needs, and caused stagnation of social development. How can the majority of cadres, who have suffered from factional struggles and face hostility from the working people, not turn to capitalism?

In fact Mao had long prepared for ingratiation with the international bourgeoisie. The "peaceful coexistence" policy was derived by Mao, and the "theory of the three worlds" was drawn up to meet the new policy of international imperialism toward China, because the latter was forced by its new crisis to seek a foot-hold in the China market. Mao's change was, in essence, the prelude to Deng Xiaoping's present policy.

But in actuality Deng's policy could only obtain a leadership position inside the bureaucracy with the fall of the Mao clique. The fall of the Mao clique and the increasing revelation of the reactionary nature of the Deng faction have objectively expedited China's independent democracy movement, which essentially is the prelude to the great movement of the Chinese people to defend the state ownership system and lead China on to socialism.

What happens in China today is not simply a reversion to capitalism. It is a struggle between the forces of the laboring people in defense of socialism and the forces of the bureaucracy, which at one time goes far to the right and at another time is forced into a certain defense of the planned economy.

For the Chinese bureaucracy, it has today undoubtedly lost self-control. In the countryside, it encourages peasants to get rich and even promotes the "contracting" of irrigation benefits (which is fostering new local tyrants to control individual farmers). In the cities it is initiating the issuance of shares. Thus in the enormous bureaucracy, quite a number of people have turned to integration with remnants of the bourgeoisie or with emerging capitalist factors in the countryside. If this trend develops, a tendency of some bureaucrats strongly demanding private appropriation of the means of production will arise. The internal transformation in China's bureaucracy today is not a simple imitation of capitalism, but the real transformation of some sectors in the bureaucracy to a capitalist class.

CONCLUSION

Of course China's destiny ultimately is not determined by the will of the bureaucracy. Why I stress that developments toward capitalist restoration have been taking place in China is to reflect truthfully an objective fact but, more important still, to call upon the laboring people and revolutionists to make a greater effort to defend China's socialist future.

I do not think that the laboring people should passively boycott the CCP's Special Zone policy. On the contrary, I think revolutionists should first exploit the favorable conditions existing in the special zones and try to revert the direction of development of the special zones, from reinstalling the capitalist order to limiting itself to principled exploitation of foreign capital. And every achievement in this work should be spread to the mainland to promote a national movement for socialist democracy.

Notes

1. Hong Kong's *Wen Hui Bao* (June 17, 1982), "A Polemic on the SEZs."
2. *Red Flag*, no. 2 (1983): 28–29.
3. Ibid., 29.
4. Report on the Conference in Hong Kong's *Wen Hui Bao* (June 17, 1982).
5. Ibid.

The Development of Private Enterprises

ZHANG KAI

NEW ASSESSMENT OF CCP LEADERSHIP ON PRIVATE ENTERPRISES

Under the CCP's leadership, China practiced over three decades of fake socialism. When this met with dismal failure, the blame was put on socialism and state ownership, and a eulogy was given to the vitality of capitalism and private property. The drastic change is reflected in the following report: The Chinese News Agency reported

> from a reliable source that a leader of the CCP, when he interviewed the head of state of an African country, said: "from China's experience, I would advise you not to practice socialism, or at least not to practice general socialism. . . ."
>
> Almost at the same time, another CCP leader, when interviewing this leader of a Black African state, also advised him not to develop a state-owned economy as China did in the past; instead, more private economy should be developed.[1]

The CCP did not deny or clarify this report. *Wen Hui Bao*'s former editor-in-chief, Jin Yaoru, wrote two articles in *Wen Hui Bao* to expound this idea, and he pointed out that the two CCP leaders were Deng Xiaoping and Zhao Ziyang.

Because the advice to other countries is not to practice socialism, it means China's past practice was basically wrong and, therefore, that China should develop a private economy.

In recent years quite a number of intellectuals in China have come to the conclusion from theory and practice that the CCP was not yet practicing socialism. It is said that Su Shaozhi, the former head of the Institute of the Study of Marxism, Leninism, and Mao Zedong Thought, an institute under

110

the Academy of Social Sciences, also held this view. This can help more people realize that putting the blame on socialism is the CCP's shirking its responsibility, imperialism's slander of marxism, and misunderstanding on the part of some of the working people.

Henceforth the CCP leadership will promote capitalist private economy more blatantly rather than doing so in the name of "socialism," as it did in the past.

OFFICIAL COVER-UP OF THE TRUTH

For several years the CCP has allowed the private economy to exist in China in violation of the Constitution. Last March a resolution was adopted by the First Session of the Seventh National People's Congress to revise some articles of the Constitution to protect officially the legal development of the capitalist economy. To what extent had the private economy grown before this legalization? Probing the situation can help observation of its development after legalization.

According to statistics compiled by the State Industrial and Commercial Management Bureau, up to the end of 1987 there were two hundred twenty-five thousand private enterprises in the whole country, employing 3.6 million workers, that is, on average sixteen workers per enterprise; their proportion within the total industrial output value of the country was less than 1 percent.

In fact the above figures were false, aiming to cover-up the real situation.

First of all it maneuvered on the definition: only enterprises employing more than eight workers were considered "private" enterprises; those with fewer than eight were defined as "individual" enterprises. There are no grounds for such a distinction. In terms of exploitation or an employer's private ownership of the means of production, there is no qualitative difference between an enterprise employing over eight workers and one employing six or seven workers; the difference is only one of degree.

It is also said that the official figures were based on reports by employers. True reports were usually unavailable due to worry among employers about official policies. The official figures were therefore far below actual amounts.

For example let us look at Wenzhou City, where the private economy is the most developed. Fewer than ten private enterprises are registered with the Industrial and Commercial Bureau, whereas Zheng Dajiong, deputy director of the Policy Research Bureau under the Wenzhou CCP Municipal Committee, pointed out that the individual and private economy has a weight of 41 percent in the industrial sector, 33 percent in the commercial sector, and about two-thirds in communication and transport.[2] How can such economic activities be those of ten enterprises? Yet the official figure of ten remains the basis for compilation of official statistics. The officials were well aware of the real situation, but politics and policies required that they cover-up this serious violation of the Constitution.

THE ACTUAL DIMENSIONS OF DEVELOPMENT

In June a national colloquium on the study of the private economy was convened in Fuzhou jointly by the China Social Sciences Periodical, the editorial board of *Rural Economy*, and *Financial Daily*. About two hundred officials, theoreticians, and representative private entrepreneurs gathered to discuss questions related to China's private enterprises. According to Cheng Xiang, a reporter for Hong Kong's *Wen Hui Bao* who participated in the colloquium, almost all participants in the colloquium agreed that the official statistics seriously underestimated the actual dimensions of the private economy. The participants could, even following the criteria set officially, partially overturn the statistics of the Industrial and Commercial Bureau.[3]

First a look at the number of enterprises: take an example from Hebei Province, where the private economy was not very developed. The province's Industrial and Commercial Bureau gave the figures that there were 17,294 private enterprises in the whole province last year. But findings by scholars showed that in just the Handang Region, one of the ten regions of the province, there were already twenty-seven thousand enterprises (based on the same official criteria). This, together with the Wenzhou statistics, should be enough to show how the official figure of two hundred twenty-five thousand enterprises for the whole country deviated from the truth.

The official term of "persons engaged in the enterprises" includes both employers and the exploited workers, thus covering up the relationship of wage employment. Although the official figure was 3.6 million persons engaged in the private economy, Professor Ge Lin of Nanjing University took into account all workers, whether they were licensed or unlicensed, employed in enterprises above or below eight persons, and gave the figure of thirty million by the end of 1987. The reporter Cheng Xiang commented that this was very possible.

Concerning the scale and percentage of workers, the official figure was an average of sixteen workers per enterprise at the end of 1987. Results of surveys on different regions provided by scholars attending the colloquium were mostly above the official figure. For example it was an average of thirty-seven workers in Wenzhou, twenty-eight in Shenyang, twenty in Changchun and Chongqing. As for the percentage, the difference is very big between the official figures and unofficial research (Figure 1).

FIGURE 1: Comparison of Number of Workers Employed in All Private Enterprises

Dimension of Enterprise	Official Statistics	Unofficial Statistics	
		Rural	Urban
under 8	>70%	2.86%	8.70%
8–20		8.57%	30.44%
21–50	>29%	25.72%	21.74%
51–100		17.14%	4.35%
101–500	> 1%	40.01%	30.45%
501–1000		5.71%	4.35%
Total	100%	100%	100%

Source: Official figures are from 1987 statistics of the State Industrial and Commercial Bureau. Unofficial figures are from the thesis by Jia Ting and Wang Haicheng, "The Rise and Development of Private Entrepreneurs in China," submitted to the Fuzhou Colloquium.

The official figure that private enterprises constituted less than 1 percent of the industrial output value is also unbelievable. Of course there is unevenness in development among different regions. However participants quoted figures to show that "within a province, there are several counties with a considerable weight of private economy. This is prevalent in almost all provinces." The examples are in Wuchuan of Guangdong Province, the output value of private enterprises constituted 48 percent of that of the whole county; in Kaiping County, it was 35 percent; 38 percent in southern regions of Jiangsu Province; in the Wenzhou region, the weight was about 60 percent in industrial output value, 58 percent in passenger transport volume, and 65 percent in freight transport volume; in Shishi City in Fujian Province, the overwhelming majority of rural enterprises are already in the private sector (Figure 2); Shishi City belongs to Jinjiang County, where the output value of private enterprises was 61.4 percent of all output value; in Chuangzhou County, it was 67.4 percent.

FIGURE 2: Rural Enterprises in Shishi City in Southern Fujian Province

	Total	Private Economy	Percent
Number of enterprises	602	561	93.2
Persons engaged	18,636	15,237	81.8
Total output value*	138.74	106.86	77.0
Total income	116.25	92.93	79.9
Accumulation for reproduction*	12.637	11.150	88.2

*In million yuan.

Source: Hua Xuezhong, "Historical Inevitability of the Development of Private Economy."

Rural enterprises have developed rapidly in the past few years. According to Lei Dong, director of China Industrial Economy Association, up to the end of 1987, there were 15.15 million rural enterprises, employing 79 million workers.[4]

As for the development of individual enterprises (official term for private enterprises employing fewer than eight workers), according to an article in *World Economic Report* of February 15, 1988, "the advantages and disadvantages of the astounding development of industrial and commercial individual economy," written by Yuan Zhang, a member of the Planning Committee of Jiangsu Province up to the end of 1986, there were already 12.11 million individual enterprises, with 18.459 million persons engaged in them, which was about 14.4 percent of workers employed in state and collective enterprises (128.19 million workers). If we compare the 1986 figures with the 1985 figures, total retail amount of commodities rose from 0.1 percent to 16.3 percent; total capital rose from 0.07 billion yuan to 27.44 billion yuan; total income from trade rose from 0.17 billion yuan to 66.59 billion yuan; net income of owners of enterprises rose from 0.08 billion yuan to 29.28 billion yuan. The article said that the above figures did not include enterprises that operated on a part-time basis or not formally or usually in operation. "Therefore, the figures are much lower than the actual situation." If enterprises with fewer than eight workers have such an "astounding" development, one can imagine the expansion of enterprises with over eight workers.

PROTECTION OF RIGHTS OF PRIVATE ENTERPRISES BY LEGISLATION

To put into practice the revised clause of the Constitution, the state council adopted two temporary ordinances and a stipulation regarding private enterprises. The ordinances are meant to encourage further the private economy to develop and to help the booming of the "planned commodity economy."

It can be foreseen that with the booming of the private economy, the state ownership system will be further eroded.

The ordinances stipulate that the private economy can exist at all levels except military, financial, and state prohibited sectors. (Still small-scale private financial companies and loan-shark credit companies already exist.) The inviolability of private ownership of property is established. Enterprises have the right to autonomy, the right to employ and dismiss workers, to decide on the system of wages and distribution of profits, and to set the prices of commodities according to state regulations.

They stipulate that labor contracts must be drawn up upon employment of workers, and the contracts should regulate the demand on the quality and quantity produced by the worker, labor conditions, and labor discipline. Most of the clauses favor the employers. As for labor insurance, it is stipulated that it only applies to "workers in trades or types of work that endanger one's health or life"; social security applies only "when the enterprises have adequate conditions." Such flexibility enables the employers to shirk their responsibilities regarding workers' rights. Yet when labor disputes arise, private enterprises go through the same procedures as state-owned enterprises, that is, to have a conciliatory committee to conduct negotiations and then to have an adjudicative bureau to make a ruling. The workers are deprived of their right to strike.

The wages for managers and directors of enterprises are allowed to be within ten times the average wages of workers in the respective enterprises. Not less than 50 percent of after-tax profits should be reserved for the development fund for production, but revenue bureaus can grant permission to "special cases" for reserving less than 50 percent. A flat rate of profit tax (35 percent) applies to all types of enterprises; the tax rate on personal income is also a flat rate of 40 percent, instead of a sliding scale.

The legislation legalizes such unjust social practices, and this is causing more and more discontent within the general population. Lately *Economic Daily* published a series of reports that reflected the masses' view on the growing discrepancy in the distribution of income. It reported that an owner of a private enterprise earned a net income of 250,000 yuan a year, whereas all income of a middle school teacher was less than 100 yuan a month.[5]

THE TREND OF DEVELOPMENT

Under such stimulation and protection by the CCP, the private economy will have an even more rapid growth at the expense of the state-owned economy.

Up to now the basic official argument that China is still practicing socialism is that the output value of state-owned enterprises constitutes the majority of the country's gross national product. Other defenses have already gone bankrupt. In the past it was said that China's land was publicly owned and so there would not be differentiation in the countryside. China's labor force was not a commodity, there did not exist a labor market, and so there was no exploitation, and capitalism could not grow; there was no inflation in China and so prices would not go in an upward spiral.

According to Lei Dong, the proportion of the total output value of state-owned enterprises in the national economy fell from 83 percent in 1978 to 67 percent in 1987; other economic sectors, including collective enterprises and private enterprises, constituted 33 percent. Lei Dong had long served as director of the planning bureau; it is not without reason that he grouped the collective economy together with the private economy—he might see the collective economy as by nature closer to the private economy than to the state-owned economy, a change that is unfolding under the present circumstances. (In the past the official version considered both the state-owned economy and the collective economy as pillars of socialism.)

The present trend is that the economy is developing to the detriment of the state-owned enterprises. China is going further away from socialism, and the factors for developing socialism are being undermined more and more.

Notes

1. *Wen Hui Bao*, CCP organ in Hong Kong, June 6, 1988.
2. Report in *People's Daily*, June 19, 1988.
3. See Hong Kong's *Wen Hui Bao*, June 26–28, 1988.
4. *Wen Hui Bao*, June 24, 1988.
5. *Wen Hui Bao*, June 5, 1988.

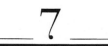

A Record of the Mass Rally at the Shanghai People's Square to Discuss Democracy

YUAN XIUMIN

The December 19 demonstration of university students in Shanghai for democracy, freedom, and human rights has temporarily subsided due to the authorities' threats. However the students' enthusiasm still ran high. They felt that the question of democracy was not only to be discussed on the campus but should be brought to society as a whole. They felt that the workers and the public should be awakened to an understanding of and a struggle for democracy. As a leadership the students did not slacken after the demonstrations. Starting from December 20, every evening at about six o'clock rallies of students, workers, and other citizens were held at the Shanghai People's Square to discuss democracy.

At six o'clock darkness had already descended over the People's Square. The only building in the square, the office of the Standing Committee of the Shanghai People's Congress, stood solitary in the chill. It was the end of the work day. Bicycles thrust on, and pedestrians walked with haste under the fragile street light. The people seemed insignificant in the vast square. Some pedestrians, wearing gauze masks and scarfs, huddled in their overcoats, walked with a quick pace and a serious expression. They headed toward one side of the square. Indeed they were going to attend rallies to discuss democracy.

It was dim in the square. Crowds gathering in circles were dispersed here and there, some numbering forty or fifty, and some one or two hundred. In the center of the circles there were ordinary workers discussing the student demonstrations, youths debating the question of democracy, and even old workers at the municipal government expressing their thoughts and showing the support for the student action. The majority of the participants were young workers.

The biggest crowd was gathered on a piece of muddy ground in the square. In the beginning about one or two hundred people gathered in a circle. About a hundred people sat on the ground in the inner rings, and the rest stood in the outer rings. In the center a young man of about thirty years of age, apparently a worker, was speaking his ideas on democracy, freedom, and human rights. He said there are two kinds of democracy—bourgeois democracy and socialist democracy, but socialist democracy is the genuine people's democracy; regrettably the Communist Party of China has always swindled the people with fake socialism and fake Marxism-Leninism. The audience applauded and cheered. He continued to say, freedom must be exercised on the prerequisite of not interfering with the freedom of others; human rights are basic rights owed to every person and must not be violated. After he spoke a young man of about twenty-five stood up to speak. He wore glasses; his hair was disheveled; his eyelids seemed very heavy; his voice was husky. Still when he spoke, his face showed a shining delight.

When this student stood up to speak, a stir was aroused. About six or seven hundred people had gathered. The student first described the cause of the student democratic movement and the course of the march, and then he gave a lively account of the negotiation between the students and the municipal government. It was a way of explaining the student movement to the public in a most direct way.

As he talked about a thousand people gathered. Young men and women, apparently workers, made up the majority. There were also middle-aged workers. Though the crowd was big, they listened to the students in a very orderly and attentive manner. Their serious expressions and looks of expectation showed that they were not there for fun. When the student criticized government policies, they nodded and smiled. When they agreed with some of the students ideas, they applauded. When the student made a brilliant remark, they cheered, and occasionally they requested or encouraged the student to go on.

When this student had finished his speech, six young men went into the center. They were also students. They sat down in the middle, and one stood up to narrate again the reason and course of the student demonstration. Then he spoke his views on democracy, freedom, the Communist Party, the multiparty system, Marxism-Leninism, the socialist perspective, and the law. Before he began a topic, he lit a cigarette and inhaled deeply, went into a moment's deep thought, and slowly exhaled the smoke. This young man—only just over twenty—showed naïveté in his maturity and captivated the audience.

It was then made known that these students had not slept nor taken a regular meal for three whole days. Fatigue and hunger tore at them, but they persisted. When they uttered in their husky voices, "We want democracy rather than bread," the audience was moved.

Over a thousand people had gathered by this time, encircling the students in broad rings. Because the students could not raise their voices any more, those standing at the outer rings wanted to squeeze in. Interestingly the crowd was divided into many layers. Those near the center sat very close to each other on the wet muddy ground. Then there were the rings for those half-squatting. Then there were those half-bending. Then there were those standing. In the outermost rings, some people stood on their bicycles, and some occasionally jumped up to catch a glimpse of the speaker. So the audience formed a natural auditorium, and a thousand pairs of eyes looked at the speaking student from different angles. Despite the vastness of the crowd, when the student spoke the crowd remained silent. Sometimes when the student spoke toward one direction, the audience on the opposite side could not hear, and they would demand that the student repeat his words to them. Those standing in the outer rings could not possibly hear, and so there was continuous pressing in. The contact between man and man was most intimate, but it could only bring understanding and help, and confrontation was impossible. Sometimes those standing in the middle layers could not bear with the pressure from behind, but they did not want to sit for fear that those in front would block their view. So they inclined to stand up during intervals of the student's speech. At those times shouts demanding others to "squat down" rose up here and there, and it was an opportunity for those in the outer rings to squeeze further in. All of a sudden, the crowd in the outer rings was like waves in the sea, moving to the right and then reverting to the left. Finally some half-squatting and half-bending sat down. When the student resumed his speech, calm returned. Those who had sat down, being blocked by those in front, would slowly rise to a squatting position. Although security agents were widely dispersed in the square to monitor them, the citizens and students seemed not to care but threw themselves into this open, free discussion.

The next student that spoke introduced himself as a student of music. He held in his hand a leaflet entitled "Letter to Compatriots," signed by "Tongji University Students." In a rhythmic but husky voice, he read the entire leaflet. The last three lines read, "Let the people throw themselves into the dynamic movement for democracy and freedom! Victory surely belongs to us! Viva the December 19 Movement!" When he finished reading them, the audience repeated the last line in unison, raised their fists, and then there was warm applause and shouts. The masses' enthusiasm reached a boiling point. The expressions of fatigue and hunger on the students' faces were covered by delight and excitement.

The discussion rally was carried out in this harmonious, open, and free atmosphere. The people followed in good order—they first raised their hands before they asked a question or made a speech. During the whole rally, there were frequent interventions from the crowd, and many penetrating ideas were expressed. The students brought up their idea of socialism. They considered that Marx was correct in his analysis of social development and that socialism can appear only after the development of feudalism to capitalism to the imperialist stage; China had not gone through the advanced development of capitalism, and so there are abuses of feudalism, bureaucracy, and privileges. At this time a young worker in the crowd raised his hand to speak and asked if this meant China should revert to the capitalist stage. The student answered no, a new road for China can be created only by genuine socialism, and for genuine socialism to be realized, the people must be the masters of the country, and democracy and freedom must be practiced.

The students also talked about democracy. They considered that they were fighting for socialist democracy, that is, democracy that expressed the interests of the majority. They considered that the people's congresses today did not represent the spirit of the people as masters of the country. They demanded direct election of the people's deputies by the masses.

At this time a middle-aged man in the crowd expressed his ideas about the Communist Party of China. He considered that there were good party members devoted to reforming the country. However there were also many capable and enthusiastic people among the masses that wanted to reform the country. These people should be allowed to join the party freely and work together with the good party members.

A young student at once raised the question of the multiparty system. He considered that the era of one-party dictatorship should end. A multiparty system should be practiced, and with competition there would be progress.

Some students mentioned their views on Deng Xiaoping's open-door policy. Basically they supported it, but they thought that it was too radical in the course of implementation. China had not been able to adapt to it, and many ordinary people did not understand the content of the reform. Yet the open-door policy brought social problems, including the upsurge of prices and the lowering of living standards. The livelihood of the public was much worse than before, and this demonstrated that a reform without democratic participation could only be disadvantageous to the citizens.

A student discussed his ideas on the law: the law is an instrument maintaining social order and protecting the lives and property of the people; however the law in China protects the superstructure and the interests of the privileged. Only when the people draw up the law collectively can the interests of the people as a whole be protected.

Some citizens expressed disagreement with the student demonstration for causing traffic disorder. A young man at once excitedly came to the center to speak and said, "The student demonstration is a reaction to the social contradictions; the action of the students is righteous. The demonstration will inevitably cause inconvenience to some people, but can we therefore give up our action of fighting for democracy and freedom?" He gave an example: if one gets a fishbone stuck in one's throat while eating rice, will he never again eat rice? This received applause from the crowd, which urged the young man to speak on.

Another student raised the question: Can democratic reform be effected just by sitting down to discuss and negotiate with the authorities? He pointed out that the action of the students alone was not enough. A social movement could be victorious only by joining forces with the workers. His speech also won warm applause from the crowd.

Thus the rally on democracy went on in vigorous discussion. The citizens' participation showed their concern for the student action and their concern for the country's future. The Shanghai citizens, always under repression in word or action, expressed their thoughts at this rally. A person even said, "Even if what I say now will cause the security men to come and arrest me, I must still do so." Their indignation had been pent up for a long time, but their attitude was like the slogan on a banner during the demonstration: "We will not keep silent!" The rally ended at about ten o'clock.

When the crowd left late that night, cold and solitude descended again upon the square. The only building, the office of the Shanghai People's Congress, stood alone in the square, looking particularly forlorn in the chill and dim street light. If only the discussion rallies could continue!

8

The Signature Campaigns for the Release of Political Prisoners and Related Incidents

XIAO DIAN

Since the beginning of this year, there has been a series of signature campaigns in mainland China demanding the release of jailed dissidents and political prisoners. There were also widespread signature campaigns in Hong Kong and abroad in support of the campaigns in China, most of which went beyond the initial demands of the Chinese campaign.

During this period two incidents occurred that attracted international attention to the way the Chinese regime handled the events.

Though the petition campaigns appear to be relatively small-scale and mild, combined with stupid actions on the part of some Chinese bureaucrats in creating the incidents, they in fact mark a turning point in the attitude of intellectuals in China and, to some extent, in Hong Kong and abroad. They highlight the acuteness of the social, economic, political, and ideological crises in China.

CHRONICLE OF EVENTS

The series of signature campaigns actually first appeared in a small Hong Kong magazine, *Cheng Ming*. In a small corner in its January 1989 issue, it published an appeal by itself and five other organizations and groups in Hong Kong and France to commemorate the tenth anniversary of the arrest of Chinese dissident Wei Jingsheng on March 29, 1989, and to demand the release of Wei, Liu Qing, Xu Wenli, Wang Xizhe, and all other political prisoners.

122

At about the same time, on January 6, 1989, Chinese dissident scientist Fang Lizhi wrote an open letter to Chinese leader Deng Xiaoping suggesting a general amnesty in China, especially the release of Wei Jingsheng and all political prisoners on humanitarian grounds in this year of the fortieth anniversary of the People's Republic of China, the seventieth anniversary of the May 4 Movement, and the two hundredth anniversary of the French Revolution.

On February 13 in Beijing, thirty-three well-known intellectuals, writers, poets, and artists wrote an open letter in support of Fang Lizhi's open letter. Then on February 19, one of the signatories and an activist in the Beijing Spring democracy movement ten years ago, Chen Jun, collected another thirty signatures among artists and democracy movement activists in support of that open letter. He also issued an open appeal to collect more signatures in China and called for solidarity from abroad. An "Amnesty '89" working group was also formed.

These bold initiatives and actions from within China immediately aroused broad support in Hong Kong, Taiwan, and overseas. Signature campaigns were started within intellectual circles with varying demands, ranging from calls for human rights, democratic elections, democratic rights, concerns for a democratic future and links among China, Hong Kong, and Taiwan, calls for attention to the human rights situation in Taiwan, attention to Hong Kong residents jailed for political reasons in both mainland China and Taiwan, appeals to Western governments to intervene in the human rights issues in China, and objections to foreign government intervention using "human rights diplomacy" as a scheme, calls to deepen the pro-capitalistic reforms in China, and, on the contrary, calls for political and economic control by the working masses, and so forth.

In mainland China the signatories and the signature campaigns were subjected to strong pressure from the Chinese regime. Individuals were harassed; the Justice Ministry came out with allegations of "influencing judiciary independence in the Wei Jingsheng case" (ten years after the "trial"!). Despite that, two significant signature campaigns were subsequently organized: one received the support of forty-two elder scientists, professors, and intellectuals; another was among forty-three mainly middle-aged and younger intellectuals and journalists.

Outside mainland China most of the campaigns were centered around intellectual circles, overseas scholars, well-known figures, etc., although they also received some support from the masses through publicity. The campaign initiated by *Cheng Ming* magazine obtained over three thousand four hundred signatures in some thirty countries and territories. Another campaign initiated mainly from among Hong Kong intellectual and professional circles obtained over one thousand two hundred signatures.

With the idea of promoting concerns for democracy and linking the democratic future of Hong Kong to democracy in mainland China, activists from the Action April 5 group organized signature campaigns in urban centers and workers' districts to approach the masses. They also promoted signature campaigns in postsecondary colleges. Altogether they distributed over 40,000 leaflets and collected over 12,800 signatures, among which about 1,000 were from students. The Hong Kong Federation of Students and student organizations in colleges and universities in Hong Kong also organized independently and collected over six thousand five hundred signatures among students.

In Taiwan over five thousand signatures were collected among university students in support of human rights and democratization in mainland China. On the other hand, declarations from progressive circles drawing attention to the abuse of human rights and democratic freedoms in Taiwan itself aroused controversies in the newspapers.

On February 26, Chinese police prevented Fang Lizhi and his companion from attending the farewell dinner organized by U.S. President Bush in Beijing, thereby creating an incident that attracted much international attention.

The end of March saw another incident that has even greater impact in Hong Kong. On March 28, a seven-member delegation from Hong Kong went to Beijing to present the over twenty-four thousand signatures collected in Hong Kong and overseas to the National People's Congress then in session in Beijing. Upon arriving in nearby Tianjin, the signatures and press release material were held by Chinese Customs officials and a member of the delegation, a reporter from *Cheng Ming*, was refused entry. The remaining six delegates went on to Beijing and were subjected to constant surveillance and harassment by Chinese plainclothes policemen numbering over a hundred at times. Widely reported by the Hong Kong and international reporters, who were themselves also harassed, the two-day incident aroused deep feelings in Hong Kong and, to an unknown extent, in China, because the incident was questioned openly in the National People's Congress with live coverage by Chinese television. The question of political prisoners, human rights, and democratic rights in China once again came under national and international focus.

As a sequel to these incidents, Chinese democracy activist Chen Jun was forced on April 7 to leave China for the United States, where he once studied and has residence rights. During transit in Hong Kong airport, he was kept in custody for ten hours by Customs officials. Four days later, Chen Jun's wife, a British subject, was refused a visa by Chinese officials to reenter China.

ANALYZING THE SIGNATURE CAMPAIGNS

One feature of the wave of signature campaigns is the large number of campaigns and various demands that appeared.

The first wave of campaigns in mainland China focused their demands on the release of Wei Jingsheng and other mainland Chinese political prisoners, and they requested an amnesty on humanitarian grounds. Subsequent campaigns inside mainland China were mostly in support of the initial campaigns. However in the case of the forty-two elder scientists and professors, over half of whom were party members, their demands were much bolder and unconcealed. They included:

1. Political democratization within the premise of continuing the economic reforms, for democracy and control by the general masses under conditions of the commodity economy;
2. The guarantee of the basic rights of citizens, especially freedom of speech and of the press;
3. The release of all prisoners jailed for their thoughts, an end to jailing because of dissident thoughts or speech;
4. Increased funding for education and scientific research and improvement of intellectuals' livelihood.

Although the first demand reflects an illusion in "democracy and control by the general masses" under conditions of the market economy, the other demands are much more advanced than the other campaigns inside mainland China.

Although the initial campaign led by *Cheng Ming* focused on the demand for the release of mainland Chinese political prisoners, the other signature campaigns initiated in Hong Kong also included the demand for the release of Hong Kong resident Liu Shanqing, who was arrested when he visited relatives of jailed Chinese democracy activists in mainland China in 1981 and was sentenced to ten years in prison.

In particular the demands of the Action April 5 signature campaign included:

1. An end to one-party dictatorship in China and the institution of party pluralism;
2. Freedom of speech, publication, and assembly; freedom to organize, demonstrate, and strike; and freedom of thought and political belief, not to be suppressed under any pretext;
3. The immediate release by the Chinese government of Wei Jingsheng, Liu Qing, Wang Xizhe, He Qiu, Xu Wenli, Chen Erjin, Hong Kong resident Liu Shanqing, and other activists of the democracy movement, and their exoneration.

The heading of the leaflet that they distributed was "Only with a democratic China can there be a democratic future for Hong Kong!" The leaflet further explained why these demands are important for the masses to become real masters under a democratic political system.

Another campaign, organized mainly in Hong Kong, Taiwan, and among mainland Chinese scholars overseas, linked together the demands for democracy and the release of political prisoners in mainland China and Taiwan, revealing also the extent of political imprisonment, including that of Hong Kong residents, in Taiwan. It emphasized the unity of the people of mainland China, Taiwan, Hong Kong, and Macao, as masters of the country and society, in incessant struggles against totalitarian rule; it also denounced the hypocrisy of "human rights diplomacy" in international politics.

Another campaign, organized mainly among ethnic Chinese scholars in the United States and intellectuals in Hong Kong and endorsed by Fang Lizhi, in a declaration urging democratic reforms in mainland China, demanded:

1. Independent civilian newspapers and journals;
2. The right of association, independent of the ruling party;
3. Democratic election of government leaders at county and regional levels and below;
4. Release of all political prisoners;
5. Separation of party and state.

The declaration itself also affirms the positive results of the economic reforms and expresses the belief that only a total removal of the obstacles to free economic development can reduce the political and economic differences actually existing on the two sides of the Strait and provide the basis for a peaceful unification of China, as well as guarantee long-term stability and prosperity for China, including Hong Kong and Taiwan.

In other words it implicitly calls for the restoration of the free market economy and unification based on the capitalist system, as opposed to some other campaigns, whose calls for political democratization and control by the masses are based on the existing nationalized property system and planned economy.

The signature campaigns that originated from Taiwan also revealed different perspectives. Although some advocated the abolition of the communist system in mainland China, there is still a minority voice that not only avoids such calls but calls for unification of mainland China and Taiwan based on democracy, freedom, and human rights, and the upsurge of the people from both sides to actively change the social and economic situation.

Also worth mentioning is the fact that the signature campaigns received wide support among Chinese and other people in the West. Besides the unprecedented support from Chinese intellectuals all over the world for the release of all political prisoners in China, another campaign initiated in France with similar calls received wide support, including from sixteen Nobel Prize winners.

WHY INTELLECTUALS IN CHINA STARTED MOVING

Although the outspoken, pro-Western dissident scientist Fang Lizhi attracted much attention in the various events, especially outside of mainland China, the real significance of the signature campaigns inside China lies in the changing attitude of broad layers of intellectuals, as partially reflected in the series of signature campaigns even after strong pressure to stop them was exerted by the regime. It is the culmination of severe social, economic, political, ideological, and cultural crises in China.

Ten years of opening up to capitalistic reforms in China have produced widespread and deep problems. By abandoning efforts to reinforce a planned economy, even if it is of the bureaucratically directed type, and changing to a policy of allowing capitalist market mechanisms to operate freely, Deng's "reforms" have resulted in:

• Extremely irrational and disproportionate economic growth, investment, and production structure, with severe shortages in electricity and energy supply, transport, raw material and productive goods, increasingly obsolete equipment, etc.;
• A severe disruption of industrial production, with many industries stopped 50 percent of the time;
• A several-year decline in the production of grain, oil seeds, and cotton;
• Disorderly markets;
• Rampant speculation, especially by bureaucrats;
• Widespread corruption at all levels of the bureaucracy;
• Severe inflation and huge price increases;
• Disintegration of the social order;
• A widespread social mood of "money first";
• A severe crisis in the educational system;
• Increased social polarization;
• Gradual concentration of land in the hands of a minority;
• A severe reduction in cultivated land area;
• Severe population pressure;
• Increased localism;
• Widened differences between rich and poor regions;
• Heightened discontent of national minorities;
• Severe environmental pollution and ecologic destruction;
• General discontent among broad layers of the population;
• An unprecedented ideologic crisis in the CCP;
• A crisis of credibility for the CCP among the population;
• A rejection of bureaucratic "socialism" by the masses;
• Discontent and confusion among the majority of the population arising from the actual negative impact of capitalism;
• Hesitation of CCP leaders to make future projections;
• Disappointment and disillusionment of broad layers of the society toward the Chinese regime; and so forth.

Facing such severe crises, intellectuals feel particularly disappointed and desperate. They feel a strong urge to speak out, to discuss, and to find a way out. With the severe political repression in China in mind, the initial focus is directed toward the fate of dissident democracy fighters who have been jailed for almost a decade and with whom they have maintained some distance until now. That explains the concern for the release of all political prisoners in China, already widespread among intellectuals abroad, but particularly deeply felt among intellectuals inside China. The depth of the crises is shown by the fact that the signatories included many long-time communist intellectuals who have been party members for over half a century and that many signatories overcame the fear arising from forty years of campaigns of repression.

THE EXPLOSIVE SITUATION UNDERLYING THE INCIDENTS

However it is precisely the series of incidents related to the signature campaigns that brought the acuteness of the situation in China into the open.

The further development of wide and deep crises have come together and created an explosive situation, as shown by:

- Rapid increases in prices, runs on banks, waves of panic buying, and widespread discontent in the second half of last year, have forced the Chinese regime to suspend some aspects of the economic reform and to cut many capital investments, housing and building constructions, loans to village enterprises, and to reduce consumer spending, etc. An immediate effect of these austerity measures is the surfacing of an excess labor force, estimated to be over 100 million in all. Because a large amount of rural land has been contracted out, many of the redundant workers cannot return to the land and have to wander from place to place in search of work, creating the grave situation of unprecedented "blind flow."
- As a result of the reduction in grain production since 1985 and partly as a result of shortages of foreign reserve, limiting the ability to import grain, the grain supply has been tight since the beginning of this year. Rampant localism and large-scale "blind flow" also added tremendous pressure on grain consumption and has resulted in partial shortages of grain in some areas.
- The majority of city workers have been hit by rising prices, decreases and halts in production, and enterprise reforms, and have been responding by widespread slowdowns and strikes.
- Long-time Han chauvinism and bureaucratic rule have created an explosive situation among national minorities, exploding around March 10 in Tibet into large-scale riots, forcing the Chinese regime to impose a curfew.
- Although the long-time discontent and disappointment among students and intellectuals have been prevented by repression from exploding on a large scale so far, under the impact of the signature campaigns, the May 4 anniversary, and other events, they may explode at any time. The prospect of a link-up of students and intellectuals with workers and other social layers is more than a nightmare for the regime.

At the same time, the many problems arising from the economic reforms have focused the attention of people toward political reforms and bureaucratic rule itself. On the other hand, the overall social, political, and economic crises in the Soviet Union and all other Stalinist bureaucratic systems have forced (Soviet President Mikhail) Gorbachev to carry out limited political reforms and *perestroika* and forced Hungary and Poland to allow party pluralism and political liberalization conditionally. These developments have exerted a certain pressure on the Chinese regime to carry out some political reforms and democratization.

However facing the grave situation and deep economic crisis in China, the Chinese regime has no room to make concessions. On the contrary it can only hope to contain the discontent and crisis in society and try to prevent it from exploding. That is why the "New Authoritarianism" has surfaced in recent months.

The Fang Lizhi dinner incident and moreover the Hong Kong delegation incident occurred precisely in this tense situation. Besides the fear that the Hong Kong and overseas signature and democracy campaigns may encourage intellectuals and democracy fighters inside mainland China, the Chinese regime could not afford to display any sign of weakness or tolerance when facing what amounted to mild but still confrontational challenges. On the other hand, the internal and international situation did not give it the free hand of direct brutal repression as has happened so often in the past. Hence the ugly and seemingly stupid bureaucratic behavior despite the strong presence of journalists from Hong Kong, Taiwan, and the world.

THE EFFECTS IN HONG KONG

For a long time, especially after the rejection by the Chinese regime of the 1 million signatures from Hong Kong against the building of the nearby Daya Bay nuclear plant, the failure of the 1987 campaign for direct elections in Hong Kong, partly because of pressure from the Chinese regime, and the blatantly fake consultation by the Chinese regime on the drafting of the Basic Law, broad layers of the so-called "democratic current" went into a crisis of orientation, though the general public remains politically apathetic, despite the increasing shadow of the 1997 question and the increasing bureaucratic political and economic intervention of the Chinese regime in Hong Kong.

However the overall severe crisis in China is also felt in Hong Kong to some extent. The response of mainland intellectuals to the signature campaigns therefore found quite a strong echo in Hong Kong, not only among intellectuals, but also among the general public, as can be felt by the good reception of the signature campaign in the street. The masses are generally receptive to the idea of "only with a democratic China can there be a democratic future for Hong Kong."

The signature campaigns in Hong Kong also aroused renewed interest and concern about the developments in China among many intellectuals, students, and, notably, the Hong Kong Federation of Students.

The explicit inclusion of Hong Kong resident Liu Shanqing on the list of political prisoners in mainland China by many signature campaigns also marked a significant change of attitude of many Hong Kong activists and students. In the past, calls for his release were not widely supported, partly because of fear of confronting the Chinese regime and partly because of the general apathy.

A rally in Hong Kong on April 5 also marked the changing attitude among activists, students, and, to some extent, the general public toward the affairs in China and toward confronting the Chinese regime.

The rally, which was legalized by the last-minute issuance a rally license by the police, although the organizers declared openly that they would not apply for one, was organized by the Action April 5 group to commemorate the thirteenth anniversary of the Tiananmen Uprising in Beijing in 1976 and the eighth anniversary of the suppression of the "Beijing Spring" Democracy Movement in 1981, as well as to support the signature campaigns in China and to protest the treatment of the Hong Kong delegation to the Chinese regime.

Some two hundred activists and students took part in the highly spirited three-hour rally and demonstration, despite some harassment from the police. The rally attracted general sympathy from the public. Its significance went well beyond its size, particularly in view of the current political climate in Hong Kong.

As a result of all the incidents, it is possible that part of the general public may feel so indignant toward the Chinese regime that they resent not just the bureaucracy but also the socialistic base of mainland China, and therefore their illusion in capitalism is reinforced. However it is all the more possible that with the rise in the struggles for democracy by the working masses in various parts of China, including Taiwan, Hong Kong, and Macao, and the concern and solidarity with the struggles in other parts of China, the working masses of all China will gradually find the system that best satisfies their interests.

At present although in no way minimizing the importance of the campaigns for democracy, it is also important to note that, by and large, they have not yet linked up with the working masses and their economic interests to any significant extent. Only by linking intellectuals and students with the working masses and combining the struggles for democracy with the struggles to protect the majority of people's standard of living from the attacks of capitalistic reforms and bureaucratic rule in China and from capitalism in Taiwan, Hong Kong, and Macao, can there be a persistent struggle capable of mobilizing the greatest number of people.

China is in an explosive situation, as the signature campaign and the related incidents reveal. That is why it is all the more important to link the social forces capable of solving the crisis in the interests of the majority of the people.

9

Learn the Lesson of Blood: Overthrow the Rule of the Bureaucracy

EDITORIAL

Beginning June 4 the Chinese bureaucracy massacred students and other citizens in the capital on a large scale: innumerable brave and outstanding militants sacrificed under rattling machine guns and rolling tanks! Subsequently the bureaucracy has massively hunted and executed student and working-class leaders!

The role of students as the vanguard in awakening the masses has been fulfilled; from this point of view, the students' movement has succeeded. However it suffered bloody repression at a time when the students' movement has developed into a revolutionary movement involving all layers of the masses fighting for democracy but before the working class can rise up to act as the central force in the struggle. The people's blood has been spilled! The red blood wakes up the people: when the rule of the bureaucracy suffers serious threats, to maintain its power to the very end, how bloody and ferocious it is! The red blood wakes up the people: peaceful means are finally rolled over by tank. Only by people's power and people in arms can a brutal regime be countered.

The tragic massacre revealed that the entire bureaucracy is the butcher, that the massacre was meticulously planned. From the very beginning, the regime refused to engage in dialogue with the students, refused to concede one inch, while at the same time, it prepared intensely the repression by the army. The pressure from the people caused serious divisions within the bureaucracy; therefore before the top leadership concentrated its fire against the people, it first had to clean up internally, unify the tone, and transmit the orders. This is the reason why it delayed the clampdown. When it had put its own house in order, the bureaucracy started the massive repression,

132

massacre, and manhunts. From this, the following conclusion should be drawn: the so-called "Deng-Li-Yang clique" is not only a few mad murderers, but the representatives who uphold the ruling power of the entire bureaucracy. The repression was carried out only after the majority of the top and middle layers of the bureaucracy expressed support for the central leadership; if dissenters want to oppose it, they must break with the entire bureaucracy and side with the people.

After the June 4 massacre, the entire bureaucracy continues to hunt down and kill prodemocracy militants and carries out a rule of terror. This further indicates that the people cannot depend on the armed forces of one faction of the bureaucracy to strike at or contain another faction. The only way out is through the struggle of the people as the central force and the winning over of the soldiers and the good people who are quitting the party to support the struggle of the people.

At present, students and workers' movement militants escaping the manhunt, as well as party members and cadres who have left the disintegrating Chinese bureaucracy, are forced to carry out their activities underground. This will directly catalyze the birth of new parties to promote future struggles. These new forces should be able to learn the lessons from the current events and understand that to overthrow the bureaucracy's rule and to realize people's power it will not be possible to use peaceful means. Revolution will be necessary.

To explain the struggle's political aims and perspectives, that is, to overthrow bureaucratic rule, it is necessary to tell the facts to the people everywhere, and especially to the enlisted ranks of the army, to draw the lessons from the Beijing massacre, especially the nature of bureaucratic rule and its irreformability. At the same time, the people need to mobilize fully and organize, in particular, to intervene forcefully by using the organized power of the working class, for resistance and self-defense. The next step is to win the army over to the people's side and eventually to overthrow the bureaucracy.

In Beijing, Shanghai, Guangzhou, Chengdu, Nanchang, Hangzhou and other places, autonomous workers' organizations have already been set up. Although some leaders have been arrested or killed and the organizations forced to go underground, the working class' strength has not been seriously reduced so far.

In the current stage, in the face of the mad counterrevolutionary attack by the bureaucracy in its death agony, in the face of attacks on living standards due to deepening economic difficulties, the people need to unite more closely to defend themselves, to fight repression, to preserve strength and unity, and to prepare for struggle in the next wave of the revolution.

The Chinese people have awakened! The people's revolutionary struggle to overthrow bureaucratic rule has made an important stride!

To overthrow the rule of the Chinese bureaucracy, to realize the rule of the people as masters, struggle to the very end!

10

The Significance and Lessons of the Antibureaucracy Revolutionary Struggle

EDITORIAL

The struggle of students, workers, and citizens in Beijing and other major cities from mid-April to early June shook not only China but also all the so-called "socialist countries" and the whole world. The struggle of the Chinese people is a severe blow to international Stalinism. It is part of the struggle of the people of all countries against the rule of the bureaucracy, and it is also part of the struggle of the world's toiling masses to become their own masters.

The crisis of world Stalinism is now extremely severe, and especially because the CCP is in decay and the tradition of bureaucratism is especially strong, this crisis breaks out in China with extreme acuteness. To maintain their rule, the Stalinist bureaucracies have to usurp the people's revolutionary gains in overthrowing the private property system and suppress the people's right to decide on the economy and society, which results in stagnant economic growth and intensified social contradictions. In China the crisis of the bureaucracy's rule worsens even more since the death of Mao Zedong. After ten years of "open door reform," the combination of capitalist economic factors with bureaucratic dictatorship aggravates corruption and decay, speculation, hoarding by bureaucrats, social polarization, and imbalances in economic development. It is precisely the breaking point of these social contradictions that forms the background to the recent massive mobilization of the masses.

One significant effect of this struggle of the students, workers, and citizens is the thorough exposure of the reactionary nature of the CCP bureaucracy and the depth of its crisis of rule. Even though the student movement from the beginning emphasized peace and reason and only raised demands for reforms within the existing system, the facts show that the CCP is reluctant and indeed unable to carry out the least reforms or make the least concessions. On the contrary it uses the army and subsequently the entire repressive apparatus to launch a reign of terror, suppress the people's demands, and beat back their mobilization. The bloody brutality is meant to declare to the people and to be written into history: the bureaucracy will not tolerate any action undermining its rule and will not consider all the serious consequences that the repression incurs. Taking part in defending this thoroughly decayed ruling caste is not just the so-called "Deng-Li-Yang Clique," but the entire bureaucracy that groups around itself all the reactionary forces and vested interests that can still be grouped together.

In fact regardless of the students, workers, and citizens' subjective wish to peacefully demand concessions from the regime, the contradictions between the rules and the ruled have reached this state: under very intense social contradictions, the people's mobilization has made a breakthrough by opening a breach in the forty years of highly repressive bureaucratic rule and is gradually gathering force together and starting to organize itself. With the masses mobilizing further, with the whole population out to block the army, with the resistance to the martial law that the bureaucracy has declared, even though the subjective force of the masses is still insufficient, objectively it has accelerated the split within the bureaucracy, further undermining the already narrowed social base of bureaucratic rule. In blocking the army's entry, erecting barricades, controlling important parts of Beijing, maintaining social order, etc., the people of Beijing mobilized massively. In some other major cities, large-scale mass mobilizations also appeared. The scale and length of this spontaneous mobilization of the Chinese urban masses is unprecedented.

The events have reached a stage when either the people's political revolution to overthrow bureaucratic rule continues to develop until it gains victory or the bureaucracy's counterrevolutionary repression succeeds. The contradiction between the bureaucracy and the people can no longer be compromised. The bureaucracy has chosen to repress. Just before the massacre, the students and masses also learned that the only way out is to overthrow the current regime. The Tiananmen Square Command Center at the last moment made "down with the Li Peng false government" the single slogan, reflecting that they had come to grips with the objective revolutionary situation.

The people of the capital have written a heroic, solemn, and tragic new chapter in the modern history of China. Despite various weaknesses in the subjective factors, which led to the defeat of this developing political revolution, the people's political revolution to overthrow the rule of the CCP bureaucracy has made an important advance, revealing thoroughly the weaknesses of the bureaucratic regime and demonstrating the main problems of the political revolution. The urgent task now is to draw a balance sheet of the tragic historical experience and learn the lessons to continue with the struggle until the victory of the political revolution.

It can be seen from the current struggle that, with forty years of one-party dictatorial rule consciously dividing and atomizing the masses' strength, it is very difficult to start to gather forces. The students successfully used mobilization tactics, first through the pretext of commemorating Hu Yaobang, then through peaceful petitioning, hunger strike protests, and other methods, to conduct independent mobilization and organization and to develop autonomous student organizations in Beijing and the provinces. Although in the beginning of the movement, some bureaucrats could have tried to take advantage of the movement for factional fights within the bureaucracy, the subsequent development of the student movement clearly shows that the students consciously avoided becoming the tool of any wing of the bureaucracy but instead actively turned to the masses for support, especially from the workers. They recognized that without the participation of the working class, the bureaucracy cannot be confronted.

The struggle in fact developed rapidly to a violent confrontation between the citizens and the regime. Citizens and workers not only mobilized on a large scale but also formed the "Beijing Autonomous Workers' Federation" and the "Federation of all sections of the people of the capital," etc. The working class independently mobilized and organized and began to display its potential strength, lead the masses to grasp the historical opportunity, and break through the many years of tight control and repression by the bureaucracy. This initially assembled force of urban masses with workers as the backbone is not subjectively well prepared, yet when the situation changed sharply, it became a major force in confronting the bureaucracy.

The massacre and subsequent reign of terror indicate that when faced with the frenzied struggle of a regime in death agony, if the people insist on peaceful means they will only be massacred arbitrarily. To overthrow a brutal regime possessing an army and a huge repressive apparatus, to remove the chief obstacle in the social and economic development of today's China, individual, unorganized, and aimless efforts are futile. It is necessary to rely on conscious and organized social forces, especially the working class, which can control the economic veins of the society, to widely and consciously organize and become active political forces. To advance the political revolution, it is necessary to have a revolutionary party with a program that clearly advocates the overthrow of the bureaucratic regime and the organization and mobilization of forces from various layers. Only through this can the army be won over and the bureaucracy overthrown.

The era of political revolution to overthrow the rule of the bureaucracy has begun. Although the struggle of the masses has been temporarily repressed, the masses have awakened and have mobilized; the bureaucracy is in its death agony. It can be foreseen that the present counterrevolutionary repression will lead the bureaucracy into even deeper crisis; economic difficulties will be more severe; concessions to regional power, foreign capital, and capitalist forces will be even greater; the oppression and exploitation of the toiling masses will be worse; and the antagonism with the people more irreconcilable. Therefore the social contradictions that have triggered this revolutionary struggle will continue to aggravate.

At the moment under the counterrevolutionary repression of the bureaucracy, the most urgent task is the defense of the militants in this struggle from persecution and execution. At the same time, it is necessary to start from the defense of the right of the people to live, combining the struggle for basic democratic rights with the struggle in defense of the people's living standards, so as to mobilize and organize workers and other social layers and prepare well for the next high tide of struggle.

11

One Year after Democracy Movement '89

YANG HAI

In the reports on the national economic plan and government budget by the Chinese State Department in March 1990, the economic situation was described as "relatively good" even though they also mentioned briefly that there were still some difficulties. However the real situation, especially since the second half of the year, is much more serious than the picture painted and can even be described as crisis-ridden.

The causes of this situation clearly include the impact of Democracy Movement '89, but deeper reasons lie with the ten years of economic reforms and with the rule of the bureaucracy.

The effects of the economic crisis on society and the people's lives are even more serious and are threatening directly the regime of the CCP.

The way the CCP regime guarded Tiananmen Square since April of this year reflects its feeling of sitting on a volcano that can erupt at any time.

THE ECONOMIC PERFORMANCE IN 1989

The official reports said that the gross national product in 1989 was 1,567.7 billion yuan (Renminbi), a growth of 3.9 percent over 1988, while the national income, gross agricultural product, and gross industrial product grew by 3.7 percent, 3.3 percent, and 8.3 percent, respectively. The foreign trade deficit has decreased; the foreign currency reserve has increased by U.S. $2.2 billion. The economic rectification process was said to have achieved results: fixed capital investments have increased, the rise in prices was less than in 1988, and social consumption demands were under effective control.

Presumably the result that the CCP regime is happiest about is the good grain harvest, whose gross amount is slightly above the historic peak of 1984, even though per capita grain production is still lower than in 1984 because of population growth. Moreover production of vegetables, fruits, meat, and aquatic products has increased although production of cotton, oil seeds, and sugar products has not reversed the downward trend.

To deal with the so-called overheated economy, the CCP continued the rectification policy started in the fourth quarter of 1988 and apparently achieved some results. The industrial growth rate that has been too high for several years has begun to come down, from 20.7 percent in 1988 to 8.3 percent in 1989. The severely unbalanced industrial production structure has improved slightly; the production of energy, important raw materials, electricity, and transportation of goods have increased between 3 percent and 7.2 percent although it is still lower than the average industrial growth rate. The value of completed fixed capital investments has decreased by 11 percent compared to 1988, still less than the reduction requested by the plan. Nonproductive construction investments have also decreased. The construction of luxury houses and apartments has also been restrained. General prices still rose very sharply in the first half of 1989 but slowed in the second half; the annual inflation rate was still a high 17.8 percent, only slightly lower than the 22.2 percent in 1988.

SURGE OF ECONOMIC PROBLEMS

At the same time that the so-called overheated economy cools off, problems that have accumulated over the years have broken out, accompanied by the impact of Democracy Movement '89, causing severe and contradictory economic difficulties. Although huge demands still exist, the market has seriously weakened, industrial production has decreased, and economic efficiency has dropped significantly.

Starting from May 1989, the consumer market has softened, with a continuous drop in sales; since August, its growth rate has become negative. The total social goods retail sales volume has actually decreased by 7.6 percent compared with 1988, after taking inflation into account. The weak market situation has continued into the first quarter of this year. As a result of the weak market, unsold goods have begun to accumulate massively, resulting in a huge increase of industrial and commercial stocks of over 100 billion yuan in 1989. Industrial and commercial enterprises have thus experienced problems in circulation funds, and there is a severe problem of debts between various enterprises.

Industrial production also began to slow down since May 1989, and in October it dropped by 2.1 percent compared with October 1988. Starting in May, light industrial production began to decease, and since September it has continuously registered lower results than in 1988. The drop in demand for productive goods from light industry, together with the squeeze in fixed capital investments and other factors, has begun to affect heavy industrial production. Starting in September, heavy industrial production has decreased each month, although the scale of the decrease was not as severe as it was in light industry.

To reverse the drop in industrial production, the CCP has released massive loans in the fourth quarter of 1989 in the amount of 120 billion yuan, twice the total for the previous three quarters. But it could only barely arrest the falling trend. In January and February of this year, industrial production dropped again by 0.9 percent, with the daily production for February dropping by 6.5 percent compared with January and by 5.7 percent compared with February of last year. Therefore the CCP has resorted to relaxing the "buying power of social groups" and other methods to stimulate production, especially light industrial production. As a result March industrial production increased by 1.4 percent compared with March 1989.

IMPACT OF JUNE 4

There are many reasons for the weak market and the decrease in industrial production and economic efficiency. Democracy Movement '89 and the June 4 massacre have in several ways accelerated their outbreak and aggravated them.

Democracy Movement '89 shook the entire CCP bureaucracy. The people generally feel extremely dissatisfied with the speculation, corruption, and conspicuous consumption by bureaucrats, forcing the CCP center to order the bureaucrats, large and small, to reduce somewhat their grandiose consumption, control the so-called buying power of social groups, and restrain the construction of luxury homes. Since June 1989 the special groups consumption retail sales amounts have dropped, especially in August, September, and October. However sales for the year still totaled 69.3 billion yuan, an increase of 4.2 percent over 1989 (a decrease of about 11 percent after accounting for inflation), still very much higher than requested by the CCP center.

Furthermore the CCP leadership has intensified the crackdown on bureaucratic speculative companies after June, closing down over seventy thousand companies, about one quarter of the total. It also increased taxes or monopolized the sale of some speculative goods, restraining speculation to a certain extent and the income and consumption resulting from it.

On the other hand, the CCP intensified its control and tax collection on individual businesses and the overhauling of rural enterprises. Under the pressure of tightening up, many people, especially those who have enriched themselves during ten years of reforms, have reduced consumption, especially high-grade consumption.

Under the influence of several factors, the sale of high-grade consumer goods has dropped severely, especially cars, color televisions, and refrigerators; the production of these three products in the first quarter of this year has consequently dropped by 34 percent, 32 percent, and 49 percent, respectively, compared with the first quarter of 1989.

As for the general masses, several factors affect their power or desire to consume. It was apparent that after June 4, the citizens' mood suffered a heavy blow, and they reduced their consumption. Since 1988 the introduction by the banks of inflation-linked savings has reduced consumer demand somewhat. Under the CCP's austerity measures, workers' wages and bonuses have been restrained; the reduction or even stoppages in factory production, as well as the government's forcing workers to subscribe to state bonds to alleviate its financial difficulties, have also seriously affected workers' incomes.

What is more difficult to estimate is the effect of the people's passive resistance in the factories, especially the workers in big cities like Beijing, to the CCP regime after the blow of June 4. In the official figures for 1989, the overall labor productivity in industry has only increased by 1.6 percent over 1988, compared with 9.3 percent in 1988, while the overall labor productivity in construction has actually dropped by 1.5 percent, compared with a rise of 1.8 percent in 1988. Together with the massive increase in enterprise losses and the drop in economic efficiency, they might reveal, besides falling or stopped production and other factors, the effect of a further drop in worker motivation.

Under the impact of June 4, income from tourism has dropped significantly. Official figures indicate a decrease of U.S. $410 million compared to 1988, or a drop of 19.6 percent. However, in contrast to a projected continuation of the 20 percent growth in 1988, the loss in income would amount to U.S. $0.8 to $1 billion.

Moreover foreign government and bank loans to China have virtually stopped after June 4, and the sanctions have only begun to be relaxed as of the beginning of this year. Figures from the State Budget Report indicate that "income" from foreign loans last year fell short of budget by 3 billion yuan, a drop of 18.3 percent, but figures released by the Foreign Economic and Trade Ministry revealed a much more serious effect: total agreed loans last year were U.S. $4.8 billion, a drop of over 50 percent from 1988, and actually used loans were U.S. $5.9 billion, a drop of nearly 10 percent.

In view of the instability of the CCP regime, most foreign capitalists have taken a hesitant attitude toward expanding investments in China. Official figures show that "actual foreign business investments" have only grown by 4.1 percent in 1989; as a close comparison, the "actual amount of foreign investments used" in 1988 grew by 16.4 percent over 1987. Had there not been a massive increase in investments in China from Taiwan capitalists looking for opportunities to divest outside of Taiwan, the situation would have been much worse.

EFFECTS OF TEN YEARS OF REFORMS

A deeper reason for the weak market and drop in production may be found with the change in industrial structure as a result of ten years of economic reforms.

In recent years all over China, many production lines for high-grade consumer products have been imported and are producing automobiles, color televisions, refrigerators, high-grade beverages, and so on, on a massive scale. These products are marketed for the consumption of bureaucrats and those who have enriched themselves during the reforms. Now there has appeared a serious excess productive capacity for these products. For example it was reported that total productive capacity for color televisions in China is now 16 million sets per year; last year 7.89 million sets were produced and 7.01 million sets sold; this year the plan is to produce 6 million sets, that is, only at 37.5 percent of total productive capacity. The distorted development of consumer goods production has become a heavy burden for the economy.

Moreover the CCP center has for years practiced a policy of granting power and the right to profit to the provinces and enterprises. To promote regionalism and to satisfy the huge demand for light industrial consumer goods that were neglected for decades, regional bureaucracies have blindly developed light industry, resulting in excess productive capacity and low efficiency.

At the same time, traditional large-scale light industry and heavy industry have been neglected, machinery and technology have become worn out and obsolete, and production efficiency has dropped. The basic production infrastructure has also become seriously unbalanced; the production of raw materials and energy, transport and road facilities, and so on, are seriously inadequate.

This is the situation behind the so-called overheated economy. It also reveals that the apparent boom brought about by ten years of economic reform is actually financed to a very large extent by massive internal and foreign loans, with distorted development fostered by high-grade consumption by bureaucrats and the nouveau riche, whose effects and influence are clearly shown now.

In reality the basic needs of the people are far from satisfied. At the same time as the market becomes weaker and some stocks increase massively, people's savings in urban and rural areas have increased by 35 percent, reaching 513.5 billion yuan, the equivalent of three-quarters of annual retail sales of consumer goods.

Ten years of economic reforms have also made the Chinese economy, especially in the coastal provinces and the processing industry, rather dependent on the capitalist world market. At the current regulated foreign exchange rate of about U.S. $1 to 6 yuan (not just the official exchange rate of 4.73), the total import and export trade amounts to an equivalent of over

40 percent of the gross national product. Last year's restriction of imports has not only affected domestic production but also restricted the capacity to increase exports; the slowing down in the U.S. economy in the second half of last year has undoubtedly also had an effect in the slowing down of Chinese exports.

All these transformations were not made overnight, nor can they be changed easily. And the entire process of change has resulted in heavy internal and external debt burdens. A great mass of workers and rural laborers have come to depend on the new economic structure for their living, and any adjustments or economic crisis will have very significant consequences.

GOVERNMENT FINANCIAL CRISIS

The weak market and the drop in industrial production and economic efficiency, combined with the changes after ten years of economic reforms, have caused extremely severe pressure on the Chinese government's finances, especially those of the central government. Not only was the government unable to get more income from taxes and profits from the enterprises, it had to increase significantly its subsidies to enterprise losses to 60 billion yuan last year. Together with 37 billion yuan of price subsidies, they used up one-third of the government's financial income.

Moreover the military and special administrative costs in repressing Democracy Movement '89, along with the reduced income caused by foreign sanctions, have altogether caused the government deficit to reach 37 billion yuan (not counting the money raised from debts as "income," as the CCP used to do), which amounts to over 10 percent of government income and an increase of 8.2 percent from 1988.

The huge increase in the deficit and the cut-off of foreign loans have forced the CCP to raise internal debts by all means, resulting in an increase of 26.2 percent above budget in 1989. Total government internal debts have now reached 80 billion yuan, excluding the debts raised by banks and enterprises. The official foreign debt is over U.S. $40 billion, which does not include the reported U.S. $70 billion in foreign loans made by companies and enterprises and guaranteed by the Chinese government.

This year the financial situation of the government is even gloomier.

Besides the economic difficulties affecting income and expenditures, the military and administrative expenses have to be maintained at a high level, and China has entered into the peak for repayment of internal debts this year. Reportedly the government has to repay 26 billion yuan of principal and interest this year, but the government budget intends only to repay 12.4 billion yuan of state bonds sold to individuals, while postponing the repayment of bonds sold to enterprises, units, and banks. Even so the

government budget deficit for 1990 is a high 42.3 billion yuan, 14.5 percent
more than the 1989 high.

This year the government will also have to borrow massively to repay old
loans. The budgeted new internal loans will be 17 billion yuan, 21.3 percent more than the 1989 record high.

What makes the CCP central government feel powerless is also the fact
that the center's control over financial income and material resources has
been greatly reduced over the ten years of reforms. Income for the center is
now less than half of the total state financial income, while all local difficulties
eventually end up as problems for the center.

PEOPLE'S LIVING STANDARDS SERIOUSLY AFFECTED

Over the last year, the drop in production, the government financial crisis, and
other economic problems have seriously affected the lives of the broad masses.

Because many factories have reduced or even stopped production, the
income of many urban workers has been significantly reduced, and workers
in factories that have stopped production receive only 70 percent of their
wages, not to mention any bonuses. The situation in rural industries and
individual businesses is even worse. It can be calculated from official figures
that the real income of the urban masses has dropped by 4.7 percent on
average, while the real income of the average peasant has dropped by 8.3
percent. The total amount of consumer goods sales has dropped in real
terms by 9.4 percent, falling back to the level of 1987.

The government financial crisis has also negatively affected the broad masses'
living standards. On one hand the government has to borrow more money
from the people, even using forced subscription of state bonds; on the other
hand, price subsidies of many important daily necessities such as meat, cotton wadding, soap oil, coal for civilian use, etc., have begun to be reduced
or even removed, increasing the hardship for people whose income has already been reduced.

SERIOUS PROBLEM OF UNEMPLOYMENT

The problem of unemployment has become more serious, causing great concern
within the CCP regime, because it would seriously threaten social stability
and the rule of the bureaucracy.

The number of unemployed and partially unemployed urban citizens has
grown significantly. In February of this year, some Chinese newspapers estimated that about 6 percent of state enterprises have stopped or partially
stopped production, affecting over 4 million workers already; it is worse in
the coastal provinces, with the ratio reaching over 10 percent in some prov-

inces. Other reports talked about 80 percent of enterprises in Guangdong province as not having enough work and an unemployment rate of over 10 percent. Official estimates say this year's "waiting-for-employment" rate in urban areas will grow from 2 percent to 4 percent or 5 percent—that is, from over 3 million to 6 or 7 million people or more.

Because of a serious drop in urban employment opportunities, especially because the construction industry has been under serious pressure, many rural laborers have returned to the countryside or moved around throughout the country, forming "blind flows." Moreover about 15 percent of rural enterprises have gone bankrupt or merged, and of the 95 million rural laborers employed by them, over 3 million have lost their jobs. Moreover, about 15 percent of the rural and urban individual businesses have also closed, eliminating 3.6 million jobs out of 20 million. Rural unemployment is thus especially serious. In Sichuan Province, which has a population of 100 million, 15 million are reportedly "waiting for employment," and several other provinces are in a similar situation.

PEOPLE RESIST BUREAUCRACY AND ARMY

The Democracy Movement '89 and the June 4 massacre have enabled the people to see clearly the true face and nature of the CCP bureaucracy, thus laying a more solid foundation for the next wave of the democracy movement. The crisis brought about by ten years of reforms has deepened the difficulties of CCP rule and forced it to shift the cost of the crisis onto the workers and peasants, causing even greater pressure on people's living standards. The people's struggles for democracy and defence of their living standards have become the main impetus to overthrow the rule of the CCP bureaucracy.

Since June 4 the relationship between the people and the bureaucracy and army has been very tense. News of people passively resisting the bureaucracy are frequently reported, for example, the boycotting of the CCP campaign to investigate democracy movement participants, Beijing citizens refusing to buy "patriotic cabbages" last winter, and so on. The success of Chai Ling and other democracy movement activists in hiding all over China for ten months, receiving broad protection from the people, and finally safely arriving in France and the United States shows clearly the people's general attitude. News about underground organizations that include students, workers, intellectuals, party members, and soldiers are also reported.

Moreover news of soldiers and their families being insulted, attacked, or even killed are often heard; the army even complains to the government about these attacks and requests that the government step up security.

The CCP bureaucracy's fear about the sharpening crisis, the bitterness of the people, and the unstable situation can be clearly shown by all the nervous measures to guard Tiananmen Square and Beijing, Guangdong, and other big cities since April of this year.

Various signs also indicate that there are many internal conflicts inside the bureaucracy: the party rectification campaign fizzled out, no common position or final judgment on the question of Zhao Ziyang, etc. In the intensified economic and social crises, the conflicts between central and regional bureaucracies, especially those in the coastal provinces and special economic zones, will only become more serious.

There are also signs of instability inside the army, to the extent that the party bureaucracy has to appeal many times in the newspapers for increasing discipline in the army, for maintaining unity, for the party to direct the army, and so on.

RULE OF BUREAUCRACY CRISIS-RIDDEN

On the other hand, the national question has broken out on a larger scale. Demonstrations broke out and were met with bloody repression in Xinjiang on April 5 of this year. Xizang can still explode any time, and there are also signs of instability in Inner Mongolia. Besides the CCP bureaucracy's Han chauvinism leading to national and economic oppression of the national minorities, the situation there could also be a result of encouragement from democratic and national movements in Eastern Europe, the Soviet Union, and Mongolia. The national question may even trigger the entire Chinese people to rise up against the bureaucracy's rule.

Another serious potential threat to the Chinese economy and CCP rule is the probability of recession or even depression in the world capitalist economy. Because of the degree of dependence of the Chinese economy on the world capitalist market today, a worldwide recession would seriously affect production inside China, especially the processing industries, and employment and entire societies in coastal provinces would be most affected.

The CCP regime is already forced into a corner by economic, social, and political crises. Facing the drop in industrial production and its consequences, the CCP has even had to resort to encouraging "consumption of social groups," using feasts and grandiose consumption to stimulate demand, thus risking the danger of deepening the hatred by the people toward the bureaucracy. The CCP certainly knows the danger and therefore constantly increases its work inside the army, because the army is now the only pillar left for the bureaucracy.

Last year's good grain harvest is indeed the CCP's only consolation. With its control and influence in the countryside greatly weakened by ten years of reforms, the CCP can only continue to look to the sky this year, praying at least that the question of food can be solved. For this reason, the

CCP center has "greatly" increased its basic investment in agriculture by 30 percent, an increase that turns out to be only 1 billion yuan, as compared to 69.3 billion yuan of "social group consumption" in 1989! The contradiction, crisis, and instability of the CCP regime are certainly revealed by this trifle.

_12_

The Future of China and Hong Kong Hinges on the Prospect for the Democracy Movement!

EDITORIAL

(This editorial was distributed as a leaflet during the June 3–4, 1990, rallies in Hong Kong.)

The repression of the Chinese Democracy Movement '89 does not mean that the democracy movement has failed. The movement for democracy is a process, and the ends cannot be fulfilled by one or two attempts. The repression only silenced society superficially, while contradictions continue to accumulate.

In fact Democracy Movement '89 has made significant achievements:

- Not only has it inherited the traditions of previous democracy movements, but an unprecedented people's mobilization has started. The students played a pioneering role and aroused a broad and long-lasting mobilization of working people in the capital and other big cities. The brave action by the students and working people has gained unprecedented support from the people around the world.
- Students and some of the working people have significantly broken through decades of suppression by the CCP and have started to organize themselves, forming Students' Autonomous Unions, Workers' Autonomous Unions, Joint Committees of Various Sections of the People of the Capital, and so on. The beginning of large-scale mobilization and organization of the people has become a severe threat to the CCP.
- More important is the political lesson: Democracy Movement '89, especially the June 4 massacre, has inexorably revealed the nature of the CCP regime as a whole. The CCP has lost legitimacy for its rule and has become the common enemy of the people and the target of revolution.

148

LESSON OF BLOOD

This lesson is learned with the blood of the people. Until the very last moment, wide sections of the people and of the movement's leaders have looked to reforming the CCP, believing that the bureaucracy and the "People's Army" will not massacre the people. That is why leaders of Democracy Movement '89 have not put forward calls for the ending of one-party dictatorship, have not analyzed the nature of the CCP bureaucratic structure, and have not seriously warned about the repression by the bureaucracy. For this reason they have insisted until the very end on the use of "peaceful, rational, and nonviolent means" to appeal to the "open-minded reformers" inside the CCP, thereby precluding the prospect that the masses might organize and defend themselves, let alone seize power.

Therefore the key tasks for today are to learn this lesson of blood, identify the enemy, and prepare for programmatic leadership of the future democracy movement.

Democracy Movement '89 and the June 4 massacre have further revealed the nature of the entire bureaucracy including the "open-minded reformers." Developments in the past year have also revealed the true face of various regimes and vested interests. From the so-called "advanced," "democratic" Western regimes to Taiwan and British-Hong Kong regimes, verbal support for the Chinese people's struggle for democracy has, after making anticommunist political propaganda gains, colluded with the CCP regime for their own real interests. The experiences of sanctions against the CCP, the "most-favored-nation status" issue, the treatment of the "Ship for Democracy," as well as the changing attitudes of vested interests and the increased repression of democratic rights in Hong Kong, are profound experiences for the people.

THE PEOPLE NEED TO ORGANIZE THEMSELVES

The task of overthrowing the CCP bureaucracy's rule and struggling for true democracy and people's freedom cannot depend on other antidemocratic forces, neither the reformers inside the party nor the Western regimes and vested interests. It can only depend on the self-organization of the toiling masses. This road is undoubtedly more lengthy and difficult than imagined, but the gains will be more solid and conform to the real interests of the masses of working people. In fact only the rise of the urban workers uniting with the peasants and other social layers is powerful enough to overthrow the rule of the CCP bureaucracy.

At the moment the Chinese democracy movement is still in a state of repression; it is still a period of accumulation of forces for the democracy movement. However the economic, social, and political factors triggering the outbreak of Democracy Movement '89 have not disappeared because of the repression, but instead they are becoming aggravated.

DEEPENING CRISES

In the past year, except for the relatively good grain harvest, most of the economic problems have been aggravating, especially since May and June of last year: the market has become and continues to be sluggish; industrial production has stagnated or even fallen, and one-sixth of the enterprises have encountered losses. The state financial deficit has risen to over 10 percent of the budget, and not only was the CCP unable to repay old debts, but it has to borrow to survive. During the ten years of economic reforms, the growth in production has been sustained by internal and external debts, driven by the high-level consumption of the bureaucracy, enriched through corruption and speculation, and the nouveaux riches, all of them aided by the policy of laissez-faire from the party center. The costs and effects of this growth are now breaking out with doubled intensity.

As a result the real income of the urban and rural masses has on average dropped by 4.7 percent and 8.3 percent, respectively, last year, and the standard of living has fallen. Many enterprises have reduced or even stopped their production. Some 15 percent of rural enterprises and individual households have gone bankrupt, resulting in a huge increase in the number of unemployed in the cities and the countryside, causing a severe social crisis.

Losing its legitimacy of rule, the CCP regime is facing a deepening of the economic and social crises. It has been unable to achieve results politically through purging the party or controlling the masses. During the anniversary of Democracy Movement '89, it acted in a particularly nervous and stupid manner: closing off Tiananmen Square, releasing a group of democracy activists, while arresting others like Liu Qing, lifting martial law in Tibet while declaring at the same time a set of special laws, etc. Contradictions within the party and the army have frequently surfaced. The safe escape of Chai Ling and other democracy activists contrasts sharply with the self-exile of Xu Jiatuan (the former head of the CCP bureaucracy in Hong Kong and a senior member of the CCP) to the West, revealing the general support of the Chinese people for the democracy movement, as well as disintegration within the CCP.

Pressure is building up toward the outbreak of the next wave of the democracy movement.

DEMOCRACY IN CHINA AND HONG KONG TIGHTLY LINKED

The movement in Hong Kong in support of the struggle for democracy in mainland China has tightly linked up the democratic future of China and Hong Kong.

The "Hong Kong people save Hong Kong" campaign, the campaign for the right of abode in Britain, the drafting of the Basic Law for Hong Kong, and so on have made more citizens of Hong Kong aware of the reality. For most of the people who cannot or do not want to leave Hong Kong, on the one hand, they are not happy with becoming a submissive subject of CCP rule and are doubtful about the usefulness of being submissive; on the other hand, with the repression of Democracy Movement '89, they do not yet foresee the rise of the people's power in the mainland, while the citizens of Hong Kong have remained in a dispersed and unorganized state. Their feelings are thus very complex.

To prepare for the future rise of the democracy movement in China, the citizens of Hong Kong need to recognize the prospect for the democracy movement and do support and organization work: on the one hand, to demand the release of all detained democracy activists, to break through the news blockade, to promote the boycott of the Asian Games (to be held in Beijing in September of this year), etc., to put pressure on the CCP regime by all means and to mobilize and organize the citizens of Hong Kong at the same time; on the other hand, making full use of the favorable information environment in Hong Kong to conduct more reflections on the course of the democracy movement and explore its prospects, in particular, by studying the political, economic, and social situation in China, by exploring the experiences of the developments of democracy movements in the Soviet Union and Eastern Europe, to be better armed ideologically and provide a way for the next wave of the democracy movement.

13

The People's Resistance Continues

ZHANG KAI

During the anniversary of Democracy Movement '89, the Chinese government made unprecedented precautionary measures to "stem any resistance in its budding stage." Security was very tight, especially around Tiananmen Square in Beijing, and the square was closed to the public on many memorial dates. The tense atmosphere was comparable to a fleeing army's suspicion of danger at the slightest sound.

Understandably under this extremely high-handed repression, the Chinese people have not carried out large-scale protests against the Communist Party regime.

Unexpectedly, however, there were still many people who were not afraid of arrests and cruel persecutions and have tried to fight to express their opposition to the rulers. The following are some resistance actions.

COURAGEOUS RESISTANCE

On April 7 an underground poetry club was discovered; over ten members were arrested and charged with illegal publishing.

On April 15 in Tiananmen Square, a man from Guizhou attempted to lay a wreath, inscribed with "In deep memory of comrade Hu Yaobang" [whose death triggered Democracy Movement '89] and "In deep memory of the brave fighters who sacrificed for democracy and freedom in China." He was arrested by the security police.

On May 7 big character posters appeared in the streets of Beijing, criticizing Premier Li Peng and army leader Yang Shangqun, demanding their resignations.

On May 11 a student tore down three progovernment wall posters in the Triangular Area in Beijing University; he was immediately beaten and arrested.

152

In mid-May some Beijing University students marched inside the campus "against sanctions against China by other countries" (a typical way of saying the opposite in China). The students were later detained by the police.

At the end of May, the recently released intellectuals Zhou Tuo, Gao Xin, and Hou Dejian intended to hold a press conference; they were all secretly arrested and not released for two weeks.

On June 1 Beijing citizens threw memorial money notes (money meant for use by the dead, an old Chinese custom) from public buses in Changan Street. Streets around Tiananmen Square were also laid with heaps of these notes in memory of the dead martyrs of last year. A woman tried to talk with a West German television crew, but was arrested.

On June 3 a man showed a placard to a foreign reporter in Tiananmen Square; while he was carried away by the security police, he shouted slogans like "the people, stand up!"

The same evening someone fired two shots at the guards in front of the gates to Zhongnanhai (where the CCP leaders reside); this news was revealed by "Internal Reference Information" circulated inside Beijing University. Later that night two thousand Beijing University students held a rally. A student, Li Mingqi, spoke to the rally, expressing the people's thoughts. He was later expelled by the University administration and arrested.

Following that students began throwing bottles (the word "bottle" in Mandarin is homonymous to Deng "Xiaoping") and breaking glasses in the dormitories, singing "The Internationale," even more so when army vehicles passed by.

At the same time, Fudan University students in Shanghai threw bottles for three hours, and similar actions were taken by students in Wuhan University.

On June 4 bottles continued to be thrown from buildings at Beijing University, even though the regime had closed off the university area. The riot police were dressed in full gear, and additional guards were placed in the dormitories. Riots also broke out in five other universities in Beijing; students from Jinan University in Guangdong threw bottles and sang songs for three hours. A man laid flowers and wreaths in front of Beijing University and was severely beaten and arrested by the security police. Two Buddhists were praying outside the gate to the Forbidden City and were arrested. A worker in Beijing bought a wreath for his deceased grandmother and was detained for twenty-four hours when the security police mistook his action for commemoration of the deceased in June 1989.

On the evening of June 5, students in People's University threw bottles, sang songs, and shouted slogans in the dormitories.

All the above news items were gathered from nonofficial sources and are by no means complete. Other acts of resistance were, in fact, not reported and are not known overseas. Although the scale of these acts was not big, their duration not long, and for the most part individual acts, they were carried out in a highly repressive and terrorized atmosphere, requiring exceptional courage and a willingness to endure arrest and even torture. The fact that many people still stood up in this manner revealed that people are angry and willing to challenge the die-hard conservative rulers, regardless of possible reprisals. This reflected the people's extreme discontent and restlessness and showed signs of a revival of the struggle for democracy.

REVEALING SURVEYS

The people's minds are more concretely and widely reflected in the results of some surveys. The way to answer these surveys is also a form of political struggle.

According to a June 3 report in *Ming Bao Daily* in Hong Kong, in March of this year the Beijing Municipal Committee and the State Education Commission conducted a "survey of the ideological state of students" in eight universities in Beijing. Regardless of possible bias in the study in favor of the government, for example, in selecting students for the survey, the results showed, at least partially, the general attitude of the students in Beijing today: many students refuse to lay to rest the events of June 4 of last year and think that the current screening process in high schools is "penalization after the events and still another political campaign."

Concretely many students judged that the "political event in 1989" was "the expression of the masses' discontent towards corruption and inequalities in distribution"; some 20 percent maintained that it was a "patriotic democracy movement," and only the least of them thought that it was a "counterrevolutionary riot."

Many students (31.8 percent) thought that, after ten years of reforms, the main problems existing in China today are "poor Party discipline, a declining in moral standards, worsening of the social mood, and worsening of crime rates." "The main reason for these many problems is the result of old institutional structures and old concepts." Only 8.8 percent of students believed that it was because of "the flooding of bourgeois liberal ideas." As for the solution, 25.4 percent looked to "political pluralism and the fight for more democracy and freedom," while only 8.8 percent believed that it depends on "the leading role of the Communist Party to lead the entire people through the crisis."

Regarding their opinion on the current leadership, 44.5 percent thought that it was "difficult to make the final judgment and necessary to further hear their words and see their deeds"; only 5.3 percent selected the answer of "correct decisions, brilliant and effective results, deeply loved by the people."

Regarding the new rules by the State Education Commission governing self-financed overseas studies, some 40 percent of students resolutely agreed and another one quarter of them disagreed. Furthermore, some one-third of the students would still "try by all means to leave the country"; some 30 percent were awaiting changes in the policy, and only some 10 percent "do not intend to leave the country."

The above results show that a great majority of students played a discordant tune to that of the ruling CCP clique. It shows once again the extreme isolation and lack of support for the ruling clique!

What seems slightly out of tune with the above results in the survey was the response to a reoccurrence of the student movement. Reportedly some 60 percent of students indicated that they would "watch from the sideline" or "be unconcerned." 10 percent would "boycott," while 9 percent would "participate actively." A possible reason for this response is that the bloody massacre and high-handed persecution of the students have demoralized many students; another reason could be on the part of those surveyed or the attempt to gain trust to facilitate going overseas or even a desire to join the party "to make life easier." Even so the 9 percent of students who frankly said that they would "participate actively" is a large number and will form the core force of the future student movement. By that time many "watchers from the sideline" or "unconcerned" would rejoin them actively.

A special article on June 3 and 4 of the Hong Kong *Wen Wei Bao* entitled, "The State of Mind of Beijing University Students, a First-Hand Report," reported a similar situation. Because it was conducted by surveys and interviews of students along with state officials, its results are somewhat different from the survey reported by *Ming Bao*. Many students would not speak out when directly facing state officials, even to the point of matching the official opinion. Even so many results are still valuable. For example regarding the social effects of the student movement, 69.4 percent had a positive judgment, whereas only 15.4 percent were negative. For the answer to the question, "What would you do when a student movement appears in the future?" 11.2 percent said that they would "boycott," 15.2 percent said that they would participate or actively participate, while 61.8 percent said that they would be unconcerned. That more students would participate than boycott is even clearer than in the reports in *Ming Bao*.

This special article also pointed out that most students thought that the rectification done by the ruling clique has brought unfavorable effects to reforms and the open-door policy or has caused stagnation or even retreat of reforms and the return of the old system. Students (63.4 percent) were pessimistic about the current economic situation. This obviously shows discontent toward the policies and practices of the CCP ruling clique and a way to show political opposition to them indirectly.

No wonder that the article ended by saying that "through this survey, the authorities think that the situation among Beijing high school students is basically stable, but unstable factors are still potent; the ideological basis for stability and unity is not firm; the task of maintaining stability in schools is still difficult and must not be overlooked." It shows, behind the beautiful phrases painting peaceful scenery, that the bureaucracy is still showing worries about the unstable situation. The acts of resistance by the people during the anniversary of Democracy Movement '89 confirmed that the worries of the bureaucracy are not excessive.

"CONCESSIONS" FROM THE RULERS

Facing the people's general discontent, the extreme worsening of the economic situation, and rising crime rates, the CCP bureaucracy has been forced to use a two-sided maneuver: on the one hand, to continue to repress the people cruelly; on the other hand, to make a "smiling," relaxed pose by lifting martial law in Beijing and Tibet and releasing by stages a small number of arrested democracy activists.

Deng Xiaoping and Party Secretary Jiang Zemin have indicated "reflections" on the events of last year: Deng "drew the lessons" of the June 4 events by saying that "we have never blamed the students or the youths; the main problem comes from within the Party" (*Wen Wei Bao*, June 4). Jiang also said that "the Tiananmen events last year cannot be solely blamed on the youths; the central leaders are also responsible" (*Wen Wei Bao*, June 2). But the facts last year contradict these "reflections": the top CCP leadership declared in the April 26, 1989, editorial of *People's Daily* that the peaceful petitions and rallies of the students were "turmoil" and were later smeared as "counterrevolutionary riots." It was no longer simply fault-finding but fabrication to carry out bloody repression! So-called problems "within the Party" and the central leadership are not at all the confession or self-criticism of Deng or Jiang for their errors and responsibilities but only an effort to put the blame onto former premier Zhao Ziyang and other "fallen dogs"!

Such acts and talk are only aimed at improving the extremely bad image of the CCP leadership, getting the complete removal of foreign sanctions and the release of loans, continuing the "most-favored-nation status" with the United States, inviting continued foreign investment in China to help ease the current economic difficulty, reduce political unrest, redress the people's grave discontent, and finally to endure the crisis and restabilize its rule.

However such minor "concessions" and empty phrases will not achieve the CCP's aims. The people of mainland China, Hong Kong, Macao, and Taiwan, as well as all the progressive people in the world, will continue the struggle for the release of all dissenters in China, for the ending of one-party dictatorship by the CCP and the establishment of a democratic political system.

14

Source Documents of the Democracy Movement

"The Death Knell for the Rule of the Bureaucratic Privileged Class Is Tolling," (Editorial of the "Theoretical Banner" of Qingdao, February 1981.)

Following the 1948 Berlin riot, the 1956 Hungarian episode, the 1968 Prague Spring, and the 1977 Czech Charter Movement, 1980 saw the eruption of the independent trade union movement in Poland. This movement differs from previous ones in that the others were suppressed by the joint forces of their own bureaucratic privileged class and Soviet socialist imperialism. But this time the Polish independent trade union has not yet been suppressed but has gained "legal recognition." Is this because the bureaucratic privileged class has "dropped its cleaver and become a Buddha," as the Chinese saying goes, or are there other reasons?

It is obvious that the bureaucratic privileged class has not become a Buddha and can never become one. On the contrary this bureaucratic privileged class, whose true nature is killing and lying while speeding up the concentration of all reactionary venom of centuries of exploiting classes within itself, is also speeding up its own decomposition. The contemporary bureaucratic privileged class surpasses all previous exploiting classes in its deceptiveness—in the guise of serving the people and struggling in the interests of the people, it engages in unscrupulous, monstrous deeds. But deceptions do not last long. For thirty years, facts written in blood and tears have finally enabled the honest people to recognize them as wolves wearing the skin of sheep! "The workers now understand that their wages are thirty times as much as the minimum wages of workers. They see special cars taking sophisticated daily necessities to the mansions of these dignitaries." "We ordinary people often die in the corridors, but the bureaucrats live in single rooms in hospitals, cared for by good doctors. The dignitaries also have special shops and exclusive sanatoriums." On average one out of six of the over 3 million party members in Poland engage in seeking privileges. "A manager of a small import/export company received a bribe of over U.S.$1

157

million just from his company's trading partner in the West, and he embezzled DM 473,370 and over $310,000. He had a bank account and a flat in London, where he lived with a mistress. He also built a luxurious villa, disguised as a training center for the building industry, for the Minister of Construction." The funny thing is that "when vice-premier Pyka represented the government to negotiate with the striking workers in Gdansk and the workers asked him how many country villas he had, he gave evasive answers and was very embarrassed." As its counterpart in China, where the economy is about to collapse after the fall of the Gang of Four, it has become common practice for the bureaucracy to build private villas! At the same time that there is not enough food for farmers and not enough housing for the people, not only are mansions built for party secretaries and generals, mansions are also built for the sons, in easy conscience! The people are obliged to ask: How did they obtain high-class villas and luxurious cars, these bureaucrats and sons of bureaucrats who never created any wealth? Is this the principle of distribution in socialism—"to each according to his ability"? When this whole lot of "red dignitaries," while boasting of the superiority of socialism, are unrestrained in corruption, wasteful spending, and privilege-seeking, can their wolf nature under the sheep skin remain unrevealed? Can the people whose blood is sucked and whose flesh is stripped not rise and defend their right to live? *The primary reason for the victory of the independent trade union in Poland is the sped-up decomposition of bureaucratic privileges and the general awakening and true solidarity of the masses.*

Moscow's tanks have rolled over Berlin, Budapest, and Prague. But the Soviet Union, which is militarily stronger, cannot roll into the headquarters of its military Pact—Warsaw. Not only is this because it is bogged down deep in Afghanistan and is held down by young brothers like Vietnam and therefore lacks the material strength to influence the situation. More importantly it has lost the moral strength of holding together allegiance, for who in the world now does not look upon the Soviet Union with hatred—the main camp where human rights are strangled? In scrambling for world resources and markets, the Soviet Union seems to be on an aggressive stance and is indeed threatening for its imperialist opponents. But the system and the class represented by Soviet socialist imperialism have been relentlessly spurned by the people! The bureaucratic privileged class has lost all popularity. The moral support for the rule of the bureaucratic privileged class has entirely crumbled. Unquenchable, fiery flames to bring down the rule of the bureaucratic privileged class are already been alight!

The present problem is: With what are we going to replace the rule of the bureaucratic privileged class? Can we replace the rule of the bureaucratic privileged class by restoring the economic basis of capitalist private ownership or depending on ideologies like Catholicism? The answer is this would be absolutely wrong. As the rule of the bourgeoisie should absolutely not be replaced by the rule of the bureaucratic privileged class, the rule of the bureaucratic privileged class must not be replaced by the rule of the bourgeoisie (although the rule of the bourgeoisie is, compared with the rule of the bureaucratic privileged class, more moderate to the people at present). The only correct outlet is to build a system of proletarian democracy suitable for this particular transitional period in history, organically and firmly linking up true public ownership with true democracy, so that they will complement and guarantee each other in the forward stride on the road to true socialism.

At this time no so-called socialist country can ignore the existence of the independent trade union in Poland. This shocks the bureaucratic privileged ruling class, but it inspires the people. The evaluation and attitude to this historic event have been clear criteria in examining the political position of different social groups. We now find the CCP, sensibly enough, still faithfully reporting the truth about the Polish events. Of course, *the truly sensible thing to do is not to alleviate the decomposition of the bureaucratic privileged ruling class but rather to stand for the people's rights and carry out fundamental reforms to the present so-called socialist political and economic system. A revolution must be waged against the feudal bureaucratic system, which has stubbornly ruled China for over two thousand years; reformism of any type is futile.* Considering that He Qiu and others of the China National Unofficial Publications Association who had been illegally detained have been released, that the Changsha student movement has been fairly handled, and that no savage intervention has been imposed on the free electoral activities of people's deputies now vigorously unfolding in some universities, we do not entirely give up hope on the party in power. China may gain radical transformations without going on Poland's road, but there is also the possibility that "the longer the suppression, the speedier the eruption," and China would accomplish radical revolution by a road more chaotic than Poland's. This will depend on whether the party in power will accomplish it by adopting a superior way or an inferior way, thus incurring blame to itself. The people, having suffered decades of hardships, do not want to repeat the same historical pattern unless there is no other way out. We hope that the party will not let the people down again on what hope they still harbor, will go with the tide of historical development, will advance society to progress, and will truly take up the task of bettering the world and carrying through to the end this proletarian democratic revolution that has started with reforms.

The death knell for the bureaucratic privileged class has tolled!

Let us closely unite under the banner of proletarian democracy and fight to eliminate all class rule, class exploitation, and class repression, and help advance China's overall modernization!

"The people can float the boat but can also overturn the boat!"
Long live the people!

Leaflets and Wall Posters during the December 1986 Student Democratic Movement in China (The following leaflets and wall posters were reprinted in *October Review*, December 1986.)

SELECTION OF LEAFLETS DISTRIBUTED BY SHANGHAI STUDENTS

LETTER TO COMPATRIOTS (distributed in the street December 23)
Citizens, compatriots!

Have you long felt that our right to democracy and freedom is so very restricted and artificial? The feudal system in which democracy and freedom did not exist, and the Cultural Revolution in which democracy and freedom were trampled on, belong to the bygone days. However the broad masses of people still live under democracy and freedom in name only. We must ask: How many people's deputies are elected by large numbers of people exercising their true rights? And can they really represent the people's wishes at critical moments? No! The answer we inevitably obtain is "NO!" In the eyes of most people, those deputies are merely lead types waiting for us to put a mark on! We must also ask: Are we free? The same answer: No. In all the major newspapers and radio broadcasts, there is simply nothing at all about the student movement in Shanghai and in other places. This alone serves to prove that the press is not free. The news blockade deceives the people, so that they cannot see the just demands of the patriotic youths and how people support them everywhere. This is tragic.

We believe that the people will not remain silent forever. After Hefei, Xian, Beijing, Kunming, Wuhan, and Shenzhen, a dynamic student movement broke out in Shanghai on December 19. Its purpose is to fight against bureaucratic repression and for democracy, and its means are legal demonstrations and sit-ins. Large numbers of students have taken to the street, and with their patriotism and the material and spiritual support of the citizens, they persisted until the early morning of December 20. At that time, large numbers of military police, in violation of the pledge of the municipal government, began to disperse the students violently. Many students were badly beaten, and often three or four policemen would attack one student (including women). Dozens of patriotic students have been arrested. The people, when they see this kind of brutality, are enraged. Faced with violence and autocratic power, we will not give up. All universities go on strike and demonstrate, and a struggle of greater scope unfolds.

Though we might temporarily be defeated, we shall not give up. We are convinced that are cause is just. History will eventually vindicate our student movement. The future and destiny of China should be grasped in the people's hands. Full democracy and freedom will become the people's rights.

Let more people throw themselves into the dynamic movement for democracy and freedom!

Victory surely belongs to us!

Long live the December 19 Movement!

Tongji University Student

LETTER TO CITIZENS

Friends, citizens!

In the contemporary era, to vote by raising one's hands is the means to express one's opinion; unanimously to adopt a resolution is the eventual result of all kinds of meetings; election is the goal of nomination. We are not at all informed, and the worker model is produced, the people's deputy is produced. Representation has lost its meaning. Have they asked for our opinion? Can they really represent the people's wishes? Our socialist country is even worse than a capitalist country on this question!

Democracy and freedom!

Democratic elections!

Tongji University Student

SELECTION OF WALL POSTERS AT UNIVERSITY CAMPUSES OR PUBLIC SQUARES

WHITHER GOES THE STUDENT MOVEMENT OF FUDAN UNIVERSITY?

The present student movement should not only talk about abstract slogans of democracy and freedom. Our movement needs a concrete goal that can be achieved. We believe that the present student union does not truly represent the great majority of students. It is the puppet of the university authorities. The small handful of student cadres are in actual fact a student aristocracy.

In some people's eyes, only we are to be educated. However why do they not also need some education? Now is the time for us to rise up to attempt to change all of this.

We propose that the student union should throw off the university authorities' administrative control and become an independent, autonomous student body.

The autonomous student body should counterbalance the university administration. Any decision involving student interests must be adopted by the autonomous student body. If the autonomous student body cannot reach an agreement with the university authorities, the question should be decided by a referendum of the whole university.

The way to form the autonomous student body is: 1. Every department will democratically elect its candidate, and then an autonomous student supervisory council will arrange an election for the whole university. 2. The autonomous student supervisory council is to be formed by two members democratically elected by each department. The duration of office is to be six months and for one term only. Any member at any time can file a motion of no-confidence in the executive committee. The supervisory council can propose a referendum on the motion. If the motion is adopted, the executive committee is to be reorganized.

Campus democracy should be the first step toward social democracy.

Fudan University Student

A LETTER TO THE VOTERS OF THE UNIVERSITY OF SCIENCE AND TECHNOLOGY

(Note: this wall poster appeared in the University of Science and Technology on December 1, and aroused a heated response from the students. Rejection of the undemocratic election of people's deputies to the provincial people's congress was the central issue in the student demonstration that broke out in Hefei, Anhui Province, on December 5. The demand of the students was granted—the election was postponed from December 8 to December 29, and students were allowed to nominate their candidates. The victory of the Hefei students stimulated student protests in other cities.)

The election is soon to be held. Voters, do you know who the candidates are? Have you seen them? Have you heard their promises? Do they have the competence or the will to serve you?

According to the Constitution, the people's congress at all levels is the power organ of the different levels. However the people's deputies' only function is to raise their hands to show approval. The people's congress is a rubber stamp for a minority of the people. As whose rubber stamp do you want to act, voters?

We are not puppets; we are not dummies. We refuse to be fooled. The people holding real power cannot be chosen by us but are appointed by a small minority. The rubber stamp provides a democratic garb for them. Now we are to give legitimacy to this rubber stamp. Voters, what is the value of such elections besides a waste of time?

It is not that we do not want elections. We just do not want this kind of election. We want real democratic elections.

We propose that: (1) The candidates must voluntarily stand up to be people's deputies, and cannot be appointed by a small number of people.

They must state clearly to the voters what they intend to do. The people's deputies must regularly report to the voters about the congress and their role and function in the congress and accept the supervision of the voters and serve the interests of the voters. (2) The power holders, such as the mayor or the district head, must arise out of direct election. Before their election, they must state their election program to the voters, report their work and achievements during their term of office, and accept the voters' supervision. The voters have the right to denounce their neglect of duty and abuse of power. Only in this way can the power holders really serve the people and not a minority of people.

Voters, support the above proposal! In the name of real democracy, boycott elections of fake democracy. Refuse to put on a check-mark, refuse to vote, or, brave voters, write on your ballot: we want *real* democracy!

A voter at the University of Science and Technology

Introducing Selected Source Documents of the 1989 Democracy Movement

During the movement for democracy that unfolded in April 1989 in Beijing and then in other major cities throughout China, culminating in the June massacre by the Communist Party of China in power, a large number of wall posters and *samizdat* (self-published) publications took the opportunity to express the political views of different sectors of society and conduct debates and discussions. *October Review* obtained a quite comprehensive collection of these source materials of the democracy movement and during 1989 published three collections of Selection of Source Documents from the Chinese Democracy Movement. Included in these collections are over three hundred color and black-and-white photographs; over three hundred articles written by students, workers, citizens, Communist Party members, soldiers; and over ten interviews conducted by readers of *October Review*.

Some of these materials have been translated into English and can be found in *Cries for Democracy* and *Voices from Tiananmen Square*. These books can be purchased from *October Review*.

Thus the translated source documents selected below from these two books and from *International Viewpoint* intend only to give a very general idea of the 1989 movement. With the "Hunger Strike Statement of the Beijing University Students," students at Tiananmen Square started their indefinite hunger strike on May 13, which ended only on May 20, when martial law was declared. The Beijing Workers' Autonomous Union was one of the most significant developments in the 1989 tide of democracy movement, for it was the first time workers came out in public, declared the formation of an autonomous trade union, independent of the ruling Communist Party, set up a tent-office on Tiananmen Square in the heart of the capital, and openly recruited members, gave interviews to the press, broadcast workers' news, distributed union leaflets, and organized workers' support actions for the students. Some key documents are reproduced here.

HUNGER STRIKE STATEMENT OF THE BEIJING UNIVERSITY STUDENTS

We commence our hunger strike in the lovely May sunshine. In the full bloom of youth, however, we leave beautiful things behind, but with great reluctance.

Yet the condition of our country is one of rampant inflation, economic speculation by officials, extreme authoritarian rule, serious bureaucratic corruption, a drain of products and people to other countries, social confusion, and an increase in the number of criminal acts. It is a crucial moment for the country and its people. All compatriots with a conscience, please heed our call:

> The country is our country.
> The people are our people.
> The government is our government.
> If we do not cry out, who will?
> If we do not take action, who will?

Our bodies are still tender and not full grown, and the prospect of dying frightens us all, but history calls us, and we must go.

Our purest and patriotic love and our most generous sentiments have been called "turmoil" with "ulterior motives," which is "manipulated by a handful of people."

We ask every Chinese citizen with a sense of justice, every worker, peasant, soldier, intellectual, celebrity, government official, policeman, and even our accusers, to look into their hearts and ask what crime has been committed. Is it a "rebellion" to strike, to demonstrate, and to go on a hunger strike? Why must we hide ourselves away? Our feelings have been treated too lightly. We live in miserable conditions as we search for truth and then are beaten up by the police. Student representatives kneel to request democracy, and are ignored. Our request for an equal dialogue is repeatedly ignored, and the student leaders are put in a very dangerous position.

What shall we do?

Democracy is a desire intrinsic to the human condition. Freedom is an inherent human right. We now must sacrifice our lives for them. Is this something that the Chinese race should be proud of?

The hunger strike was forced upon us as a last resort. We face death resolutely, although we are fighting for life. We are still very young. China, our mother! Look closely at your sons and daughters. Hunger is ravaging their youth, and death is near. Can you stand unmoved?

We do not want to die. We have a passionate desire to live on in the prime of our lives. We want to live and to learn. Our motherland is poor, and we do not want to leave her so. No, we are not seeking death, but if death could lead to improved conditions and prosperity for our country, then we ought not shun it.

Though we are starving, dear parents, do not despair. When we bid farewell to life, dear uncles and aunts, do not be unhappy. We hope only that you will live better. Remember always that we were not looking for death and that democracy is not the product of a few, nor the accomplishment of a single generation.

Death awaits. Farewell. To our colleagues who share our loyalties. To our loved ones, whom we would rather not leave, but whom we must. To our mothers and fathers, for whom we cannot be both patriotic and filial at the same time. To the people of our country, from whom we ask permission to pursue this final act of loyalty.

We make a commitment with our lives, to make the sky of the republic clear and bright.

Reasons for the Hunger Strike: First to protest against the casual attitude of the government toward the demonstration of the Beijing students. Second to protest the government's continued refusal to engage in a dialogue with the representatives of Beijing's institutions of higher education. Third to protest against the government's condemnation of the patriotic movement as "turmoil" and the distortions of the media.

Demands of the Hunger Strikers: First that the government quickly enter into equal, concrete discussion with the Dialogue Group of the Beijing institutions of higher education. Second that the government retract its statements concerning the nature of the Student Movement, and evaluate it fairly and honestly as a patriotic and democratic movement.

May 13, 1989

BEIJING WORKERS' AUTONOMOUS FEDERATION PROVISION MEMORANDUM

Based on the initial guiding principles, prepared by the preparatory committee of the Beijing Workers' Autonomous Federation, issued on May 25, 1989.

Preamble: In the entire People's Patriotic Democracy Movement, led by the students in mid-April, the majority of the Chinese workers have demonstrated a strong wish to take part in politics. At the same time, they also realize that there is not yet an organization which can truly represent the wishes expressed by the working masses. Therefore we recognize that there is a need to set up an autonomous organization that will speak for the workers and that will organize the realization of the workers' participation and consultation in political affairs. For this purpose, we put forward the following preparatory guiding principles:

1. The organization should be an entirely independent, autonomous organization, built up by the workers on a voluntary basis, through democratic processes, and it should not be controlled by other organizations.
2. The fundamental principle of the organization should be to address political and economic demands, based on the wishes of the majority of workers, and it should not remain solely a welfare organization.
3. The organization should possess the function of monitoring the party of the proletariat—the Chinese Communist Party.
4. The organization should have the power, through every legal and effective means, to monitor the legal representatives of all state and collective enterprises, guaranteeing that the workers become the real masters of the enterprise. In other enterprises, through negotiation with the owners and other legal means, the organization should be able to safeguard the rights of the workers.
5. Within the bounds of the constitution and the law, the organization should be able to safeguard all legal rights of its members.
6. The organization's membership should come from individuals on a voluntary basis and also group or collective membership in branches of various enterprises.

Tiananmen Square, May 28, 1989

TEN QUESTIONS FROM THE BEIJING CITY WORKERS' UNION

1. How much did Deng's son bet on a horse race in Hong Kong, and where did he get the money to place the bet?
2. Mr. and Mrs. Zhao Ziyang play golf every week. Who pays the greens fees and other expenses?
3. How does the Central Committee [of the CCP] judge the ongoing reforms? In his New Year Address Premier Li Peng said that there have been mistakes. What are they? What exactly is the situation now?
4. The Central Committee has proposed a reform for the control of prices, yet inflation continues, with the people's living standards declining. Can they explain this?
5. China must begin the repayment of foreign loans in 1990. How much must each citizen contribute to this? Will it affect basic living standards? Please answer us.
6. Deng Xiaoping has suggested raising the status of intellectuals from "stinking ninth" to "top rank." What is a top-ranking person? Would that be a landlord? Or a landlord's father?
7. How many residences and retreats do top party officials have spread around the country? What do they cost? Can this be made public? Please answer us.
8. Make public the personal incomes and possessions of top party officials.
9. How is the party going to respond to approaches from the government of Taiwan for peace talks?
10. Would the party be so kind as to explain the meaning and implications

of the following terms: (i) Party, (ii) Revolution, and (iii) Reactionary?

Would the party please publish its responses to the above ten questions as soon as possible?

April 20, 1989

DECLARATION OF THE BEIJING WORKERS' AUTONOMOUS UNION PREPARATORY COMMITTEE

The working class is the most advanced class, and we, in the Democratic Movement, should be prepared to demonstrate its great power.

The People's Republic of China is supposedly led by the working class, and we have every right to drive out the dictators.

The workers know best how to use knowledge and technology in the production process, so we will not permit the destruction of the students, who are of the people.

To bring down dictatorship and totalitarianism and promote democracy in China is our undeniable responsibility.

In the Democracy Movement, "we have nothing to lose but our chains and a world to win."

May 21, 1989

PUBLIC NOTICE I FROM THE BEIJING WORKERS' AUTONOMOUS UNION PREPARATORY COMMITTEE

The BWAF is a spontaneous and temporary organization formed by the workers of Beijing in response to the unusual current situation. Its objectives are to fight for democracy, bring down dictatorship, support and protect the student hunger strikers, promote democratization in alliance with the students and citizens from all walks of life. We call for:

1. A general strike in Beijing (with the exception of electricity, water, gas, mail, and communications), beginning at noon on May 20, and lasting until the military withdraws from the city.
2. Opposition to the entry of troops into the city, defense of the Democracy Movement, the maintenance of discipline in Tiananmen Square, the blockage of all main roads into the city and subway exits with vehicles, the maintenance of the normal operation of radio and television broadcasting.
3. The cooperation of all citizens in informing the troops in Beijing concerning the true situation.

May 20, 1989

PUBLIC NOTICE II FROM THE BEIJING WORKERS' AUTONOMOUS UNION PREPARATORY COMMITTEE

This afternoon, the Standing Committee of the BWAF called an emergency meeting on our special role in the present situation. As the leading group they set up a secretariat, a public relations section, and a liaison and support section.

1. The BWAF is a Beijing workers' autonomous organization with the objective, democratically and legally, of promoting a Patriotic-Democratic Movement. It invites all workers in the capital to participate actively in our union.
2. Given the present situation, the meeting decided specifically: (i) that the present task of the workers' picket group is to maintain a close cooperation with the Students' Autonomous Union, and to guarantee the safety of the students and the stability of Beijing society; and (ii) that the workers' picket group also ensure the movement of the city's resources and daily needs of the citizens, such as transportation and food.

May 21, 1989

LETTER TO COMPATRIOTS (A Text from Beijing Independent Workers' Union produced before the Tiananmen massacre)

The despotism and greed of the corrupt officials and mandarins has reached new heights! There is not a scrap of truth left in the whole of China! No reactionary power is any longer able to hold back the waves of the anger of the whole people; the people can no longer believe the poisonous words of the authorities who deceive the people. Therefore we write on our banner: science, democracy, liberty, human rights, a legal system.[1]

On April 21, 1989, in Beijing, we officially founded the Workers' Union of the city of Beijing to protect the interests of the workers and issued two documents—"Letter to the people of the City" and "Ten Questions." In an editorial on April 26, 1989, the *People's Daily* nevertheless treats us as reactionaries. Our reply is, Since you do not dare to publicly answer our ten questions, publish our two documents. Have you not put forward for forty years the slogan "have confidence in the broad masses"? We demand the total repudiation of the editorial of April 26 and the severe punishment of whoever was responsible for this article, along with their clique behind the scenes.

We have carefully established the facts about the exploitation of the workers. The mode of exploitation has been analyzed according to the method taught by Karl Marx in *Capital*. We subtracted from the value of production: the workers' wages, premiums and benefits; socially necessary accumulation; the social facilities; and the expenses for the expanded reproduction of capital; and we have discovered to our amazement that the "people's public [state-owned] enterprises" are expropriating the whole of the surplus-value extracted from the sweat and blood of the people! The rise in exploitation is unheard of! Atrocious! Such is the flavor of the "specificities of China." Throughout the country, the "people's public enterprises" build, out of our sweat and blood, luxurious villas (protected by the army under the pretext that they are forbidden military zones) and deluxe automobiles. The functionaries organize pleasure trips (supposedly inspection visits), on which the officials take along their children and even their nurses! Women functionaries spend hours making themselves beautiful, while the male officials run after pretty women, and so on. It would take too long to recount all their villainies, not to say crimes.

Starting from the interests of the people and the nation, comrade Fang Lizhi expressed a correct point of view on the question: "What good does it do us to attract foreign capital?" We support and agree with him, because, as in the past, this "foreign capital" will be transformed by legal means into the individual fortunes of the degenerate officials. It is the nation that pays, while a "tiny handful" profits. It is the broad masses of the people who pay the debts. It is they who must do the accounting!

"The Great Market of the Mandarins" We are opposed to that brutal violation of human rights, the forcible sale of Treasury Bonds.[2] We demand the publication of the income and expenditure of Treasury Bonds in recent years and how they have been used. We demand that the whole value of the Treasury Bonds currently in circulation among the population be restored and the closing of the market in Treasury Bonds. This is the great market of the mandarins, the great financial resource of the degenerate bureaucrats.

We repeat: To raise wages and stop inflation, it is necessary that the two, even three generations have similar wage levels. We call for the opening of an inquiry into the Heads of State and government, the Military Commission of the Central Committee (CC), all the Commissions of the State Council [government], and the Central Committee and Secretariat of the CC of the Chinese Communist Party (CCP).

The first group of people who should be investigated for misappropriation of public funds are—Deng Xiaoping, Zhao Ziyang, Li Peng, Chen Yun, Li Xiannian, Yang Shangkun, Xi Zhen, Wan Li, Jiang Zemin, Ye Xuanping, and their families. It is necessary to investigate at once the whole of their fortunes, inspect the national registers of accounts, and publish the accounts for the whole population to see.

The students have matured! In front of Tiananmen, it is clear that millions of people uphold revolutionary order! The people have awakened! They have understood that in any society, in any epoch there are only two classes, the dominant class and the dominated. Those classes, parties, and organizations that follow the current of history are progressive and revolutionary, those that resist are retrograde and reactionary.

This is the fundamental reason that, from the time of Qin Shi Huangdi[3] to our days, the Chinese people has cherished "upright officials," and needs, praises, and commemorates them.

At the present time we must be especially vigilant that political opportunists from the CCP do not profit from this democratic movement to achieve their objective of an autocratic usurpation of supreme power. Deng Xiaoping used the "April 5" popular movement[4] and its repression to reveal his true colors after mounting the throne. The "successes of the reform" that they talk about are false and superficial. The reality is that the standard of living of the majority has fallen, while borrowing increases, on the assumption that the people will pay it back!

Comrade workers of the broad masses, it is urgently necessary to unite around the workers' unions, under the leadership of the workers' unions of the cities and push the present democratic movement to a new level. Our union is calling for a big workers' demonstration of the whole city to support the student movement and to launch a peaceful petition campaign. The slogan of the demonstration is "There is not a scrap of truth left in the whole of China!"

Notes

1. *Legal system*: due to the weight of tradition and the effects of pseudomarxism, there are very few written laws in China, thus the insistent demand for a legal system with written laws.
2. The state forces employees to "invest" in state-issued bonds that then depreciate in value.
3. The first Chinese emperor, 221–208 B.C., infamous for his exceptional cruelty, tyranny, and bloodthirstiness.
4. April 5, 1976, uprising against the "Gang of Four" after the death of Zhou Enlai.

15

Marxism in Twentieth-Century China

ZHANG KAI

It is the hundredth anniversary of Marx's death. Marx's thought has been tested ever since. As a scientific ideological system, it has shown great vitality; its analysis of historical developments has been confirmed by practice, and so it has gained more support from the laboring masses and revolutionists.

However at the same time that marxism is continuously developed and enriched, it is distorted and vulgarized by those in power who claim to be its followers.

In twentieth-century China, marxism has also been tested and confirmed. This article attempts, by basing itself on the development of the Chinese Revolution, to explain how marxism has been confirmed by revolutionary practice, where it has been developed by later marxists and where attempts to revise it have been made (such as on the question of the role of the proletariat in backward countries). The first part of this article discusses the revolutionary practice in overthrowing capitalism in China before 1949, and the latter part discusses the party in power, how true marxists have persisted on them and developed them, and how the Chinese revolutionary masses have striven for their realization.

Before marxism was systematically introduced into China, the first Chinese revolution—the 1911 revolution—had taken place. The revolution, however, only overthrew a corrupt monarchy but did not at all solve the bourgeois-democratic tasks. The prerequisites for solving these tasks were created only after the introduction of marxism into China and the exertion of its strong influence.

In China, marxist ideas came mainly from the Soviet Union. The victory of the Russian October Revolution had a strong impact on China. The CCP was set up in 1921 with the direct aid of the Communist Party of the Soviet Union (CPSU). The CPSU leadership had a decisive influence on

171

the CCP political line in the 1920s. The polemics in Russia on the revolution were later taken up in China and were closely related to the practice of the Chinese revolution. Moreover the Chinese revolution and the Russian revolution faced similar problems concerning the socialist revolution in backward countries. Thus it is necessary to refer first to the experience of the Russian revolution.

EXPERIENCE OF THE OCTOBER REVOLUTION

The victory of the 1917 October Revolution is the first example of the practice of marxism on a national level. The revolution proves the correctness of marxism: the proletariat is a revolutionary class; it has led the peasants, after repeated class struggles, to overthrow the rule of the bourgeoisie by a violent revolution, to fulfil the task of socialist revolution, and to open the possibility of transition to socialism.

The fact that the socialist revolution did not first take place in an economically advanced capitalist country in Europe but in economically backward Russia has often been quoted to prove Marx's "error." But the nature of this error is not of principle or methodology but an incorrect estimation of a concrete process. A revolutionary or prerevolutionary situation had existed in many countries in Europe. Their failure was due to the unripeness of the necessary conditions (for example, a weak party leading the revolution or an incorrect program or policy). It is not true that there was no objective necessity or possibility of a socialist revolution in these countries.

Marx and Engels had not excluded the possibility of revolution in backward countries (including Russia). For example they said in the preface to the Russian edition of the *Communist Manifesto*: "If the Russian revolution becomes the signal for a proletarian revolution in the west, so that both complement each other, the present Russian common ownership of land may serve as the starting point for a communist development."[1]

Besides the ripeness of objective factors, one important subjective factor for the victory of the Russian Revolution was the correct leadership, founded on marxism, of the Bolshevik Party.

Before the revolution, there were many theoretical polemics among the Russian marxists. One significant principled polemic concerned the task, motive force, and future of the Russian revolution. This brought about the division between the Bolshevik (majority) and Menshevik (minority) factions.

The Mensheviks considered that the immediate task of the Russian revolution was for democracy, so the leadership of the revolution naturally fell to Russia's liberal bourgeoisie; a bourgeois–democratic system was to be instituted after the revolution. The proletariat could not jump over this stage to make its own revolution but had to support the bourgeoisie in its seizure of power. The Mensheviks quoted Marx's words as justification: "No social formation disappears before all the productive forces have developed for which it has room." They then argued that Russian capitalism still had good prospects for development. Such a viewpoint read Marx from the position of one single country and failed to see that Marx was elaborating the continuation and change of general social systems.

Lenin, with Marxist methodology, considered that the central task of the Russian revolution was land reform. Yet the bourgeoisie allied itself with the landowners and feared the proletariat, and so it could not fulfil its historic task and could not lead the revolution. The motive force of the revolution was not the bourgeoisie but the proletariat and the peasants.

Trotsky agreed with Lenin's above idea, but one rather big difference between them in the early years of the twentieth century was that Lenin proposed a "democratic dictatorship of the proletariat and peasantry" (whether the peasantry had an independent role in the dictatorship was not clarified); Trotsky, on the other hand, proposed the dictatorship of the proletariat (leading the peasantry). Concerning the future of the revolution, Lenin considered it capitalist, while Trotsky considered it noncapitalist, that is, socialist.

After the February 1917 revolution, Lenin produced his "April Theses," which abandoned the slogan of the democratic dictatorship of the proletariat and peasantry and proposed that "the Soviets of Workers' Deputies are the *only possible* form of revolutionary government," that is, he "considered that the best political form for the dictatorship of the proletariat in Russia is a republic of the soviets."[2]

Thus Lenin's views converged with Trotsky's. The "April Theses" rearmed the Bolshevik Party and helped the party and the proletariat to draw up a clear revolutionary line, guaranteeing the victory of the October Revolution. Practice confirmed who was correct and incorrect in previous polemics.

These theories of Lenin and Trotsky were a further development of marxist theory. As early as 1850, Marx had put forward related theories, though at the time he was basing himself on the experience of the 1848 revolution in Germany.

In the "Address of the Central Authority to the League" that Marx and Engels drafted, they pointed out that

> it is our interest and our task to make the revolution permanent, until all more or less possessing classes have been forced out of their position of dominance, the proletariat has conquered state power, and the association of proletarians, not only in one country but in all the dominant countries of the world, has advanced so far that competition among the proletarians in these countries has ceased and that at least the decisive productive forces are concentrated in the hands of the proletarians.
>
> But they themselves [the German workers] must do the utmost for their final victory by making it clear to themselves what their class interests

are, by taking up their position as an independent party as soon as possible and by not allowing themselves to be misled for a single moment by the hypocritical phrases of the democratic petty bourgeoisie into refraining from the independent organization of the party of the proletariat. Their battle cry must be: "The Revolution in Permanence."[3]

In *Results and Prospects*, written in 1905, and *Historic References on the Theory of "Permanent Revolution"* (1905–17), Trotsky developed Marx's idea of permanent revolution:

> In a country economically more backward, the proletariat may come to power sooner than in an advanced capitalist country.
> The Russian revolution cannot solve its democratic problem, above all the agrarian problem, without placing the working class in power.
> It is only the depth of the agrarian problem that opens the immediate prospect of a dictatorship of the proletariat in Russia.
> The day and hour when the power will pass to the hands of the working class depend directly not upon the level obtained by the productive forces but upon the relations in the class struggle, upon the international situation, and finally upon a series of subjective factors—traditions, initiatives, preparedness for fighting.
> The fate of the most elementary revolutionary interests of the peasantry—even of the entire peasantry as a caste—is bound up with the fate of the whole revolution—that is, with the fate of the proletariat.
> The idea was . . . of an uninterrupted revolution, linking up the liquidation of absolutism and of civil serfdom with a socialist revolution, thanks to multiplying social clashes, uprisings of new layers of the masses, unceasing attacks of the proletariat upon the political and economic privileges of the ruling classes.[4]

In a word the permanent development of democratic revolution to socialist revolution is not divided into stages.

Twelve years later the Russian revolution confirmed the foregoing idea. Marx's theory of permanent revolution was confirmed in Russia. In China where the task of the revolution was similar to that in Russia, the practice, however, soon negatively confirmed Marx's theory of "permanent revolution."

LESSONS OF THE SECOND CHINESE REVOLUTION

The 1925–27 Chinese revolution could very possibly have been victorious if not for the wrong policies of the Comintern under the Stalin-Bukharin leadership. The revolution was strangled by the Guomindang (KMT) and suffered a tragic defeat. The mistakes of the Comintern were basically these:

1. It carried out a right opportunist line and asserted that "the only significant national revolutionary group in China is the KMT. It relies on

liberal bourgeois democrats and the petty bourgeoisie, and on the intellectuals and the workers."[5] It was tantamount to Stalin's assertion that the KMT was "a bloc of four classes."

2. It directed the CCP to restrain itself and give up political and organization independence. The Comintern sent two directives in July and August 1922, asking the CCP to "practice 'intra-party cooperation' with the KMT, ie., CCP members should join the KMT as individuals."[6]

3. At the high tide of revolution, it opposed the setting up of soviets of workers, peasants, and soldiers but instead considered that the KMT could replace the soviet. It was tantamount to refusing the formation of an organizational center of the revolution to unite the workers, peasants, and soldiers and to lead the masses in rebellion and seizure of power.

4. When the revolution was bloodily repressed and totally defeated, it directed the CCP to adventuristic armed riots, causing serious destruction of remnant revolutionary forces and aggravating the extent of defeat.

Stalin's attitude to the Chinese bourgeoisie and its political party, the KMT, was an exact reproduction of Russian Menshevism. It caused immeasurably greater harm than the latter. Stalin had not drawn any lesson from the polemics and historical experience in Russia.

The Chinese bourgeoisie was itself weak and timid. Its close interests with the imperialists prevented it from promoting a national revolution; its collaboration or even fusion with remnant feudal landowner forces prevented it from waging a radical land reform. It was not revolutionary and could not lead any national democratic revolution. One strong evidence is the fact that KMT leaders such as Chiang Kai-shek and Wang Ching-wei had repeatedly strangled the revolution and massacred CCP members, workers, and peasants.

But given its illusions in the Chinese bourgeoisie and the KMT both theoretically and politically, the Comintern on the one hand gave the KMT massive financial, material, and military aid and moral support to build up its strength, and on the other hand imposed discipline on the CCP to join the KMT and to accept conditions such as refraining from criticism of Sun Yat-sen's "Three People's Principles." Despite the repeated request of some CCP leaders to withdraw from the KMT, the Comintern line persisted, and thus the CCP's political activities were strait-jacketed and its independent leadership role was nullified. At the same time, the Comintern "not only did not give material aid to the CCP, it did not even give it theoretical help"[7] and so the CCP was unable to resist the KMT offensive. Although the Comintern's resolution said that "this must not be done at the cost of annihilating the CCP's unique political bearing; the party must maintain its original organization,"[8] this was mere empty talk. The CCP paid a high price for deviating from Marx's theory of permanent revolution.

On the above four key issues, Trotsky's ideas and propositions were diametrically opposed to those of Stalin and the Comintern. However his ideas were suppressed by Stalin and could not be realized.

CONFIRMATION BY THE THIRD CHINESE REVOLUTION

The 1949 victory confirmed the correctness of marxism in the following aspects:

1. The bourgeoisie of semicolonial, backward countries is not the motive force of revolution and not even a participant; it is in fact the target of revolution. The entire revolutionary process was a direct life-and-death struggle with the bourgeoisie's political representative—the KMT regime.
2. The bourgeois-democratic tasks of land reform and national independence were not fulfilled by the bourgeoisie (it did not even attempt their fulfillment); they were fulfilled only during and after the overthrow of the bourgeois regime.
3. The tasks of socialist revolution were not to start only after the completion of democratic tasks and after a long period of capitalist development; it was a continuous, concurrent process. At the same time that the old regime collapsed, bureaucrat capital, which constituted the majority portion of China's industrial, commercial, and financial capitalist enterprises, was confiscated and nationalized, and the remaining private industrial and commercial enterprises were gradually "transformed" until nationalization was basically completed in 1956.

The above general developments had been anticipated by Trotsky early in this century when he elaborated Marx's idea of permanent revolution, although he did not specifically discuss China.

However there are at least three differences between the 1949 revolutionary victory in China and the 1917 Russian revolution.

1. The 1949 revolution did not base its chief motive force on the Chinese proletariat. In the whole revolutionary process of the third revolution, the proletariat in KMT-ruled areas, despite individual strikes, in general did not rise up to intervene in the events.
2. It did not take the form of uprisings by urban workers to seize power. Instead it took the form of a civil war waged by peasant armed forces against China's ruling class after a prolonged resistance war against Japanese imperialism.
3. The CCP, as leader of the revolution, was in its overwhelming majority composed of peasants. Its program before the revolution and during the victory was the promotion of "new democracy" and not the prompt establishment of socialism.

It seems that these differences have revised, and even overthrown, Marx's related theories, and that Mao Zedong's road of rural guerrilla warfare—

"the siege of the cities by the countryside"—has replaced Marx's idea of the proletariat's seizure of power by means of an urban uprising and has become the general rule for revolution in backward countries, as boasted by CCP propaganda. If this argument can be established, the appraisal of the proletariat's role in Marx's teachings will have to be fundamentally negated (even if it can be maintained in relation to advanced countries). But historical experience in China proves otherwise.

Let us sum up this experience by dividing it into three phases.

INITIAL FAILURE OF "SIEGE OF THE CITIES BY THE COUNTRYSIDE"
1. FROM AUTUMN 1927 WHEN THE RURAL ARMED STRUGGLE BEGAN,
TO 1937, EVE OF THE RESISTANCE WAR

In this period, the road of "siege of the cities by the countryside" proposed by Mao was a failure. He quickly noted it and proposed a change of direction. For example he said:

> In the past year we have fought in many places and are keenly aware that the revolutionary tide is on the ebb in the country as a whole. . . . Wherever the Red Army goes, the masses are cold and aloof. . . . We have an acute sense of our isolation, which we keep hoping will end. Only by launching a political and economic struggle for democracy, which will also involve the urban petty bourgeoisie, can we turn the revolution into a seething tide that will surge through the country.[9]

Although the Mao Zedong leadership, through its land reform, instigated the peasants to rise up in struggle and join the Red Army, and at the same time exploited the gap in the struggle between the Chiang Kai-shek regime and the warlords, they were frequently besieged and attacked by Chiang's army. Finally in 1934 when defense of the bases was impossible, they had to abandon soviet bases, break through the encirclement, and shift the forces to regions in northwest China. The so-called "25,000-mile Long March" was in fact a retreat of serious defeat. The army of three hundred thousand that broke out of the siege in October 1934 shrank to less than thirty thousand on arrival in northern Shaanxi in October 1935.[10] This indicates the severity of defeat suffered by the Red Army. It was not the successful siege of the cities by the Red Army but the contrary.

At the end of 1935, Mao Zedong reviewed the previous line at the Wayaopao meeting: "The kind of impatience that was formerly displayed will never do. Moreover, sound revolutionary tactics must be worked out; we will never achieve great things if we keep on milling around within narrow confines."[11]

After admitting that the line of "siege of the cities by the countryside" was "inapplicable," Mao again proposed a turn to democratic struggle in the cities and on a national scale, and "concentrate on the movement for a

national assembly and a constitution."[12] "'Why do we place so much emphasis on a national assembly?' Because it is something which can affect
every aspect of life, because it is the bridge from reactionary dictatorship to
democracy . . . the essential thing is still the national assembly and freedom
for the people."[13]

   The "inevitable road" Mao discussed was in fact the line of struggle proposed by
former CCP leaders such as Chen Duxiu (founder of the CCP) and Peng Shuzhi
after the defeat of the 1927 revolution. At that time they were in complete
unison with Trotsky's viewpoints and proposals concerning the Chinese revolution. Their opposition to joining the KMT and their later demand for
withdrawal from the KMT coincided with Trotsky's ideas. They therefore
supported Trotsky's positions and considered that after the defeat of the
revolution, adventuristic, putschist riots should not be conducted; the work
should be mobilization of the masses in struggle for democratic rights (the
central demand being the calling of a universally elected, all-powerful national assembly) and against Chiang Kai-shek's military dictatorship to prepare for the next revolutionary tide. The criticisms and proposals made by
Chen and Peng and their comrades persisted in a marxist line in the interim
between two revolutionary tides. But their correct ideas were rejected by
the CCP leaders, who followed the Stalinist line. They were charged with
"liquidationism" and were expelled from the party. Later they formed the
Bolshevik-Lenin Group. In 1936 it was renamed the Chinese Communist
League and became the Chinese section of the Fourth International in 1938.
The name was changed to the Revolutionary Communist Party of China in
August 1948.

THE GROWTH OF CCP FORCES DURING THE RESISTANCE WAR
2. FROM JULY 1937, WHEN THE RESISTANCE WAR STARTED, TO AUGUST
1945, WHEN THE WAR ENDED

The invasion of China by Japanese imperialism and the massacre, looting,
repression, and enslavement of the Chinese people incited the latter's indignation and patriotism. Mass movements surged everywhere. The CCP made
use of this opportunity to mobilize, organize, and arm the masses, and it led
the resistance war. Its forces grew rapidly.

   The following figures show the speed of growth: at the beginning of the
resistance war, the CCP sent its chief Red Army regiments, the Eighth
Route Army (30,000 troops), to the front; later it sent the New Fourth
Army (10,000 troops). So the total number of its forces was only 40,000.
But in April 1945, the CCP announced that its People's Army had increased
to 910,000, the militia to 2.2 million, the self-defense army to 10 million,
and there was a total of nineteen liberated regions covering a total area of
950,000 square kilometers, with a total population of 95.5 million people.[14]

This significant development was based on the upsurge of the mass movement. Without the masses' active support, the CCP's guerrilla activities would not have scored such successes, and its forces would not have grown so rapidly.

Because this was total war and the whole population was seriously affected, active resistance was necessary to save the country from annexation. National contradictions, social confrontations, and class struggles were interwoven and acutely intensified. Marxism has always asserted that war leads to revolution, the main reason being that war causes all social contradictions to intensify acutely and the base of rule to weaken seriously. This also was the outcome of China's resistance war. The mass upsurge was very favorable to the armed struggle that the CCP led.

The above factors provided "the siege of the cities by the countryside" with very favorable conditions. But "siege" alone could not destroy the enemy decisively. A radical revolutionary program is more important to mobilize fully the people to gain an early victory. Yet such a program was lacking in the CCP.

The Fourth International and its Chinese section put forward their proposals at the very beginning of the resistance war in China. For example the Executive Bureau of the Fourth International proposed the following in August 1937 in "Resolution on the Sino-Japanese War":

> The world proletariat . . . should resolutely defend China against Japan. . . . In order to mobilize the Chinese masses to the revolutionary war of resistance and to the Third Chinese Revolution, a program with definite social and political demands must be drawn up: arming of the masses, freedom of publication and organization, election of councils of workers, peasants, and soldiers, confiscation of landowners' land, redistribution of land, abolition of heavy taxes, elimination of shark loans, workers' supervision of production, shouldering of war costs by the bourgeoisie, preparation for the revolution to transfer power from the KMT to the workers and peasants, the extension of hands by workers and peasants to the laboring masses of Japan and Manchuria, democratic election of a constitutional assembly and national assembly of councils of workers, peasants, and soldiers, only by which China's destiny will be determined.[15]

In May 1940 a Statement of the Emergency General Meeting of the Fourth International declared:

> The war [against Japan] has gone on for almost three years. It could have ended with the infliction of a catastrophe for Japan, if China had waged a true people's war based on land reform and burning the Japanese soldiers with its flames. Yet, the Chinese bourgeoisie is more afraid of its armed masses than the Japanese bandits. Chiang Kai-shek, the fiendish butcher of the Chinese revolution, although obliged by circumstances to wage the war, maintains his previous program, which is based on repression of the Chinese workers and compromise with imperialism.[16]

The bourgeois KMT naturally could not practice any revolutionary program. The CCP, at the start of the resistance war, made big concessions to the KMT in order to secure the Second Cooperation with the KMT. This was expressed in the ideas of the July 15, 1937 CCP Central's "Statement on KMT-CCP Cooperation":

1. Sun Yat-Sen's Three People's Principles is necessary for China today. Our party is willing to struggle for its complete realization.
2. All rioting policies and reddening movement to overthrow the KMT will be canceled; the policy of confiscating land of landowners by violent means will stop.
3. The present soviet government will be abolished.
4. The name and designation of the Red Army will be canceled and re-organized into the National Revolutionary Army to be commanded by the Military Commission of the Nationalist Government.[17]

The Three People's Principles was the program of the bourgeois KMT and was "an altogether reactionary idea" (in Lenin's words).[18] The CCP's proclamation to strive for its "radical realization" and glorification of it could only help the KMT disseminate its poisonous ideas and facilitate the prolongation of the KMT reactionary regime.

The interruption of land reform and the practice of very limited reformist measures such as reduction of rent and interest were objectively favorable to continued invasion by Japanese imperialism.

The thoroughly reactionary aggressive war by Japanese imperialism could not escape the fate of ruin. In early May 1945, Germany surrendered unconditionally, leaving Japan in complete isolation. Three months later the Soviet Union and the United States inflicted a most serious blow on Japan. On August 6 and 9, the United States dropped two atomic bombs on Hiroshima and Nagasaki. The Soviet Union declared war on Japan on August 8. "The Soviet army entered the northeast areas, eliminated the main force of the Japanese army, captured 510,000 Japanese soldiers, and *decisively* brought about Japan's collapse and surrender."[19]

"Because of the strength of the Soviet Red Army and the speed of attack, the northeast crack troops of the Japanese Army were rapidly eliminated; Japan was forced to announce unconditional surrender on August 14."[20]

The end of the resistance war in China or, so to speak, the initial success of the CCP's "siege of the cities by the countryside" was due not only to the rise of the Chinese mass movement and the prolonged armed struggle based on peasant forces that caused serious defeats of Japanese imperialism on the Chinese arena but also to international factors. (According to the above assertion of the Xinhua News Agency, the Soviet Union factor was "decisive.") Without these coordinated favorable conditions, the mere resort to peasant guerrilla forces could not have ultimately defeated Japan and laid the basis for the CCP's later victory.

SPECIFIC CONDITIONS LEADING TO THE 1949 CCP VICTORY
3. FROM THE OUTBREAK OF THE CCP–KMT CIVIL WAR (1946) TO THE COLLAPSE OF THE KMT REGIME (1949)

This was the period of general confrontation between the CCP and the KMT and the period when the CCP proclaimed the strategy of "the siege of the cities by the countryside" and later acted with more resolution to seize political power in the whole country. It was not a true reflection of the reality of one designated the countryside as the CCP's sphere of influence and the cities that of the KMT. The fact was that at that time, both sides occupied vast areas, which included both cities and countryside. Moreover the CCP's central tactics at that time had shifted from guerrilla warfare to mobile warfare.

Actually as soon as Japan surrendered, the CCP's army, in coordination with the Soviet army, liberated the northeast areas. The Soviet army transferred large amounts of Japanese weaponry to the CCP's army, thus significantly strengthening the CCP forces. According to the CCP, in the two months after Japan's surrender, it had recovered three hundred ten thousand square kilometers of territory, 190 cities, and occupied vast areas in the northern and central parts of China. The main KMT government forces were initially stationed in the hinterland; they gradually moved to the east and attacked areas (in particular cities) occupied by the Liberation Army. The CCP announced that in the first year of generalized civil war starting from July 1946, the government's army had seized one hundred ninety thousand square kilometers of land and 84 cities from the CCP, yet the liberated areas were still 2.2 million square kilometers, holding 420 cities, with a total population of 130 million. What happened was the two confronting powers began seizing cities and territory from the other after the complete withdrawal of Japanese and Soviet armies. (In the first year of the civil war, the offensive was taken by the government army and the contrary from the second year on.) It was not merely a question of the CCP footholds in the countryside besieging the KMT cities. It was a class struggle between two forces representing different class interests and developing to an intensive generalized civil war. (The KMT represented the interests of the bourgeoisie and the landowners and the CCP the interests of the peasants.)

That the revolution achieved overall victory was the outcome of a convergence of the following specific historical conditions:

1. The bourgeois KMT regime was corrupt and incompetent to the core. It had been severely weakened in the two wars (of different nature) fought over a decade, especially in the later period. The industrial and agricultural

output was very low, the budget and deficits soared, the value of the currency plunged, and the people's suffering intensified. The regime had become the object of hatred and opposition by the whole population (including the soldiers). Struggles by workers, peasants, students, and the masses against civil war and hunger surged one after the other and put the regime in absolute isolation. Its internal structure disintegrated. Its army was tired of war, and large numbers surrendered to the CCP army. Faced with the despair and irreversible decline, even a force as strong as U.S. imperialism could do nothing to rescue it.

2. The rapid development of the CCP forces in the period of the resistance war had been described previously. In the early stage of the civil war, although the CCP still wanted negotiation with Chiang Kai-shek to set up a coalition government, the attack by Chiang's army caused even Yanan—the heart of the revolution—to fall in March 1947. The CCP was then forced to issue the manifesto "Down with Chiang Kai-shek, for a New China" and proclaim the decree on land reform to confiscate land for redistribution to the peasants. A year after the proclamation, 100 million peasants in the liberated regions were allocated land. This was a strong stimulus that played an important role in the CCP's victory over the Chiang regime.

However in this revolution, the Chinese proletariat, which should have been the revolutionary class in leadership, had not played its role. Despite its sufferings under Chiang's rule and some struggles, such as strikes, during the civil war, it had not been mobilized by the CCP; it was only asked to defend the factories and mines and wait for liberation. This abnormal development of the revolution and distortion of the permanent revolution by the CCP was due to the CCP's bureaucratism and neglect of marxist theories.

The CCP leadership claimed that the CCP was the vanguard of the proletariat, "representing" the proletariat to fulfil its revolutionary tasks. Yet marxism considers that the liberation of the proletariat is the affair of the proletariat itself; the proletarian revolution is an act of the whole class and not to be done in proxy by a minority (even if the minority is the vanguard of the proletariat).

Concerning the actual relationship between the CCP and the Chinese proletariat, the CCP was a working-class party in the 1920s in program and composition. It worked among the workers and had a close relationship with the workers. However after it had shifted to the countryside to engage in armed struggle, the CCP became alienated from the workers. The CCP's work in the cities in the KMT-occupied regions was almost completely destroyed or voluntarily abandoned. The CCP's worker members and sympathizers were mobilized by the party to the rural soviet regions. This caused an extreme weakening in the links between the CCP and the urban proletariat.

PRAXIS NEGATED THE SCHEMA OF NEW DEMOCRACY

The CCP's theoretical framework and political program had become very peasant-oriented. It was epitomized in "On New Democracy," written by Mao in 1940. Mao wrote:

> Stalin has said that "*in essence,* the national question is a peasant question." This means that the Chinese revolution is essentially a peasant revolution. . . . Essentially, the politics of New Democracy means giving power to the peasants . . . the strength of the peasants is the main strength of the Chinese revolution.[21]

The above position of Mao and Stalin on the peasant question has nothing in common with the position of the *Communist Manifesto* on the question of the peasants and the revolution. It was in actuality a degradation (or negation) of the role of the proletariat. The process of the 1949 revolution was the practice of this attitude of the CCP toward the proletariat.

In the same article, Mao Zedong asserted that "China's national bourgeoisie has a revolutionary quality at certain periods and to a certain degree" and proposed that the new democratic republic to be set up, "according to its social character," would be neither a republic under bourgeois dictatorship nor a republic under the dictatorship of the proletariat but "a republic under the joint dictatorship of several revolutionary classes." In such a republic, to develop a new democratic economy, there would only be nationalization of big banks and big industrial and commercial enterprises, and "the republic will neither confiscate capitalist private property in general nor forbid the development of such capitalist production as does not 'dominate the livelihood of the people.'" "The Chinese revolution cannot avoid taking the two steps, first of New Democracy and then of socialism. Moreover, the first step will need quite a long time."[22]

Mao's New Democracy schema was in fact a varied form of Menshevism. It was put into practice after the 1949 victory, yet frustrations soon compelled "socialist transformation" of private commercial and industrial enterprises. The political and economic schema of his New Democracy theory failed to materialize. The CCP officially recognized this later.

The Political Report adopted by the Eighth CCP Congress in 1956 declared:

> The setting up of the People's Republic of China signifies the basic end of the stage of bourgeois democratic revolution in China and the start of the stage of proletarian socialist revolution. It signifies the beginning of China's period of transition from capitalism to socialism.

This was the official negation of the possibility of a mode of development as envisaged in New Democracy.

In December 1958, at the Sixth Plenary Session of the Eighth CCP

Central Committee, the "Resolution on some questions on the People's Commune" admitted:

> We are followers of the Marxist-Leninist theory of permanent revolution. We consider that between the democratic revolution and the socialist revolution, and between socialism and communism, there does not and must not lie a Great Wall.

This means that Mao's division of "new democracy" and socialism, with the former having a "considerably long period of development" was not accepted.

In 1959 Zhou Enlai wrote that since the revolutionary victory, the confiscation of bureaucrat capital "had economically surpassed the scope of democratic revolution."[23] That the confiscation of bureaucrat capital had been accomplished before land reform in newly liberated areas shows that socialist tasks did not start only after the completion of all democratic tasks. This overthrew Mao's previous theory of "two revolutionary stages": "The revolution is divided into stages, that we can proceed to the next stage of revolution after accomplishing the first."[24]

The theories and propositions of the CCP (under Mao's leadership) before the victory of the revolution reflected its underestimation of the historical role of the proletariat. Yet under the pressure of each significant historical event, it was forced by its empiricism to make changes and revise some theories or policies. The inconsistencies and contradictions illustrated that the CCP leadership was not composed of truly conscious marxists. They had attempted to get rid of the rule of the revolutionary law as explained by Marx but in vain. Marxism has manifested its objective correctness.

Although the 1949 Chinese revolution relied on the peasant army as the dominant force, the peasants were not politically independent nor could they play a leadership role. The CCP, the leader of the revolution, had been influenced by the following factors relating to the proletariat: the CCP initially had the nature and tradition of the working class; it had always claimed allegiance to Marxism-Leninism (while at the same time it parallelled Mao Zedong Thought with Marxism-Leninism in order to elevate the former); it was inspired by the Russian October Revolution and had links with Soviet or East European "fraternal countries"; it reacted to the corruptness and despair of the capitalist world; it waged a prolonged struggle with the KMT; and it was under the pressure of the proletariat when it moved close to or into cities. All these factors had obliged the CCP to opt for a revolutionary road at critical conjunctures to overthrow capitalist property relations. Thus the victory of the revolution and the fulfillment of revolutionary tasks were not the result of the direct action of the Chinese proletariat, and yet basically they were somehow related to the proletariat. The proletariat functioned in an indirect manner.

But the fact that the revolution had undergone such a deformed development and that the proletariat had not directly played an active leadership role further facilitated the crystallization of the Chinese bureaucracy, which caused the laboring people of China to pay a heavy price, the socialist construction to encounter many obstacles and defeats, and the speed of transition to socialist society to be retarded.

MARX'S THEORY OF THE TRANSITION PERIOD AND CHINA'S REALITIES

The transition period is a period of struggle between waning capitalism and growing communism. A country in the transition period must continue to struggle with capitalist forces. What were Marx's propositions for such a country to come to communist society? How has the practice in China tested these propositions?

An important assertion of Marx was "between capitalist and communist society lies the period of the revolutionary transformation of the one into the other. Corresponding to this is also a political transition period in which the state can be nothing but the *revolutionary dictatorship of the proletariat*."[25]

Marx had expounded his propositions on the transition period, basing them on the experience of the Paris Commune. In *The State and Revolution*, Lenin summed them up: "The dictatorship of the proletariat, the period of transition to communism, will for the first time create democracy for the people, for the majority, along with the necessary suppression of the exploiters, of the minority." "Democracy signifies the formal recognition of equality of citizens, the equal right of all to determine the structure of, and to administer, the state." "*Against* their transformation into bureaucrats the measures will at once be taken which were specified in detail by Marx and Engels: (1) not only election but also recall at any time; (2) pay not to exceed that of a workman; (3) immediate introduction of control and supervision by *all*, so that *all* may become 'bureaucrats' for a time and that, therefore, *nobody* may be able to become a 'bureaucrat.'"[26]

In China after the nationalization of the major means of production, productivity was still very low, the economy backward, and the material supplies insufficient. The people's lives were difficult. Yet the CCP claims that such a society is already a socialist society, which in marxist terms is the first stage of communist society.

Politically the CCP practices one-party dictatorship—the several small parties in the Political Consultative Committee do not play any real role. There does not exist any soviet form of organization such as the congress of deputies of workers, peasants, or soldiers. The National People's Congress is only a rubber-stamp organization. All officials are CCP-appointed. The people do not have the power to elect, recall, or supervise the officials. On the contrary the laboring people are deprived of basic democratic rights. In their daily life or work, they are subject to the control of cadres. The higher the rank of the cadre, the more political privileges, pay, and material benefits he enjoys.

What is practiced in China's political system has nothing of the content of the dictatorship of the proletariat in marxist terms.

REVOLUTIONARY MARXISTS PERSIST IN MARX'S PROPOSITIONS

As a workers' party adhering to marxism, the Revolutionary Communist Party (RCP) of China is diametrically different from the CCP in its evaluation and conclusions on the above questions. It believes that the classic ideas of marxism are still valid: China has not yet developed to a socialist society; it is still a transitional society between capitalism and socialism. In the strict sense of the word, China should be delineated as a deformed workers' state and not a socialist state; the nature of China's political power is not a genuine dictatorship of the proletariat but a bureaucratic dictatorship repressing the proletariat.

The RCP of China and its major leader for many years—Peng Shuzhi— have put forward many theoretical and political analyses and propositions concerning China's development in the past three decades. Their positions can be summed up as follows: staunch defense of the gains of the Chinese revolution; full democratic rights for the working masses; improvement of their living and working conditions; workers' management of production, reorganization of the communes, and production brigades according to the peasants' will; democratization of all organizations and institutions; establishment of a congress of deputies of workers, peasants, and soldiers; right of autonomy and separation for the national minorities; a foreign policy of proletarian internationalism and world revolution; preparation and carrying out of political revolution to assure realization of the above goals; and establishment of a socialist, democratic political system.

The RCP's political ideas and positions can be found in detail in its programmatic document, "The Development of New China an Our Tasks."[27]

Peng Shuzhi's writings on questions concerning new China have been collected in *Peng Shuzhi, Selected Writings* (Chinese edition), volume 3, and in the English edition of his writings—*The Chinese Communist Party in Power*, published by Monad Press, in 1980.

Here we quote some of his main ideas:

On December 1, 1954, in "The Third Chinese Revolution and Its Perspectives," Peng anticipated: "China will resemble the deformed workers' states of Eastern Europe in all essential features. If this happens, China will have to go through a political revolution to achieve genuine socialist construction, just as the Eastern European countries and the Soviet Union itself must."[28]

In April 1960 in "On the Nature of the CCP and Its Regime—Political Revolution or Democratic Reform," Peng said: "In my 'Report on the Chinese Situation,' written in 1951, I pointed out that even before the CCP took power, a stubborn and self-willed bureaucracy had taken shape in the rural area it occupied. After taking power, this bureaucracy, because of the monopoly and concentration of all political, economic, military, and cultural organization and power, rapidly crystallized into a privileged caste."[29] Peng then analyzed the bureaucracy in different aspects and quoted examples of the bureaucratic privileges. His analyses and conclusions were later repeatedly confirmed by the broad masses and various contending factions during and after the Cultural Revolution.

Peng's conclusion was "at present in China, as in the Soviet Union, the Eastern European countries, North Korea, and North Vietnam, it is impossible to carry out democratic reforms. The right road, and the only possible one, is political revolution."[30] The tasks of the political revolution are to end the bureaucracy and its privileges and practice genuine dictatorship of the proletariat with full socialist democracy, while maintaining the system of public ownership and planned economy.

On economic policy Peng Shuzhi and his comrades have proposed concrete ideas and criticized the CCP's following mistakes: stress on heavy industry at the expense of light industry and agriculture, stress on production at the expense of the people's standard of living, stress on accumulation at the expense of consumption, stress on investments in capital construction at the expense of scientific and technological reforms, stress on quantity and not the quality of products, stress on high quotas and high rates while neglecting effectiveness, resort to administrative compulsion and commandism while repressing the voluntarism of the masses (especially during the communalization campaign in 1958), dependence on political incentives as against the principle of reward according to labor input (especially during the Cultural Revolution). All these extremely wrong practices have caused a vicious cycle in which the people's enthusiasm for production remains very low, serious discrepancies exist among different economic sectors, and a sometimes regressive stagnation to persist in China's economy.

In recent years although the CCP has admitted the above mistakes and embarked on economic readjustment, there have not been radical changes in many false policies, despite the correction of some. While some ultra-"leftist" policies have been abandoned, they are replaced by rightist policies (such as the present get-rich movement in the countryside). This has expedited the growth of capitalist factors both in the cities and in the countryside and has increased the danger of capitalist restoration.

THE PERSISTENCE OF THE MASSES IN MARXISM

The broad masses of China have waged numerous struggles to strive for improvements in their work and living standards, for democratization, and against bureaucratic dictatorship. The politically conscious workers and revolutionary intellectuals, when they compare the teachings of Marx, Engels, and Lenin with China's realities, with the CCP's mistakes, and with the situation in the Soviet Union and other workers' states, find themselves confronted with unanswered questions and with the urge to seek a correct road for China's socialist construction.

Yet with the CCP's high-handed repression, the people generally do not have the freedom of speech and publication to express their dissent toward the CCP, nor the freedom of assembly and organization to form political groups that can exist openly and carry on political activities. The CCP's strict censorship has, moreover, prevented the existence of dissidents and their organizations from being known by the general public, not to mention the people outside of China.

Nevertheless many times when there was political turmoil and relaxation of CCP control, or when contending CCP factions needed mass support in their struggle with other factions, the mass movement had an opportunity to rise up, and revolutionists stood up to express their political ideas and even to form political organizations to fight for their demands.

Here are some events in the history of new China.

1. In 1957 after the CPSU condemnation of Stalin's crimes, the revolution in Hungary, and the Poznan uprising in Poland, the CCP, to alleviate people's discontent and social tensions, was obliged to call on the people to express their opinions in the "Hundred Flowers Bloom" campaign to help the party rectify its evils—"bureaucratism, subjectivism, and sectarianism." The people, especially young students, revolutionary intellectuals, and some CCP members and Youth League members, made an extensive and ongoing criticism of CCP bureaucratic arbitrariness and privileges and expressed strong discontent and opposition. The revolutionary tendencies at that time were reflected in the opinion of the movement's leaders, the most representative of whom was Lin Xilin, a student at the People's University and a Youth League member. She considered that "the superstructure in today's China is not compatible with the system of public ownership." "The party and state institutions have become a set of bureaucratic organs ruling the people and without democracy." "Reformist measures cannot be applied to the shortcomings! Our aim is well delineated—to build genuine socialism, to lead a genuine people's life." So, "radical reforms are necessary."

   Dai Huang, a CCP member and a Xinhua News Agency reporter, clearly proposed the setting up of new parties "to practice democracy and freedom and to eliminate the bureaucratic class."[31]

This was the first group of revolutionary leftists that publicly appeared in new China. But the CCP and Mao Zedong quickly repressed the Hundred Flowers Bloom Movement, labeled all the critics as "rightists," and jailed many of them. For example, Lin Xilin was jailed for fifteen years. According to official figures, those labeled "rightists" in 1957 and rehabilitated in the several years after the fall of the "Gang of Four" amounted to four hundred thousand. This reveals the extent of the bureaucracy's witch hunt of progressive elements (though there were some true rightists among those repressed).

2. The "Cultural Revolution" that started in 1966 was initially Mao's maneuver to call upon the strongly discontented students and youth to form into Red Guards and rebel to pull "capitalist-roaders" down from power. But this campaign objectively unleashed a fervent mass movement throughout the country, which quickly got out of Mao Zedong's and the CCP's control. Mao, having brought down the major members of the old faction in power and secured supreme power for himself, at once compromised with the rest of the old cadres and promoted "an alliance of three forces" (i.e., old cadres, the army, and Red Guard leaders). Then he turned to repress the Red Guards, disbanded them, compelled them to go into the countryside, and jailed or even executed Red Guards (especially the leaders) who refused to obey. This further expedited the awakening of the young generation and shattered their illusions in the Mao Zedong-Jiang Qing faction. In the several years of the Cultural Revolution, there were many Red Guard publications, the most representative of which was *Whither Goes China*, the programmatic declaration of the Red Guard group Hunan Province Proletarian Alliance, whose leader was Yang Xiguang. It represented the rethinking of the radical young generation and its demand for carrying the revolution to the end. Although the program attempted to explain Mao's contradictions by Mao Zedong Thought itself, it expressed discontent with Mao's perfidy and explored the question of "whither goes China." It considered that "China cannot go in the direction of the Revolutionary Committee's bourgeois reformism; it will be capitalist restoration. China can only go in the socialist direction of radical revolution—the 'China People's Commune' declared by the Beijing People's Commune of the 1960s." "China must go towards a society without bureaucrats. Now, 90 percent of the high-ranking cadres have formed into a special class ... the privileges and high pay of the 'red' capitalist class are based on repression and exploitation of the broad masses. This class must be overthrown if 'China People's Commune' is to be realized."[32]

This document was labeled "counterrevolutionary" by the Central Cultural Revolution Group that same year. The Hunan Province Proletarian Alliance was disbanded, and Yang Xiguang was imprisoned.

3. During the 1974–76 "Campaign to criticize Lin Biao and Confucius," revolutionary youths who had undergone the ordeal of the Cultural Revolution went through an ideologic rethinking and theoretic exploration.

At that time the most well-known, influential writing was the Li Yi Zhe Wall Poster—"On socialist democracy and legal system"—which appeared in Guangzhou. (The authors of the poster were *Li* Zhengtian, Chen Yi*yang*, Wang Xi*zhe*, and Ge Wenzhi.) Formally it proposed six points for the consideration of Mao Zedong and the Fourth National People's Congress. Essentially it was the program of their marxist ideological system and their statement attacking the "bureaucratic caste" and the "newborn bourgeoisie." It is worth particular attention that this document reflected the hopes of revolutionary youths for breaking the reins of traditional leadership, and it alluded to the reorganization of a revolutionary political party in China to coordinate social strength to struggle against the bureaucratic caste. Despite its declaration of allegiance to Mao Zedong, it was an historic document and had a far-reaching impact inside and outside China. The slogan of socialist democracy and legal system that it proposed has become the central demand of the democracy movement that emerged later within the Chinese population.

THEORETICAL CURRENTS IN THE DEMOCRACY MOVEMENT OF RECENT YEARS

4. The democracy movement from the end of 1978 to April 1981.

This movement had its stimulus directly from the rehabilitation of the 1976 Tiananmen uprising. The uprising, in which one hundred thousand people participated, was a prelude to the political revolution against the entire bureaucratic system. It was an angry explosion of the masses' discontent with the bureaucratic dictatorship (besides Beijing, there were mass uprisings in Nanjing and Zhengzhou). The bureaucracy headed by Mao accused it of being "counterrevolutionary," yet mass actions did not subside because of repression, and they ultimately compelled the faction in power to revoke the Central resolution of April 1976 and recognize it as a mass revolutionary action. It was a new antibureaucratic victory for the masses, and it greatly enhanced their mood for struggle. Wall posters were posted up everywhere; *samizdat* publications were published, and spontaneous street rallies and demonstrations of the masses took place. They made political proposals: the CCP's one-party dictatorship and bureaucratic privileges became the focus of criticism, and the demand for democratization became a common, central demand. To sum up they wanted to realize the Paris Commune principles elaborated by Marx.

In this emerging tide, revolutionists all over the country put forward their political ideas, and over a hundred *samizdat* publications joined in the political forum. The main ideologic current among them was marxist. They consider that what is practiced in China today is not socialism or marxism but a distortion of marxism. This society is transitional. The major antagonism in society is the antagonism between the CCP bureaucratic rulers and the people. Common ideas among them are continued maintenance of state ownership of the means of production, power to all working people, practice of Paris Commune–style government, full socialist democracy, and improvement of the people's standard of living.

Among the representative well-known personages, there are differences on individual concrete problems. For example:

He Qiu, the chief editor of Guangzhou *samizdat* "People's Path," considered that the democracy movement opposes bureaucrats and bureaucratic privileges in the government and defends marxism and socialism. He wanted the people to discard the last illusions (including illusions for the "reforming faction"). His important writings include "My Bibliography" and "Open Letter to the National People's Congress Standing Committee and the People of China."

Wang Xizhe, writer for Guangzhou *samizdat* "People's Voice" and the chief writer of the 1973 Li Yi Zhe Wall Poster, considered that the obstacles to Four Modernizations in China are the ossification of the economic system and the bureaucratization of the political system. The cause is Mao Zedong's personal autocracy and dictatorship of the bureaucratic privileged class that tried to realize Mao's "program for agrarian socialism." Mao was not a marxist, Wang asserted. Wang still harbored hope for the CCP's reforming faction, but he proposed the people's democratic supervision of the Paris Commune type. His important writings include, "Strive for the Class Dictatorship of the Proletariat," "The Direction of Democracy," "The Dictatorship of the Proletariat is a Dictatorship of Humanity," "Mao Zedong and the Cultural Revolution," and "The Party's Leadership and Democratic Supervision."

Wei Jingsheng, the chief editor of the Beijing *samizdat* "Explorations," considered that the obstacles to China's development in various fields came from the lack of democracy in the social system and the Mao Zedong–type dictatorship. The characteristics of marxism lie in its "achievement of the ideal through the integration of general democracy and dictatorship with concentration of power"; marxism, whose revolutionary essence has been extracted and discarded, is then used by the rulers as an excuse to enslave the people. Wei proposed "democratic socialism," that is, all power to the whole people organized in a democratic way. His important writings include, "The Fifth Modernization—Democracy and Others," "For Democracy or For a New Dictatorship," "The 20th Century Bastille in China, and "Self-Defense Speech at the Court Trial."

Xu Wenli and Liu Qing, founders of the Beijing *samizdat* "April 5 Forum," had similarly moderate positions. They considered that China's laboring class is basically in a passive position, yet the regime's authority is also decreasing, and the acute confrontation of social contradictions cannot be concealed. The revolution is approaching, but because they considered that China could not stand any more upheavals, they hoped that the "reforming faction" among the power holders could carry out reforms. Xu's important writings include "The Most Urgent Task Today," "Analysis of Contemporary Social Reforms in China," "The Present Situation and Our Viewpoints," and "Proposals for the 1980 Reform." Liu's writings include "The Necessity of Institutional Reforms in the Light of Zhou Enlai's Fate" and "Prison Notebooks—I Appeal to the Social Court of Justice."[33]

Because they had a common understanding and aim—for democracy and against the bureaucracy—and it was necessary to gather strength to confront the bureaucracy, twenty-one samizdat publications organized themselves as the "China National Samizdat Publications Association" in September 1980 and published the organ Duty. Over ten other samizdat publications later joined the association.

On the other hand, the bureaucratic and dictatorial nature of the "reforming faction" in power was increasingly exposed, and the repression of the samizdat publications and organizations intensified. Wei Jingsheng was arrested in March 1979 and sentenced to fifteen years' imprisonment. Liu Qing was arrested in early 1980. From April 1981 onward, the main samizdat editors or activists all over the country were arrested, and over thirty of them known to the outside. About a year later, it was known that Xu Wenli was sentenced to fifteen years (it was reported that one of the charges on Xu was initiation of a national organization, "The China Communist League," and planning of a political organization, "Association to Promote Democracy and Unification in China"), Wang Xizhe to fourteen years, and He Qiu to ten years. There was no news about the other arrested militants.

The general repression was a strong blow to the democracy movement and to revolutionists who thought independently and put their intellectual abilities to work for a better future for society. Yet it also shattered any remaining illusions in the "reforming faction." The regime's repression did not eliminate the people's resistance. Revolutionists that have not been arrested have turned underground and continued their activities clandestinely. For example since late 1982, a Guangzhou samizdat called "Wild Grass" has been circulated abroad. These democracy movement militants will continue their theoretical expositions to contribute to the development of marxism. In the future with the accumulation and intensification of social contradictions, with changes in the domestic and international situation, and with a new awakening of the working class and the upsurge of its struggles, the Chinese revolutionists and masses will again be active on the political scene.

POLITICAL REVOLUTION IS A NECESSARY SUPPLEMENT TO MARXISM

The thirty years of Chinese history, similar to the history of other bureaucratized workers' states, has been the usurpation by bureaucratic dictatorship of the proletariat's power to manage the country and production. This has caused the working class to remain for long periods in powerlessness and passivity. It has caused the development of productive forces in China to be impeded and the people's material and spiritual life to be impaired. Marx's correct assertion that the proletariat must become the ruling class in the transition period has not been put into practice, though the CCP and the various Communist parties have been obliged to give it lip service.

Lenin's summary of Marx's political propositions concerning the transition period that we quoted earlier in this article could have been put into effect if the leading party had truly followed Marxism-Leninism and remained faithful to the laboring people. If these propositions had been followed, bureaucratization in state institutions could have been prevented, as well as the numerous losses and waste caused by wrong policies of the bureaucratic dictatorship. These propositions are the touchstone for determining if a political party is faithful to the working people and to the Marxist-Leninist program.

The CCP's practice has completely violated Marx's recommendations. The party's praxis is neither marxism nor scientific socialism.

After the fall of the "Gang of Four," and especially in recent years, a number of people in China's theoretical circle have proposed the theory of socialist alienation, which promotes the idea that in China, in areas like ideology, politics, economics, and labor, realities alien from and opposite to socialism exist. This means that many CCP theories, policies, and practices are deviant from marxist and socialist principles and have become alien from or opposite to socialism. Theorists of socialist alienation have referred to Marx's theory of alienation. Although Marx discussed the alienation of labor in capitalist society and did not talk of socialist alienation, such a theory as applied to China and other so-called "socialist societies" is a remarkable development of marxism. The realities of alienation that they point out expose the hypocrisy of the CCP's self-representation of marxism.

It is a serious misconception to mix the CCP's deeds with marxism or socialism. However, this misconception is quite common among the people and even among the workers. This distortion of the teachings of marxism and scientific socialism has led to a relative lack of interest among workers in production and politics. To overcome this indifference, the original countenance of marxism must be restored so that the working class will be ideologically armed to seize full control, management, and political power over the economy and society.

There are deep social roots for the bureaucratic degeneration (in the Soviet Union) and deformation (in China, Vietnam, North Korea, and Eastern Europe) of workers' states. A common root is economic backwardness. Rapid change of the backwardness requires economic aid from other countries (in particular, the advanced countries). To achieve this world revolution must be extended to other countries. However, the CCP and the Communist parties of other workers' states have developed their own narrow nationalism—socialism in one country—and reject the foreign policy of proletarian internationalism—world revolution. These indicate that the existence of the bureaucracy can only further impede the effort of workers' states to overcome their backwardness.

Only through political revolution by the working class to overthrow the bureaucracy can all serious domestic questions be decisively solved. This basic objective need gives rise to the necessity of political revolution. It is a necessary supplement to socialist revolution.

China is inseparable from the world as a whole. The future of China's antibureaucratic political revolution depends on the one hand on the growth of the Chinese working class's strength, the enhancement of its political consciousness, and the development of its struggle with the bureaucracy, and on the other hand on the outcome of confrontations between antagonistic class forces on a world scale. Any serious defeat suffered by the Chinese and international proletariat will give a strong push to the restoration of capitalism in China. On the contrary any decisive victory of the world revolution will give strong impetus to China's antibureaucratic political revolution and open up the road toward socialism.

Analysis of the Chinese bureaucracy in the transition period and the conclusion that is drawn—political revolution—are a new development of marxism in China after the 1950s. This idea was first applied by Trotsky to the Soviet Union after the 1920s and later by Trotskyists to the Eastern European countries that came into being after World War II. After its political break with the CPSU, the CCP made a 180-degree turn, from flat denial of the existence of a privileged caste in the Soviet Union to recognition and even to the extreme of labeling it as "social-imperialist." In past decades, the Chinese people, and especially revolutionists, have recognized that a similar bureaucratic privileged caste exists in China (some mistake it to be a privileged "class"). Although the CCP itself does not recognize this, it has officially admitted that there exist in China phenomena such as privileged bureaucrats, bureaucratism, and even bureaucratism and privileges in the party and state leadership system. These developments show that the theory of privileged bureaucratic caste is objectively true and cannot be denied by the bureaucracy's leaders.

There have been several antibureaucratic political revolutions or preludes by the people of workers' states: the Hungarian revolution and Poznan workers' uprising in Poland in 1956, the Berlin workers' revolt in 1953, the Tiananmen rebellion in China on April 5, 1976, the Polish revolution that started in 1980, and others. These events show that the working masses are putting the theory of political revolution into practice. It has shown its validity and necessity.

The victory of political revolutions in bureaucratized workers' states will signify a new victory and a general revival of Marxism. These victories will expedite revolutionary victories in the capitalist world. Doubts about marxism will then be dispelled.

Notes

1. Marx and Engels, *The Communist Manifest,* English edition (Penguin, 1967), 56.
2. "Tasks of the Proletariat in the Present Revolution," Lenin, *Collected Works,* English edition, vol. 24, 23, and *Selected Works of Lenin,* Chinese edition, vol. 3, 863, n. 10. Emphasis in original.
3. Karl Marx, and Engels, *Collected Works,* English edition, vol. 10, 281, 287.
4. Excerpted from Trotsky's *History of the Russian Revolution,* English edition, appendices to vol. 3 (Pluto Press, 1977), 1259–64.
5. "Resolution of the Executive Committee of the Comintern Concerning the Relations Between the CCP and the KMT," January 12, 1923. See *Documents and Materials of the Comintern on the Chinese Revolution,* Chinese edition (China Social Sciences Publishers), 76.
6. Huang Xinrong's article in "Jiang Han Lun Tan," no. 1 of 1983.
7. Ibid.
8. Cf. n. 5.
9. "Struggle in the Chingkang Mountains," *Selected Works of Mao Tsetung,* English edition, vol. 1, 97–98.
10. *History of Contemporary Chinese Revolution,* ed. He Ganzhi (Higher Education Press), 178.
11. "On Tactics Against Japanese Imperialism," *Selected Works of Mao Tsetung,* English edition, vol. 1, 163.
12. Ibid., "Tasks of the CCP in the Period of Resistance to Japan," 268.
13. Ibid., "Win the Masses in Their Millions for the Anti-Japanese National United Front," 289.
14. Cf. n. 10, 218, 278.
15. *Questions on the Chinese Revolution* (Chun Yan Publishers), 205.
16. Ibid., 203.
17. Wang Jianmin, *History of the CCP,* vol. 3, 115.
18. Lenin, "Democracy and Narodism in China," *Collected Works,* English edition, vol. 18, 167.
19. "Monthly Chronology of the CCP-KMT Civil War," compiled by the Xinhua News Agency and published by New Democracy Press, 3. Emphasis added.
20. Cf. n. 10, 284.
21. "On New Democracy," *Selected Works of Mao Tsetung,* English edition, vol. 2, 366–67. Emphasis in original.
22. Ibid., 348, 353, 358.

23. *The Ten Glorious Years* (Joint Publishers), 35.
24. Cf. n. 21, 360.
25. Karl Marx and Frederick Engels, "Critique of the Gotha Programme," in *Selected Works in One Volume*, English edition, Lawrence and Wishart, 1968, 331. Emphasis in original.
26. Lenin, *Collected Works*, English edition, vol. 25, 463, 472, 481. Emphasis in original.
27. The full text was reprinted in *October Review*, September and December 1978.
28. *The Chinese Communist Party in Power*, English edition (Monad Press, 1980), 169–70.
29. Ibid., 236.
30. Ibid., 262.
31. Ibid., 260, and "Democratic China," ed. Students' Union of Chinese University of Hong Kong, 7.
32. "Whither Goes China," *Democratic China*, 34, 43.
33. The important writings of Wei Jingsheng, Liu Qing, Xu Wenli, Wang Xizhe, He Qiu, and other democracy movement militants are almost all collected in *Democratic China* and in *Collected Works of Wang Xizhe* (Hong Kong: Seventies Publishers).

16

The Rise and Fall of Maoism

LIN YIFENG

It is almost undisputed that Mao Zedong occupies a place in contemporary Chinese political history and exerts an influence unparalleled by anyone else in contemporary China. It is also generally known that Mao professed himself to be a marxist and the CCP has always proclaimed Maoism (or Mao Zedong Thought) as marxism applied to China's specific circumstances.

Nonetheless following the gradual exposure of Mao's mistakes, many partisans of Maoism become critics, and some go so far as to denounce Marxism-Leninism, saying that Mao's mistakes are largely to be blamed on his belief in Marxism-Leninism.

Is this the real picture?

This article attempts to compare and contrast Lenin's basic positions on revolution in backward countries with those of Mao, to look at the different roles of Maoism in various periods from the rise of the resistance war against Japan to the death of Mao, and to identify the characteristics of Maoism.

MAO'S BASIC POSITIONS ON REVOLUTION IN BACKWARD COUNTRIES DEVIATED FROM LENINISM FROM THE START

The socialist movement in China spread quickly from the Soviet Union. Like many CCP members of his generation who were inspired by the victory of the October Revolution, Mao turned from an admirer of Western bourgeois democracy to a partisan of Marxism-Leninism and committed himself to the socialist movement.

However historical facts prove that Mao did not understand the experience of marxist practice in Russia. He did not understand Lenin's analysis of the basic problems of the Russian Revolution, and in particular, he did not understand the lessons of the October Revolution.

Lenin's positions on the above question can be summarized as follows:

1. At first Lenin, Plekhanov, and others pointed out that backward Russia

197

did not possess the economic foundation for realizing socialism. They denounced the populists for their vague and harmful illusion that socialism could be at once realized under Russia's very backward conditions.

2. Lenin and others pointed out that the immediate tasks of the Russian Revolution were to overthrow the tsar and to carry out a land reform. The nature of such tasks could only be considered those of the bourgeois-democratic revolution. In other words they were not tasks of the proletarian socialist revolution.

3. However Lenin had common positions with Plekhanov and others (i.e., the later Mensheviks) only on the above two questions. On the crux of the question of the Russian Revolution, fundamental differences arose between Lenin and Plekhanov. The crux of the problem was this: in Russia, which class could act as the leader of the revolution—the bourgeoisie or the proletariat?

The Mensheviks' answer was that the leader of such a bourgeois revolution could only be the bourgeoisie. The Russian revolution would inevitably be divided into two stages—first the stage of democratic revolution led by the bourgeoisie, and then, when capitalism was fully developed and the country had the economic foundation for realizing socialism, socialist revolution could proceed.

Lenin, on the other hand, thought that this Menshevik proposition went against the principle of marxism, for according to marxist principle, the actual development of a society was determined by the concrete conditions that formed this society, especially by the actual class relations and not by a preconceived schema. When Lenin made a close inspection of Russia's actual class relations, he concluded that the Russian bourgeoisie had thoroughly degenerated—it colluded with the landowners and feared major reforms. It could not act as leader of the revolution, but on the contrary it was an obstacle to the revolution's advance. Precisely because the bourgeoisie colluded with the landowners and stood in direct opposition to the proletariat, the workers and peasants could and should form an alliance, with the workers leading the peasants, to promote the revolution and to set up a "democratic dictatorship of workers and peasants" upon the victory of the revolution.

The 1905 Russian Revolution confirmed Lenin's judgment, because in this revolution the workers and peasants jointly formed soviets (workers' councils) in opposition to the tsar, the landowners, and the bourgeoisie.

Yet how did the October Revolution confirm Lenin's formulations?

It is fair to say that Lenin only correctly dealt with the problem and found the correct answer within the framework of his exposition. When the workers and peasants indeed formed an alliance and seized power, two questions arose: first would the bourgeoisie be included among the targets of the dictatorship under the "democratic dictatorship of the workers and peasants," and second would this society develop toward capitalism or socialism?

Lenin's exposition obviously did not answer either of these two questions.

On the theoretical level, following on Lenin's analysis, one can infer that when the proletariat leads the peasants in seizing power, it will and it must expropriate the property of the bourgeoisie and advance society toward socialist development. This is true because, if the bourgeoisie can succeed in alleviating social opposition, the situation of workers' and peasants' joint seizure of power will be precluded. On the other hand, when actual class struggle forces the proletariat to realize that it must seize power, it will not limit itself simply to carrying out a democratic revolution. The conclusion inferred from this can provide more comprehensive answers to a series of related questions, such as the nature, motive force, or orientation of the revolution, than the answers given by Lenin. Trotsky gave those answers. The 1949 Chinese Revolution served as another confirmation, which will be discussed later.

Why did Lenin not make a further theoretical inference so that his answer could be comprehensive? One view is that Lenin strictly limited his exposition to the scope of known conditions and avoided a purely theoretical inference before there was sufficient concrete experience of actual class struggle related to the question. In any event the October Revolution's victory and later development definitively answered the question.

4. After the victory of the October Revolution, the Bolsheviks at first did not expropriate all the bourgeoisie's property. But on the one hand, as Trotsky had predicted, the proletariat (including its vanguard, the Bolshevik Party) leading the revolution would no longer confine itself to democratic tasks. On the other hand, the actual class struggle had by this time developed to the stage of a life-and-death conflict between the proletariat and the bourgeoisie. If the state did not generally control the means of production and expropriate the bourgeoisie's property, the infant Soviet regime could not be maintained, and the workers and peasants might starve as well. Thus a democratic revolution led by the working class directly developed into a socialist revolution to build a system of state ownership.

After state ownership had been established, Lenin announced to the whole world that the victory of the proletarian revolution in Russia showed that "the capitalist chain first broke at its weakest link." In "Theses on the National and Colonial Questions," Lenin placed the revolutionary movements of these countries in the context of the world proletarian revolutionary movement; he appealed to the proletariat of the world, and especially the proletariat of the backward countries, to draw experience and lessons from the October Revolution. This demonstrates that after the October Revolution, Lenin considered that previously unanswered questions had been answered and that the experience of the October Revolution was applicable to other backward countries.

However, when we look at the CCP after its formation, the Comintern's directives to the CCP concerning fundamental questions of the Chinese Revolution ran completely contrary to Lenin's opinions.

In fact the directives to the CCP given by the Comintern, which was controlled by the Soviet Communist Party Central Committee under Stalin's leadership, were the "national revolution" should be promoted by the active building of a "coalition of four classes (the national bourgeoisie, the proletariat, the peasants, and the intellectuals)" to be led by the Nationalist Party (KMT). It defined China at that time as a semifeudal, semicolonial country. Therefore the immediate tasks of the Chinese Revolution were to overcome the feudal remnants and the imperialist forces. The revolution at that stage, according to the Comintern leadership, was a bourgeois one; thus it should be led by the bourgeoisie.

Can it be said that the Chinese bourgeoisie was more progressive than the Russian bourgeoisie and that it would promote the revolution? The answer is *no*.

The reality was the contrary. In fact the Chinese bourgeoisie, many of whom were landowners, were either subordinate to imperialism or in deep collaboration with it. Imperialism by that time had economically dominated the whole of China through finance capital and other activities. Hence if one recognizes that China had the status of a semicolony, one should practically define that China at that time was a country of underdeveloped capitalism dominated by imperialism. The Stalinists deliberately circumscribed the crux of the question by avoiding a definition of the Chinese economy as dominated by capitalism; they merely asserted that capitalism in China was underdeveloped.

What the Comintern offered to the CCP was the worst reproduction in China of the Mensheviks' so-called "revolution by stages." The CCP's carrying out of the Comintern's positions can be viewed as the beginning of the CCP's deviation from Marxism-Leninism.

As for Mao himself, because his role in the CCP leadership at this time was not significant, his acceptance of the Comintern's false positions was not particularly significant, unless it was related to his later positions. Still it can be shown that in the *Xiangjiang Review*, of which he was editor-in-chief, Mao wrote and stressed that the "merchants" (in fact, the bourgeoisie) were revolutionary. This indicates that from the start he had consciously accepted positions contrary to Leninism on the basic questions of revolution in backward countries.

THE RISE AND DECLINE OF THE CCP IN THE 1920S

After the First World War, China's international status changed for the worse. The imperialist aggression against China intensified. Domestically there was civil strife among the warlords, bankruptcy in the countryside, and a generalized decline in the people's living standards. Meanwhile nationalism and class consciousness on the part of the workers, peasants, and intellectuals continued to increase. In 1925 a revolution shook the world.

The course of the revolution showed that the victory or defeat of the revolution was directly determined by the leadership's understanding of fundamental political questions. This, in turn, determined the opportunities of development for the leadership itself.

The CCP played a real leadership role in this revolution. At the time this infant party consciously criticized the KMT for its alienation from the masses. It devoted its efforts to organizing the urban workers' movement, and it conducted educational work for socialism. Thus it quickly and broadly won the trust of the workers, peasants, and intellectuals and became the leadership of the mass movement in China at the time. The proletariat was obviously the central force of the mass movement. Two things were thus proven: (1) Lenin's assessment of the nature and motive force of revolution in backward countries could be fully applied to China; and (2) no party other than that which grouped revolutionary vanguards with a socialist perspective (i.e., the CCP at that time) could mobilize and organize the masses. And only by actively mobilizing and organizing the masses could the CCP rise so rapidly in the 1920s.

The revolution could have had a very good chance of success if the CCP had done the following: (1) independently proposed a clear democratic revolutionary program, (2) called on the people to rise in resistance to imperialism and the warlords in a struggle for national liberation and unification, and (3) carried out a land reform. Such a course of action could have consolidated the alliance of workers and peasants and led to the election at the grassroots level of democratic councils capable of taking power.

Unfortunately the CCP at the time took an opposite course. It executed the directives of the Comintern, which ordered the CCP to join the KMT. This not only liquidated the CCP's role as leader of the revolution but also caused the CCP to abandon land reform as a condition of compromise with the KMT (because many KMT generals were landowners). And what the Comintern at first sponsored and armed was not the CCP, but the KMT! The CCP only called for land reform after Chiang Kai-shek and Wang Ching-wei had successfully disarmed the urban workers' movement and slaughtered thousands of worker militants. By then it was too late.

In sum the defeat of the Second Chinese Revolution was a result of the Comintern's deviation from Leninism on the fundamental questions of the Chinese revolution. The CCP, which executed this wrong line, was the first to suffer. Its forces were severely weakened, and it had to retreat to the countryside.

How the CCP Understood the Lessons
of the Second Chinese Revolution

Could the CCP correctly understand the lessons of the defeat of the Second Chinese Revolution? Actually it did not try. The retrospective review made by the Comintern and the CCP was essentially a search for scapegoats. They attributed their so-called "opportunist line" to Chen Duxiu and the "putschist line" to Li Lisan. However the CCP and Comintern failed to answer whether Chen and Li formulated or simply carried out the false policies. They attempted deliberately to cover up the Comintern's and to promote the idea that the "Party Central" was always correct, that those committing serious mistakes were merely individual leaders, and that the party was capable of "redressing" the mistakes. The CCP and Comintern even resorted to distorting historical facts.

Can one conclude that the defeated CCP could not draw any lessons from its defeat? If it could not, then why could it rise again during the resistance war against Japan and seize power in the civil war?

The CCP partially drew lessons, which could be summarized in two points:

1. It realized that it had to maintain the party's independence and should not readily give up the party's struggles or subordinate to collaborators. Put into practice, this idea meant persistence in independent armed struggle.
2. It realized that to preserve and develop itself, it had to join with the masses. It was also obliged to recognize that the proletariat was the leading force in the revolution.

In the party's subsequent developments, it applied this experience.

Yet it must also be pointed out that although at the time the reiteration of the socialist perspective and stress on the proletariat as the leading force of the revolution were necessary for upholding the convictions of the militants, the CCP could not implement this in practice. The CCP did not rebuild the workers' movement in the cities and build working-class support. Thus the formulation that the proletariat was the leader of the revolution was distorted into the notion that the CCP represented the proletariat or even that the CCP *was* the proletariat. This was the beginning of the CCP's overriding the working class, to which it continued to give lip service as the leading force of the revolution.

Even more critically, after the Zunyi Meeting in 1935, the CCP adopted the model of the Soviet Party in setting up a system of bureaucratic centralism. Following the practice of the Stalinized Soviet Communist Party, all major decisions were made autocratically by the central leadership, and leaderships of different levels were appointed by those above. When such a party system was integrated with the concept that "the party represented the proletarian class," the inevitable result was that the party dominated the people and the leader dominated the party.

THE RISE OF THE CCP IN THE RESISTANCE WAR, THE SECOND KMT-CCP COLLABORATION, AND THE ADVERSE CONSEQUENCES OF THE REVOLUTION DISTORTED

After Japan invaded China, a broad mass resistance movement developed throughout the country. The KMT regime waged a half-hearted struggle against Japanese imperialism but put all sorts of constraints on the mass movement. As a consequence, more and more people flocked to the CCP's banner to fight the resistance war. According to documents of the Seventh CCP Congress, when the war was drawing to a close, the CCP guerrilla troops had increased in number to 1.2 million, and the militia had increased to 2.5 million. This shows that the mass upsurge in resistance to the Japanese was the objective factor in the CCP's rising again. The subjective factor in the CCP's development was its recognition of the necessity of mass mobilization and organization and of its own independence.

When the resistance war started, the CCP took the initiative to propose KMT-CCP collaboration, that is, the so-called "United Front." The CCP also openly accepted Chiang Kai-shek's leadership. Though this is sometimes viewed as a CCP maneuver, historical facts show that the formation of the United Front not only did not help relax the KMT regime's hostility to the CCP but served to diminish the CCP members' vigilance against KMT repression. During the resistance war, the KMT forces did not concentrate on fighting the Japanese but instead struck at the CCP; the entire New Fourth Army was, for example, destroyed by the KMT. Actual experience compelled the CCP to conclude that, though the KMT-CCP collaboration was not to be abandoned, "struggles also existed within the United Front."

As the CCP evolved in its struggle against the KMT, the Japanese, and the Japanese puppet regime, it was faced with a number of questions: How would it deal with problems of nationality? What was its proposal for waging the resistance war? What sort of regime should be established after the war? What was the nature, motive force, and orientation of the Chinese revolution? These questions were no longer posed only in the abstract but had become immediate practical problems.

Mao wrote quite a number of articles on these questions. The most important ones were "On Prolonged War," "On the Coalition Government," and "On New Democracy."

Both in form and in content, the coalition government that Mao proposed simply combined all the existing elites in society so that they could compromise with each other. He did not seek replacement of the rulers or mobilization of the people's strength in a democratic way to change the state's political structure and advance the country toward political democracy. Because such a coalition government had never existed in China, it would be enough just to remember that Mao never identified himself with the principle that the government should be elected by the people; he even rejected this principle.

Still it cannot be denied that Mao's guerrilla war strategy was effective. It is necessary to understand why the CCP could achieve a victory by applying this strategy, whether it could be extended to other countries and whether it produced negative consequences.

It must first be pointed out that the CCP forces were able to grow during the resistance war and civil war because its armed struggle enjoyed broad mass support. In fact the CCP's armed struggle had remained in an adverse situation for a long time. Had it not organized a prolonged national liberation movement with an adequate supply of troops from the masses of landless peasants, combined with the CCP's ability to carry out a policy of joining forces with the masses to have cover and support, the CCP might not have been able to build up its forces, and it might not even have survived. Armed struggle detached from the masses or lacking the support of the masses does not correspond to China's experience. It could only be regarded as putschist armed adventure.

Second the military situation during the resistance war showed that Japanese imperialism obviously dominated North China and the major coastal cities by its absolutely superior ammunition, and the KMT regime controlled the remaining cities. However the Japanese army was unable to generally control the regions that it occupied; it had to join with the bourgeoisie, landowners, and local bullies of these regions to scrape together the necessary resources to maintain its war of aggression. Hence the people's forces gathered under CCP leadership had no other military option than guerrilla warfare. Moreover due to the superiority of the enemy's firepower, the CCP forces could only adopt expedient tactics (such as, in Mao's words, "we advance when the enemy withdraws; we withdraw when the enemy advances"). This saps the enemy's strength while allowing one's own forces to be built up, avoiding large-scale battles while the enemy's forces gradually collapse. (The strategy and tactics that Mao prescribed in "On Prolonged War" had their origin in the judgment that "Japanese imperialism will eventually collapse"; more precisely this concept was developed by militants who persisted in the resistance war, drawing conclusions from the actual situation and their actual experiences, and Mao simply summarized them.)

In any event from the actual class relations shown in the course of the resistance war, it can be seen that the bourgeoisie, landowners, and local bullies of the Japan-occupied regions colluded with the enemy and took the opportunity to extort from the people and to benefit from a further vicious concentration of land. Even in areas controlled by the KMT, bureaucrat capital, the bourgeoisie, landowners, and local bullies also made use of the opportunity to extort from the people and profit from the nation's calamity.

The behavior of these reactionary classes both in occupied regions and in KMT-ruled regions served to disrupt China's war against Japan and push China's society and economy toward disintegration. Could it be denied, therefore, that the people's forces had to remove these reactionary obstacles before the resistance war could gain real victory?

However what attitude did the CCP take toward the bourgeoisie and its political representative the KMT? In fact it persisted in the policy of the People's Front, that is, attempting to deny the class struggle within the nation. It did not draw a clear distinction between itself and the bourgeois KMT. (For example it could have gone beyond the limitation of fighting the resistance war together with the KMT.) The CCP, in a supra-class effort, attempted to "unite" opposing class forces to conduct social reform. When the resistance war ended and the civil war immediately ensued, and even when the CCP seized power, it never gave up its attempt to collaborate with the bourgeoisie—not even today when it declares that it "practices socialism" in China and when the bankruptcy of the People's Front is undeniable.

Another question is the CCP took power with a strategy of "besieging the cities by the countryside"—is this a valid strategy for general application?

It must first be pointed out that such a formulation in fact contains the presupposition that the crucial determination of victory is in the cities and not the countryside. Thus if this strategy is employed with the objective of advancing a revolution, it is obvious that when the revolution is advanced from the countryside to the cities, the existing armed struggle must be co-ordinated with an immediate call to the urban masses (of course with the workers as the key force) to mobilize. This must be combined with the general implementation of land reform in the rural areas. Thus military strength is still a major factor for achieving victory, but it is not the only one. In particular the force to advance social reforms is mass mobilization that seeks class liberation and not military force which is constrained by the subjective intentions of the commanders. On the contrary to link "siege of the cities by the countryside" to "political power growing out of the barrel of a gun," one will come up with the practice of achieving victory by relying on armed struggle and not on a broad class mobilization. Such a practice will cause the self-isolating military struggle to be a very arduous one or even to suffer defeat. Even if circumstances permit a revolutionary victory, adverse consequences likely will follow, such as the terrifying bureaucratic rule that emerged in China.

FROM "NEW DEMOCRACY" TO "GENERAL LINE"

In his "On New Democracy," Mao Zedong rather systematically discussed questions of the nature, motive force, and orientation of the Chinese revolution.

Mao considered that "since the invasion of foreign capitalism in China and the gradual growth of capitalist factors in Chinese society, ie., from the Opium War to the Sino-Japanese War, for a century China has gradually become a semi-colonial, semi-feudal society. . . . Whether in occupied areas or in non-occupied areas, feudalism is predominant in society" (see "On New Democracy," Chapter 3: "China's Historical Features").

Precisely because Mao considered that capitalism's development in old China was not predominant in relation to feudalism, it implied that capitalism still had much room for development, and so Mao judged that the Chinese revolution could not at once go on the socialist road; instead it should go on the road of "new democracy," that is, the Chinese revolution was to be divided into two stages which did not link up with each other.

Why, then, was the democratic revolution distinguished between the old and the new?

Mao thought that before the victory of the October Revolution in Russia, "the Chinese bourgeois democratic revolution . . . was part of the old world bourgeois democratic revolution. After this . . . it changed to the category of new democratic revolution; in terms of the revolutionary front, it has become part of the proletarian socialist revolution." The leader of this revolution was to be the Chinese proletariat.

Here Mao changed the previous CCP version, that is, he no longer thought that the bourgeoisie served as the leader of the Chinese democratic revolution. At the same time, he considered that the Chinese national bourgeoisie had a "dual" nature: on the one side revolutionary, on the other side weak and even reactionary.

In the chapter "Politics of New Democracy," Mao proposed building a "New Democratic Republic": "Such a . . . republic is different, on the one hand, from the old type, European bourgeois-dictatorship type of capitalist republic. . . . On the other hand, it is different from the most modern, Soviet, proletarian-dictatorship type of socialist republic." "It is a third form, . . . but it is also an unchangeable form."

Furthermore in the chapter "Economy of New Democracy," Mao proposed that the state should only control economic sectors that "affect the national economy and people's livelihood," and class relations should be addressed according to the principle of "caring for both the public and the private, and benefiting both the laborers and the capitalists."

From this one can see that when the CCP had developed into a powerful force, Mao began to find theoretical justification for the CCP's seizure of state power and to sketch the model of how this power was to be exercised. According to this model, he would place China under what he termed "new" democratism, that is, the track of capitalism.

However soon after the CCP seized power and formally wrote Mao's above propositions into the "Common Program," regarding them as long-term state policies, Mao proposed the "General Line" and then carried out "socialist transformations." Why?

The answer is in the international political situation. The imperialist bloc headed by the United States imposed a severe military siege and economic embargo on China. Domestically apart from those who rolled up their capital and productive equipment and fled abroad, the remaining capitalists were engaged in speculation, profiteering, and hoarding rather than producing normally. Despite the CCP's willingness to maintain capitalism, despite its insistence that foreigners' property in China would be protected, and despite the advantage of land reform, in theory, to the development of capitalism, the international bourgeoisie considered that the Chinese revolution was inimical to their interests. If they were not allowed to dominate China's economy and seize huge profits, then they would not invest at all, and they would impose an economic embargo to force China to surrender to them. In the eyes of the Chinese bourgeoisie, their property mattered most, and the expropriation of the landowners' and bureaucrat-capitalists' property also threatened them. (It must be remembered that many of them were concurrently landowners, and they had myriad ties with foreign capital, bureaucrat capital, and the landowning class.) In other words the question at this time was not whether capitalism had fully developed in China; it was already proven that capitalism was not feasible in China, and its collapse was a reality. At that time if the major means of production were not nationalized, the CCP might find it hard to hold onto power, and the national economy might also go bankrupt. Thus the Chinese revolution in effect repeated the experience of the October Revolution in Russia, that is, the evolution of the actual class relations determined the orientation of social development in China. Although the CCP had intended to maintain capitalism in China, it had to change its course and nationalize property.

If we recognize that backward countries do not possess the economic basis for realizing socialism, and yet the proletariat of backward countries, in solving democratic tasks, advances the revolution to socialism, then, when the revolution in backward countries has overthrown the rule of the bourgeoisie and established state ownership, how should its social nature be defined? To this question revolutionary Marxists respond: the nature of society at this time is transitional, which means it can advance toward socialism or it can retreat toward capitalism. This is a practical answer, because at this stage, state ownership to raise productivity is the first step to catching up with the level of productivity in advanced capitalist countries and to laying the foundation for the realization of socialism (what we generally call "to build socialist primitive accumulation; this task is not necessary in the advanced countries). At this stage socialism cannot be immediately realized. In addition due to the arduousness of this task, if there is no support from the international proletariat or if there is serious isolation, then the planned economy that this society relies on to go toward socialism will meet with big and small difficulties or even regress toward capitalism.

When Mao Zedong proposed the General Line, he totally overlooked China's backwardness. He declared that a country as backward as China could at once practice socialism. The CCP's propagandists and theorists considered that the bourgeoisie had been eliminated, that state ownership had been established, and therefore China was practicing socialism, and it could even "build communism in one country"!

The reason why Mao and the CCP propagandists told such a gross lie to the people is that the CCP wanted to impoverish the people indefinitely in the name of socialism, so that the bureaucracy could obtain maximum material conditions to underpin its rule. By implication it means that Mao at first proposed "learning from the Soviet Union" and later imposed the Great Leap Forward and the People's Communes in order that the CCP could control the nation's means of production and means of living, then control the state power and social power from above, and build up an autocratic rule of the bureaucracy acting as a parasite on state property. Such measures cannot promote socialism.

CHARACTERISTICS OF MAOISM AND ITS RISE AND FALL

We can sum up the characteristics of Maoism and its role in the contemporary Chinese revolutionary movement as follows:

In appearance Maoism generally identifies with Marxism-Leninism; in essence it concretely identifies with Stalin's positions on international and Chinese questions. Thus it has the same characteristics as Stalinism in its abstract affirmation yet concrete negation of and deviation from Marxism-Leninism.

As an ideology it reflects the consciousness of petit-bourgeois intellectuals who, going through rapid fall and placed in the crevice between capitalist forces and the worker-peasant forces, attempt to get rid of the oppression of the capitalist forces and yet also to override the workers and peasants. It has the characteristics of making use of acute, actual class struggles to build up its strength and then to rise above society.

Maoism's aforementioned characteristic went through a process from concealment to open exposure.

Starting from the time when it affirmed the CCP's turn toward armed struggle in the final stages of the Second Revolution, it made use of this form of struggle, on the one hand, to group together party members who dared not criticize the Comintern after the defeat of the revolution and yet who continued to carry out revolutionary work and, on the other hand, it followed the example of the Soviet Communist Party to set up a party system of bureaucratic centralism.

It made use of a strong advance of the movement against the Japanese invasion to reiterate "KMT-CCP collaboration" on the one hand and expand its armed forces on the other. It blended together whitewash of the Chiang regime and promotion of class collaboration with the declaration that it would not give up its communist convictions. It stressed the urgency of conducting a national liberation struggle, and with this covered up its position of abandoning the mobilization and organization of the masses to carry out class struggle. On the other hand, it ingratiated itself with the bourgeoisie, declaring its position of resisting Japan and building China in joint effort with them, and with this it covered up the irreconcilable opposition between the KMT and the rising CCP.

In the course of the resistance war and the civil war, it stressed "taking the path of the masses" and "serving the people"; with this it inspired the spirit of sacrifice of militants in struggle and enabled the CCP to grow rapidly and to shine with dazzling brightness for a certain period. However it functioned only to strengthen the CCP and not to develop (in fact it restrained) the people's autonomy.

It directed the CCP first to expand its armed strength in the countryside, hence grouping together large numbers of landless peasants, workers, and intellectuals, who had fled from the cities to the countryside. The rapidly expanded armed forces served as the chief basis for seizing power. This, of course, had its function of bringing down the enemy, yet it also strengthened the CCP's own bureaucratic party system and intensified the CCP's control over the masses. This eventually caused the CCP to sink into bureaucratic megalomania from which it could not recover.

It systematized the Menshevik "theory of revolution by stages," fragmentarily quoted Lenin's ideas on revolution in backward countries (in this, Mao also learned from Stalin), and then came to the conclusion that China's democratic revolution should be led by the proletariat (in effect, the CCP). This reflects that the rapidly expanding CCP was reluctant to act in subordination to the Chiang regime and that it regarded itself as the leader for defending and advancing the development of Chinese capitalism.

For a long time, it directed the CCP regime to be content to remain in the Liberated Zone, and only when the situation became critical—it would be eliminated if it did not mount an offensive to replace the Chiang regime—did it call for land reform and the "liberation" of the whole country. And it was only under the circumstances of siege by U.S. imperialism abroad and a vicious offensive by the landowners and bourgeoisie domestically (social disintegration would have resulted if the major means of production were not nationalized and the major means of living were not controlled by the state) that it hastily declared the implementation of the General Line.

Yet this General Line carried with it from the start antimarxist characteristics: it thought that socialism could be realized simply by placing national production under the control of state ownership or collective ownership. The so-called "constructing socialism according to China's specific circumstances" in reality allowed the CCP to dominate all power and resources in a general and strict way, to set up an autocratic bureaucratic rule that governed everything, to change the CCP from a leader of the workers and peasants to an oppressor and a ruler in opposition to the workers and peasants.

In sum its actions were contradictory. When the CCP was besieged and persecuted by the landowning bourgeoisie, it directed the CCP to join with the people in a limited way through armed struggle, so that its characteristics of anti–Marxism-Leninism and overriding the workers and peasants could be covered up. When the CCP rose to power, Maoism directed the CCP to go into opposition against the workers and peasants through a series of measures aimed at building and consolidating the rule of a privileged bureaucracy, so that its characteristics became increasingly explicit. Hence the CCP and Maoism itself also rapidly declined and came to be treated with contempt and rejection.

Maoism handled the actual class struggle in an empirical way and would give up its principles in exchange for immediate concerns. For example it initially thought that again proposing KMT-CCP collaboration would be advantageous to the CCP's public recruitment activities, and so it even dawned on the Chiang regime. When the Chiang regime joined with the Japanese puppets to strike at the CCP, it was compelled to respond, because cover-up was no longer possible. Another example is that at first it thought that by stressing China's backwardness, hence postponing the task of socialist revolution to the distant future, it could join with the bourgeois democrats; later it hastily deviated from the reality to practice the General Line. The "experience" to which it resorted was simply that when the CCP was in a position of being repressed, it stressed the arduousness of the revolution to cover up its compromise with the landowning bourgeoisie; when it was in a ruling position, it used the pretext of "building socialism" to carry out policies breeding bureaucratic privileges and infringing on the interests of the workers and peasants.

Thus though Maoism contains numerous internal contradictions as a theoretical system, there is one consistency among the many variations: it has been the ideological schemer for establishing a bureaucratic party and ushering it on to power. For the CCP, which sought to dominate the workers and peasants, these ideologic schemes were not only "appropriate" but indispensable. Precisely because of this today, when many of Mao Zedong's mistakes can no longer be covered up, the CCP still treats "Mao Zedong thought" as its guiding principle.

Needless to say when the people reject the CCP, they also reject Maoism, and vice versa.

17

The Beijing University Students and Trotskyism

JUN XING

Since Deng Xiaoping, at the Central Work Conference last December, gave the directive that "the state apparatus of people's democratic dictatorship must be strengthened," the Chinese Communist Party has stepped up its repression of dissidents, and arrests have been made across China. The hardest hit are the activists of unofficial publications and organizations.

University and college students have also come under repression. AFP reported from Beijing on May 3: "During a local election campaign, some activists of the Beijing University were arrested for their criticism of the regime. The number of arrests is not known."

In the same report, it quoted that day's *Beijing Daily* that in a political report, a Beijing University Party Committee member charged that the ideas of a small number of politically active students of the university originate from the ideas of the western bourgeoisie, Trotsky, and the Chinese Trotskyists.

The party leadership at the Beijing University linked the university activists with Trotskyism in order to mold public opinion for the repression, but this linkage is not without reason or objective significance.

Since the May 4 Movement of 1919, students of Beijing University have always stood at the forefront of the national student movement and have acquired a long tradition of struggle for democracy. After 1949 Beijing University has been one of the most active centers of antibureaucratic struggles. In the recent election movement to elect deputies for the People's Congress, their active participation in campaign activities and the acute political ideas expressed are seldom paralleled by other colleges.

Among student candidates for deputy, most of them think that the issue in today's China is that anyone who voices ideas considered by the rulers as unfavorable to them is labeled a counterrevolutionary. Some think that there is no freedom of speech in China, and, therefore, one aim of the election campaign is to promote freedom of speech and publication. Some candidates think that socialism equals public ownership plus democracy; without democracy socialism is illusive. Some think that bureaucratism is a problem of the system. Some openly point out that Mao Zedong is not a marxist and that the CCP is not a proletarian party. On the whole the emphasis of the campaign activities has been from the start analysis of overall political, theoretical, and social problems.

On the part of the "electorate," a public opinion poll shows that 48.2 percent are "very concerned and participates actively" in political life, 46.2 percent are not too concerned and do not participate too actively, and only 5.6 percent are not concerned and do not participate. The common wish of the electorate is for social reforms. Some favor "big operations": 36.6 percent of the electorate hope that the elected deputies will be for radical social reforms; 19.5 percent hope that moderate social reformers will be elected; 18.8 percent hope that steady people will be elected. (The above information is taken from Gong Pa's article on Elections in Beijing University published in Beijing University "Thought" Magazine.)

After the campaign activities, twenty-two Beijing University students proposed a "Publication Law (draft)" and collected signatures to demand that the government adopt it in lieu of the unreasonable Publication Ordinance of 1952. This document in defense of the people's right to free speech and publication has gained broad support both in China and in Hong Kong.

The foregoing shows the considerable radicalization in thinking and action of Beijing University students. Some leading party members have referred to certain students as "dissidents," and Deng had denounced "dissidents" for being "against the Party and socialism." It is known that some have been arrested.

But the more brutal the repression, the more the CCP exposes itself, and the stronger the resistance. The Beijing University students reacted promptly to the government's recent criticism of the famous novelist and screenplay writer Bai Hua, whose film *Pained Love* has been criticized as violating the Four Principles and disseminating hatred for the mother country. The students put up wall posters and rallied to show their support for Bai Hua and to demand the public screening of this banned film so that the people may judge it for themselves. They demanded that different opinions be allowed to be expressed and that the person criticized be allowed to defend himself.

The students have shown their courage and uprightness when they still stand up to defy power despite the recent increase in repression.

The fact that the names of Trotsky and his Chinese comrades are linked with these progressive militants of Beijing University or that their thinking has something in common is not accidental. The fall of the Gang of Four, the bankruptcy of Mao Zedong Thought, and the disappointment that all CCP factions in power have caused the people have helped to liberate the thinking of the Chinese masses, especially the thinking of the more progressive elements. Many of them maintain a Marxist-Leninist perspective and utilize the marxist method to analyze problems. Thus they have points in common with Trotskyism, which is the development of marxism, in particular on the subject of the bureaucratized workers' states.

Although the CCP knows well that Trotskyism has nothing in common with the Western bourgeoisie or with former Stalinists who have become anti-Communists like Milovan Djilas, it still muddles them together in an attempt to smear the image of Trotskyism. The CCP only quotes the example of some Beijing University students comparing the CCP regime with "a new ruling class." But Trotsky and his comrades have always defined the bureaucracy in workers' states as a privileged, parasitic ruling *caste* and not an independent ruling *class*. But despite some distortions, many of the Beijing University students' ideas are close to Trotskyism.

Trotsky's analysis of the Stalinist bureaucratic dictatorship of the 1930s and his proposals for fighting it have always been applicable to China. The analysis truly reflects the objective realities, and the proposals represent the interests and demands of the people. When the Chinese people, especially the Beijing University students, analyze the situation in China, they may come to conclusions similar to Trotskyism, though they may not have studied Trotskyism. However in the 1950s, China had published Trotsky's *The Revolution Betrayed*, which analyzes the bureaucratized Soviet Union, and in recent years, several other writings by Trotsky have also been published. It is therefore not surprising if some people react sympathetically after reading them.

Of course the number of people in China who can read Trotsky's writings is still very limited, because his writings are only for internal reference and as "negative" material for criticism. But from some unofficial publications circulated abroad, we have seen articles that are specific discussions of Trotskyism, and they show that the authors of these articles, having read Trotsky's writings, sympathize with or accept many of Trotsky's ideas.

Thinking that represents truth, once accepted by the masses, will turn into immense strength. Today the number of people who accept Trotskyism is still not big, but it will continue to grow so long as Trotskyism reflects truth and represents objective need. The *Beijing Daily* said that only "a small number of students" are criticized, but it admitted that at Beijing University, "their wrong ideas [i.e., Trotskyism, which is what the rulers consider wrong but what the ruled consider correct] have certain influences" (Hong Kong *Wen Hui Bao*, May 4). This reflects that its influences are not small; it also reflects the rulers' fears. And if these influences exist at Beijing University, they should also exist elsewhere in the country. This is the beginning of a promising development, presaging the trend of future developments and symbolizing the bright prospects of revolutionary optimism!

18

Trotskyism in the Eyes of the Democracy Movement

XING YING

Despite decades of censorship, disinformation, and slander by the Communist Party of China, Trotskyist ideas still exert a positive influence in China, especially among young activists in the democratic movement. The bankruptcy of Mao Zedong Thought and the CCP's discredited practice of "socialism" have stimulated an active search for historical truth, theoretical explanation, and political perspectives. It is in this context that Trotskyism has become an area of interest for young activists.

WANG XIZHE ON TROTSKY'S IDEA OF INTRAPARTY DEMOCRACY

In the relatively free and outspoken atmosphere of 1980, Trotsky and his ideas were a topic of open reference and discussion. For example on April 4, 1980, at a forum organized by the Guangdong Provincial Youth League Committee, Wang Xizhe (the chief writer of the Li Yi Zhe Wall Poster in 1974) mentioned Trotsky in his speech, and in an interview in July 1980 with a Hong Kong magazine, he further expounded his views on Trotsky's ideas: "Trotskyism has a more distinct critique of Stalinist bureaucratization"; "Trotsky considered that tendencies should exist in the party to reflect different interests of different strata both inside the party and in the class represented by the party. This point deserves our consideration . . . I personally think that open opposition should be allowed . . . the party should allow different views and even different tendencies." On the other hand, Wang stated his difference with Trotskyism: "I do not agree with the Trotskyist idea of permanent revolution; I agree more with the theory of revolution by stages." (See *October Review*, October 1980, p. 23.)

There have also been serious discussions of Trotskyism among unofficial publications in China. Two significant articles are "On the Trotskyist

Opposition—An Initial Probe into the Ideological Struggles in the RCP(B)"
by Chen Fo-shen, published in *Hua Xia Chun* (*Spring in China*) of Sichuan
Province, founding issue, October 1980 (reprinted in *October Review*, March
1981, pp. 50–58), and "Abandon Prejudices and One Will Discover Ra-
tionality" by Shi Hua-shen, published in *Ze Ren* (*Duty*, official organ of the
Chinese National Unofficial Publications Association) no. 4, January 30, 1981
(reprinted in *October Review*, April 1981, pp. 27–28).

"ABANDON PREJUDICES AND ONE WILL DISCOVER RATIONALITY"

Wang Xizhe expressed his disagreement with Trotsky's theory of permanent
revolution, but Shi Hua-shen's article recommended studies on this theory.
The article started with:

> The name Trotsky is not at all foreign to us, but it is another matter as
> regards independent studies of him.
> Trotsky told us that in the notes to Vol. XIV, Part 2, of Lenin's *Col-
> lected Works* published while Lenin was alive (second edition), it is stated
> that "even before the 1905 Revolution he [Trotsky] advanced the origi-
> nal and now especially noteworthy theory of the permanent revolution,
> in which he asserted that the bourgeois revolution of 1905 would pass
> directly over into a socialist revolution, constituting the first in a series of
> national revolutions."
> Indeed, the process of social reality again arouses attention to the the-
> ory of permanent revolution, and studies on it by us young people are
> more forceful because in our consciousness, there are fewer prejudices left
> from past epochs.
> It must be explained that the theory of permanent revolution is a con-
> siderably unique system. I have at hand a book *The Permanent Revolution*
> in which are included *Results and Prospects* (1904–1906) and *The Permanent
> Revolution* (1932); the latter, written by the author outside the Soviet Union,
> gave an overall refutation on attacks of the theory of the permanent revo-
> lution and explained the "differences" between the author and Lenin.

Shi Hua-shen quoted extensively from the book. He quoted Trotsky's
general ideas on socialism, that

> in respect of the technique of production, socialist society must represent
> a stage higher than capitalism. To aim at building a nationally isolated
> socialist society means, in spite of all passing successes, to pull the pro-
> ductive forces backward even as compared with capitalism. To attempt to
> realize a shut-off proportionality of all the branches of economy within a
> national framework means to pursue a reactionary utopia.

Shi Hua-shen then gave his opinion: "Evidently, here, the author, like Marx and Lenin, believes firmly in scientific socialism and has not succumbed to pragmatic socialism."

Shi Hua-shen expressed disagreement with Lenin's and Trotsky's assertion that "world economy in its entirety is indubitably ripe for socialism." He felt that "monopoly capitalism may take quite a long time before it reaches its summit, and during this period, one cannot say that world economy has reached the level of ripeness for the practice of socialism; one can only say that it is breeding socialism that is ripening. In this respect, the theory of permanent revolution has its weaknesses."

The article also expounded Trotsky's evaluations of the Russian Revolution, his idea of the skipping of historical stages, and most importantly, his opposition to the theory of "socialism in one country." Shi remarked after quoting Lenin's words in 1922 that common effort of the proletariat of several advanced countries is necessary before socialism can be victorious:

> Trotsky told us that during the period of the October Revolution, he stood together with Lenin to oppose hesitancy or opportunism in the central institution of the Bolshevik Party. I tend to believe in his words. . . . Here, I truly see that Trotsky and Lenin are unanimous in their basic theories of socialism. It was only in 1952 that Stalin pointed out that economic rules cannot be created; it was already too late, and moreover, it was far from reaching the depth of Trotsky's ideas.

Shi's article concluded with the following:

> There are mistakes in Trotsky's theories, but there are also shining elements of truth in them. He persists in the entirety of the world economy, and so, on the one hand, he considers that world economy is ripe for the practice of socialism, and this is the condition for the combined development of backward Russia; on the other hand, Russia itself is not ripe and its revolution must depend on international revolutions. He thinks the practice of democratic dictatorship in Russia has a reactionary nature, and so he wages a persistent struggle against the representative of this reaction—Bukharin—and he fundamentally opposes Stalin's theory of "constructing socialism in one country." I think that people should independently study Trotsky's ideas because Trotsky, like Bukharin, provides a theoretical basis for the socialist cause from different angles.

"ON THE TROTSKYIST OPPOSITION"

While Shi Hua-shen parallelled Trotsky and Bukharin in their contribution to socialist theories, Chen Fo-shen's article "On the Trotskyist Opposition" noted a distinct difference between the two by assessing Trotsky and Bukharin as "one leftist and the other rightist" in the opposition.

In this twenty thousand-word article written in September 1980, Chen Fo-shen discussed the following questions: (1) origin of the differences; (2) concerning new economic policies; (3) Bukharin's theory of class struggle; (4) bureaucratization; (5) democracy and others; (6) the theory of "socialism in one country"; and (7) unresolved case in history.

The introduction to the article read like this:

> For many Chinese, the names Trotsky and Bukharin are not foreign. Most people know that these two persons are famous opportunist and revisionist heads, but very few people concretely know why and how they become opportunist and revisionist heads. This is understandable because the distance of space and time creates a foggy barrier to our limited vision, and prejudicial and abstract dogmatism forces prohibitions on our thinking so that it is limited in an enclosed consciousness.
>
> Very fortunately, I recently had an opportunity to read the newly published "Trotsky's Writings," and thanks to the generosity of a friend, I also read an old edition of "Bukharin's Writings" and writings of other famous opportunists and revisionists like Zinoviev, Kamenev, Shlyapnikov, and Osinsky. After reading them, I was overwhelmed and moved by many feelings, the most outstanding among them being that: Trotsky, Bukharin, and others are in fact not a group of notorious, scandalous "counter-revolutionaries" or ambitious "plotters" as described in our old school textbooks. When I thought of the propaganda we received in the past and the tragic state created by this propaganda, I suddenly felt an urge to communicate some of my feelings to others. But as soon as I conveyed this idea to one of my friends, he at once wrote to warn me not to touch this big issue, because, he thought, what is involved here is not only Trotsky's personal viewpoints but the entire question of Trotskyism, the Fourth International that underwent several changes after Trotsky, and their ideology and theories. And all these are what I do not and cannot understand. Besides, there is one other question that my friend has not dwelt on: Trotskyism is to this day a terrible, frightening criminal charge in China. We have heard that several years ago when President Tito visited China, he guaranteed to some of our country's leaders that Kang Sheng was a Trotskyist! From this can be seen that it is still very sensitive to touch on this problem. Although I do not quite mind this charge—because I consider that I am only engaging in studies of a certain theory, and "there is no restricted area in the field of science," social science theories being also science—I cannot but admit the reasons and difficulties mentioned by my friend. However, I also cannot deny a new fact, that is, the charges leveled by Stalin against Trotsky, Bukharin, and others were not true! They were the mixed product of prejudice, dictatorship, superstition, and cunning malignancy. Facing this fact, any conscientious theoretical researcher cannot help being overwhelmed by a sense of duty to be responsible to history, that is, to seek the truth and restore history to its true countenance.

Therefore, I thought, even if I cannot make an overall analysis and assessment of the entire thinking of Trotsky, Bukharin, and others, it should be all right if I simply describe (even if the description is shallow and brief) how their differences with Stalin originated and what their views, ideas, and theories concerning the differences were?! And so, I have added a subtitle to my article in order to restrict its scope and thinking. I hope that this can be a start for detailed studies in this area.

BETWEEN TROTSKY, BUKHARIN, AND STALIN

In the chapter on "Origin of the Differences," Chen Fo-shen refuted the concept of grouping the opposition as one bloc. "Within the opposition, the most representative are the ideas of Trotsky and Bukharin; the two of them, one leftist and the other rightist, form a very distinct contrast." After describing the development of the opposition until Trotsky's assassination in 1940, Chen then quoted the October 1923 "Statement of 46 Persons" drafted by Trotsky as the first publicized program of the opposition. He remarked that

> Trotsky has touched a deep root of bureaucratization, which means he saw the terrible threat of a bureaucratic system that was being institutionalized or was ripening through being institutionalized. Therefore, his criticisms involved some basic problems with the party's leadership. . . . But Stalin's view replaced essence by phenomena; his view later prevailed in China, that is "the Central is correct and all mistakes are committed by those below; the party's policies are sage and mistakes rest with people who execute the policies" . . . Trotsky's criticisms were very acute and sensitive criticisms on the burgeoning, later aggravating, and finally crystallized totalitarian system. The essence of the criticisms are, speaking in our terms today, the demand for collective leadership in the party, prevention of one-person dictatorship, and guarantee for democratic life within the party. From the experience of historical developments, those criticisms were very timely and had a deep significance.

In the following three chapters, Chen Fo-shen analyzed the different proposals of Trotsky and Bukharin on economic development, Bukharin's views on class struggle, and Trotsky's acute analysis of the party's bureaucratization, centralization, and degeneration. In the chapter titled "Democracy and Others," Chen discussed the opposition's insistent demand for democratization of the party life and then said, "In 1936, Trotsky published his book *The Revolution Betrayed* abroad and the book, from a new angle, probes the relationship between class and political party, and sets the theoretical basis for the question of bi-party or multi-party system." Chen quoted from the 1963 Chinese edition of *The Revolution Betrayed* printed by the Joint Publishers, the CCP-sponsored bookshop.

In the next chapter, which dwelt on the theory of "socialism in one country," Chen considered that "the question of whether or not one country can build socialism is another basic difference between Stalin and Trotsky." After quoting both Stalin and Trotsky on this question, Chen summed up that "here, I do not intend to make a conclusion on who's right or who's wrong in this polemic. Stalin's 'victory in one country' has been negated by practice, and Trotsky's theory of world (or many) revolutions has not yet been proved by practice." But the way Chen presented the polemic revealed his sympathy with Trotsky's argument.

FAIR REVIEW OF TROTSKY'S CASE

The conclusion of the article expressed the author's wish that Trotsky's case be clarified and resolved. The conclusion ran as follows:

> In the 1938 *History of the Communist Party of the USSR* (*Bolshevik*) compiled by order of Stalin, the Trotsky and Bukharin opposition was labeled with a series of filthy charges. Under the pen of this book's authors—that is, the victors of the struggle that we just examined—the opposition is no longer prisoners of conscience or political prisoners who cannot be tolerated by Stalinism, but are a gang of imperialism's "hackneys," "renegades," and "spies" betraying the country and the people and plotting to overthrow the Soviet regime, and a gang of "murderers," "rogues," and "gangsters" assassinating Lenin, Kirov, and Gorky, and planning to assassinate Stalin. Several years ago, this series of astounding accusations deceived quite a lot of good, childish people. But today, basically no one believes in them any more. With Stalin's brutal crimes being exposed, the people gradually awaken, and many people are already convinced that the brutal suppression and persecution of the opposition were gravely false cases personally forged by Stalin, and were very rare tragedies in the history of the international communist movement. The catastrophic consequences have been proved by the painful experience of the Chinese, Yugoslav, and other Eastern European Communist Parties. However, due to the lack of forceful evidence, this false case is still unresolved, and the people, up to now, still cannot make a precise, fair historical assessment on the true countenance of the opposition, let alone a correct conclusion. In China, this point has even become the basic barrier to studies on Trotskyist theories. . . .
>
> For history, facts are important. It seems that thorough clarification of this problem, redress of the false case, and settlement of this unresolved historical case can only wait for the further revelation and discovery of new files and materials. Not long ago, the Harvard University in the U.S.A. announced that it would publish large amounts of Trotsky's letters and materials kept by the university. This has aroused concern and interest all over the world. We wait in expectation for these materials to provide new facts and bases to clarify and settle this historical case.

Articles like those by Chen Fo-shen and Shi Hua-shen reveal a new phenomenon among Chinese youth in searching for the truth. They have only read a few of Trotsky's writings, but they already disagree with the official version given by Stalin and the Communist parties and sympathize with Trotsky's views on many important political, theoretical, and historical questions. And although the Trotskyist question is still officially a "forbidden zone," the unofficial publications publish these articles in a daring spirit of persisting in the truth.

In recent years the official Chinese press has published several of Trotsky's writings. Although they are intended to serve as "texts for criticism" and are circulated only internally in the party, their publication often plays an objective role of disseminating Trotsky's ideas and liberating the thinking of militants. The spread of Trotsky's analysis of the bureaucratized workers' state and his recommendation of political revolution will provide revolutionary theory to the heroic revolutionary action of the Chinese masses to overthrow the CCP's dictatorial rule and build genuine socialism.

19

Can the CCP Rely on the Working Class?

ZHANG KAI

The collapse of the Communist parties in Eastern Europe and the Soviet Union has severely shaken the CCP. To avoid going down the same path, the CCP leadership is trying to strengthen its work toward the working class, at least on paper.

In an article entitled "Strengthen and Improve the Work of the Party Towards the Working Class Under New Historical Conditions," appearing in the May 1, 1991, issue of the CCP theoretical journal *Qiushi*, a provincial party secretary pointed out that "the intense international class struggle cannot help affecting and impacting the worker masses, and the flooding of bourgeois liberal thoughts cannot help causing some ideological confusion among the worker masses."

The article further said that "in recent years, people promoting bourgeois liberalization advocate the separation of the working class and the Party, thus destroying the relationship between the two, and call for 'trade union autonomy and independence,' saying that leadership by the party is obstructing the working class from becoming masters of society."

It went on to urge the working class to "resolutely oppose the idea of 'everything for money,'" to "obey the constitution and laws," to "consciously accept [modern enterprise] management," and to "exercise self-restraint."

Such criticisms and demands reflect growing discontent among the workers and their antagonistic mood against the CCP, constituting, with the changes in Eastern Europe and the Soviet Union in the background, what the article referred to as the "new historical conditions."

REEMPHASIZE RELYING ON THE WORKING CLASS

Faced with such "historical conditions," the article stressed the need to strengthen the work of the CCP toward the working class and to improve the relationship of the CCP with it, specifically by "wholeheartedly relying on the working class" and "further expand[ing]" the channels of workers' participation in politics and social management, and so on.

After the failed August coup and the banning of the Soviet Communist Party, the "new historical conditions" are even more severe for the CCP! Another article, entitled "Several Problems to Be Solved so as to Give Workers Full Play to Become Masters—A Study on the Situation in Some Enterprises" and published in *Qiushi* one month after the coup, highlighted the concern of the CCP on the work toward the working class.

In the article the two authors from the CCP Central Policy Study Unit explained the results of their survey of how the policy of relying wholeheartedly on the working class was applied in the enterprises. Overall some big state enterprises have applied it better, while many enterprises still lacked effective mechanisms, and although some enterprises have set up a system, it has not been functioning normally.

Specifically during the enterprise director responsibility system and contracting system reforms, quite a few leading cadres have behaved problematically, "resulting in the weakening of the idea that the leadership should rely on the workers to run the enterprise." "Some leading cadres still think today that the call by the Central to rely wholeheartedly on the working class is only a slogan arising out of the need for political stability: some are worried that too much talk on respecting the master status of workers would affect the scientific management of the enterprise. According to a survey by a city-level trade union federation, 58.8 percent of workers think that their enterprise leaders 'think of the workers only during difficult times and forget about them during good times.' A few enterprise leaders see themselves as 'owners' of the enterprise and the workers as employees, resulting in a tense relationship."

The above-quoted response of the workers effectively explains why the CCP is resinging the old song of relying on the working class: it is facing severe political problems today. The party has failed over the last forty years in its attempt to improve its relationship with the working class. How can such empty calls on the enterprise cadres resolve the ever deepening conflicts between the CCP and the workers today?

PROBLEMS OF THE WORKERS' CONGRESS SYSTEM

Both of the above-mentioned articles talked about setting up a democratic management system inside the enterprise to "give full play" to the functioning of the workers' congress system. This system was set up ten years ago by a "provisional law on workers' congresses in state enterprises" by order of the CCP Central and the State Department in July 1981. The second article in *Qiushi* revealed some facts on its situation today.

"According to a survey in a city at the end of last year," the article said, "of all basic enterprises and units in the city, only 76.4% have set up a workers' congress. Even among those set up, some workers' congresses only exist formally. According to surveys, only 20% of the workers' congresses in this city play a better role, 60% are fair, while 20% are poor. It is broadly felt that the least applied rights of the workers' congress are the rights to democratic elections and monitor controls. In one city, 76% of the enterprises have not applied the right to democratic election." Furthermore "in some enterprise workers' congresses, the deputies are mostly party and political cadres of various grades and categories; even in the advanced enterprises, production line workers only constitute about 5% of all deputies."

Thus the article revealed that most if not all of the workers' congresses in fact function as organs monopolized and controlled by the party cadres. Although the article raised not only the question of improving the election procedures to ensure representation of the deputies but also the problem of how the deputies can be monitored and made accountable to the workers, it did not say how these could be done.

UNFAIR INCOME DISTRIBUTION IN ENTERPRISES

The survey also revealed that income distribution in "some" enterprises are not fair. Specifically "some small enterprise contractors and leaseholders have unruly income and unclear accounts; enterprise assets seem to have become private property, spent at will without mass supervision. Some contracts have amassed huge wealth without an improvement in productive efficiency. Secondly, the income of many enterprise contractors differs too much from that of the workers. In many poorly performing enterprises, the contractors have income over ten times or even tens of times more than the workers, . . . severely undermining the enthusiasm of enterprise workers." Such a statement reflects the strong sentiment of the workers against unfair income distribution and the corruption and embezzling of the contractors and hints at a general slowdown by the workers.

The article's authors thought that it is important to safeguard the workers' interests and rights so that they can be enthusiastic in production. They also suggested guaranteeing the rights of the workers' congresses: (1) to contract the enterprise from the state by all workers and let the workers select an operator to manage the enterprise; (2) to have a say on the question of cadres (in their survey, 60 percent of workers in one city thought that the main sign of being an enterprise master is "the right to choose the enterprise leader"); and (3) to distribute income and interests.

CCP EFFORTS IN VAIN

Such suggestions reflect to some extent the pressure from the workers, but they run against the whole bureaucratic system and the fear that giving more power to the workers will endanger the CCP. Thus while the articles revealed some facts and made some suggestions, these suggestions will remain mainly on paper.

Regardless of reforms from above, the Chinese working class has been fighting for a long time to improve its living and working conditions through its own efforts. The recently released *White Paper on Human Rights in China* revealed an "incomplete" figure. During 1990 the national and local enterprise work disputes mediation committees have received 18,573 cases of work disputes. This figure obviously did not include those cases in which workers bypassed these committees and took slowdown or strike action themselves; however, it did reflect that workers' disputes are frequent and that the workers are fighting to safeguard their own interests.

Despite calls on paper from within the CCP to strengthen its work toward the working class and to improve its relationship to the working class, the need of the bureaucracy to maintain its monopoly of power while speeding up the economic reforms and increasing production at the expense of the workers will mean that social, economic, and political contradictions between the bureaucracy and the working class can only get worse, thereby triggering a new wave of struggle for democracy and a rising workers' movement, to eventual confrontation and revolutionary struggle. The bureaucracy's efforts to stem this tide will prove to be in vain!

20

On the Second Anniversary
of Democracy Movement '89

ZHANG KAI

On the eve of the fifteenth anniversary of the April Fifth Tiananmen Uprising and the second anniversary of Democracy Movement '89, at a time when the Chinese rulers were celebrating the "correctness" of their repression, the overseas edition of *People's Daily* has failed to censor a poem with an embedded phrase: "Li Peng, step down to placate people's anger."

Then on April 1, there was a wall poster in a street near Tiananmen Square calling for Li Peng's resignation.

Later according to a news dispatch by UPI from Beijing on April 22, a statement signed by students from at least four Beijing colleges pointed out that those who participated actively in Democracy Movement '89 are quietly continuing their resistance against the repression by the government and are persisting within the campus with ingenious acts of such resistance. "The shedding of blood has moved us from fanaticism to soberness and awakening." This sentence expresses the general feeling of a wide cross-section of the people.

According to an intellectual paraphrasing a public security official, anti-government posters and leaflets appeared in many places in Beijing in April, and the authorities believe that underground organizations have been set up on the campus. Liu Yanbin, a student at People's University, was arrested recently for publishing the underground journal *Democratic Discussions*, which called for reforms of the communist system (Reuters, Beijing, May 5).

In Shanghai, Gu Bin, Yang Zhou, and others have reportedly set up the first human rights organization and organized "underground journals."

PEOPLE'S RESISTANCE CONTINUES

These sketchy pieces of news may reflect only the tip of the iceberg of the Chinese people's resistance to totalitarian rule, despite the fact that under the constant surveillance and repression by the authorities, democracy movement activists generally do not want to act recklessly in order that they might preserve strength for future struggles.

The anti-Li Peng poem and its message became widely known inside China because of the response of the government and the *People's Daily* and their reporting on television and newspapers. It became a mockery of the regime's repression as well as its claim that the people support the government and its repression of the democracy movement.

When answering questions of foreign reporters, Li Peng tried to play down the incident as "a small matter not worth mentioning," thus contradicting the open accusation by the Public Security Minister that the publication of the poem is "a severe matter" that will be investigated. Interestingly it was revealed by the chief of *People's Daily* that, of the 32 percent of his staff who took part in Democracy Movement '89, only 1 percent have so far been punished due to "a lenient policy adopted because too many people took part." The poem incident may cause many staff members to be persecuted for their 1989 activities.

In his report to the National People's Congress, the head of the Supreme Court said that 490 cases related to Democracy Movement '89 have been heard in Beijing, involving 750 persons. In addition, 72 persons were tried in 62 cases on more serious charges of incitement and plotting to destabilize the government. He also claimed that trials of Democracy Movement '89 activists "have basically finished."

In fact new arrests have been taking place. Liu Yanbin, Gu Bin, and Yang Zhou, mentioned earlier, have all been detained. Others have been summoned for questioning; for example the recently released writer Wang Ruowang and his wife have again been questioned for thirty-six hours.

On April 4 university graduates in the city of Wuhan were sentenced to death on charges of forming "a secret society" in June of 1990 and "killing a taxi driver" in November 1990. As usual, no details were reported in the newspaper.

REPRESSION DOES NOT BRING STABILITY

Li Peng tried to justify the June 4 massacre by saying that, without such repressive measures, there would not be stability and economic prosperity in China today.

However the reality is quite different. What followed the June 4 massacre was a year of the "most difficult period" in the economy, which was not just due to the rectification and adjustment policy of the regime, but also partly due to passive resistance and negative attitudes toward work on the part of the workers, and foreign sanctions on loans and investment.

Since then, although production has increased again, it was only because the state pumped in large loans to jack up production and create demand, while the market remained sluggish, inventories continued to build up, economic efficiency continued to drop, the proportion of enterprises suffering losses increased to two-thirds, and their indebtedness increased 120 percent over the previous year.

This is partly reflected in the worsening of the government's financial situation. Taking into account the income from domestic and foreign loans, the state budget deficit was 42.3 billion yuan (about U.S. $8 billion at 5.3 yuan to U.S. $1) while the actual deficit was 50.9 billion yuan. The budget deficit for 1991 is 47.6 billion yuan. The finance minister reported that the state financial difficulties have increased in 1990 to "a state not known for many years" and "the 1991 situation is very grave."

Because of the worsening financial difficulties, the government has decided to issue 10 billion yuan of state bonds "to be subscribed by fixed proportions by citizens and individual businesses," along with other special bonds to be subscribed by various enterprises and institutions.

In the area of public order, crimes have increased significantly over the last two years. Official figures showed an increase of over 10 percent in 1990, with over six hundred five thousand persons arrested nationally for criminal offenses, where "gang crimes were more rampant and most of the offenders were youths."

WORKERS' RESISTANCE INCREASING

The resistance and struggles by the working class are important factors in the political unrest today in China. Since the June 4 massacre, the discontent of the working class toward the regime has been increasing. An immediate cause is the austerity policy of the government leading to a large increase in the number of unemployed and underemployed. This has resulted in urgent appeals for concern from the official All China Federation of Trade Unions and in *Workers' Daily*.

According to an article entitled "Workers Are Not Weak" in the April issue of *Zheng Ming*, a journal in Hong Kong that claimed to have insider news in China, the State Security Ministry reported to the CCP central that in the first eight months of 1990, there were over forty-two thousand cases of "reactionary slogans," explosions, sabotage, assassinations, and other acts of resistance in industrial and mining enterprises throughout the country and that workers' secret organizations were discovered in Hunan, Liaoning, Sichuan, Shanxi, Hebei, and other provinces. The article also described several concrete cases of workers' strikes and other struggles.

If such reports are true, the actual situation in China would be much more serious and causing a much greater threat to the regime than people have thought. The reaction of the official trade union federation and newspapers could further confirm the grave situation.

Therefore claims of stability and prosperity by Li Peng are only an attempt to show a brave face, as was his unprovoked statement that "the political stability of China includes also the stability of the Chinese government. Therefore, for the terms of this government, I see that my post as prime minister will not be changed."

The recent appointment of Zhou Jiahua and Zhu Rongjui as deputy prime ministers may reflect a factional struggle and reorganization of power in face of the sharpening social and economic difficulties.

What is worth noting is the "important explanation" Li Peng gave for their appointment: they were "firm and unequivocal in their position during the struggle to quell the counterrevolutionary riot in 1989, keeping in line with the Party central and supporting all measures taken by it." The emphasis on their position two years ago could reflect that there is still strong dissent and opposition within the party, such that Li wants more people to share the blame and responsibility.

In summary although at the time of the second anniversary of Democracy Movement '89, the democracy movement in China has not yet risen again to the surface, there are many signs that the social and economic crises are deepening, and that the masses are gathering their strength and waiting for an opportunity to mobilize again.

21

In Memory of the Marxist Militant Peng Shuzhi: Evaluation of His Political Thinking and Activities

THE EDITORIAL BOARD

The life of Peng Shuzhi was the militant life of a great proletarian revolutionary who undauntedly combated various adverse political currents. From 1920 when he devoted himself to the communist movement, Peng Shuzhi had uninterruptedly persisted in his political belief and had fought for it for sixty-three years. His long devotion to the revolutionary movement, the numerous difficulties and attacks he had suffered, his strong will to persist in struggle, and his enduring consistency as a revolutionary are indeed very rare in the history of revolution.

Peng's rarity is inseparable from his rich marxist theoretical understanding and experience, his conviction in communism, his revolutionary optimism, and the outstanding qualities of his personality. He had devoted his whole life to the cause of human liberation, and his contributions are significant. Here we shall draw a balance sheet on his major political ideas, activities, and contributions in the three main periods of his political life.

1. 1920 TO 1928: JOINING THE CCP AND LEADING THE SECOND REVOLUTION

Peng Shuzhi's political thinking in this period was based on marxism and basically derived from Bolshevism and the experience of the October Revolution, although it was not yet mature. Just as the CCP was still very young, Peng was also very young and had only a few years of experience in politics. Nevertheless in 1925 he already shouldered important leadership tasks in the party central leadership and was one of the five Central Bureau members as well as the head of the Propaganda Department—that is, he had the major responsibility in ideologic political work. In this period the Second Chinese Revolution broke out; Peng was one of the practical leaders of the revolution and participated in the planning of the successful worker uprising in Shanghai.

The revolution could have had high chances of success. But the Comintern formulated an opportunist line on the Chinese revolution and compelled the CCP to accept it—to join and cooperate with the Kuomintang (KMT), which greatly enhanced Jiang Jieshi's (Chiang Kai-shek) strength but suppressed the development of the strength of the workers, peasants, and CCP. The revolution was then betrayed by Jiang and subsequently by Wang Jingwei and suffered a tragic defeat. Although Chen Duxiu, Peng Shuzhi, and other leaders of the CCP had to bear, to varying degrees, the responsibility of executing a wrong policy, which led to the defeat of the revolution, the main responsibility should be borne by the Comintern and in particular by Stalin, who was the formulator and commander of the false Comintern line at that time.

Even while they were carrying out the Comintern policy, leaders such as Chen Duxiu and Peng Shuzhi had actually put forward opposing ideas and proposals. Although these opposing ideas and proposals were rejected by the Comintern delegates and could not overrule the decisions from Moscow, and although Chen and Peng erroneously did not persist in them and thus could not break the iron discipline of the Comintern, they had had progressive significance and positive influence.

Much of Peng Shuzhi's contribution in this period was worthy of credit. Some examples follow:

First in the preparatory stage of the second revolution, he made three important proposals to the CCP Central: (1) to reject Sun Yat-sen's demand that the Comintern's resolutions and directives to the CCP be examined by the KMT Central or a Liaison Committee set up by the KMT. Peng's proposal was accepted,[1] which helped the CCP change its total obedience to the KMT; (2) to set up a committee of the workers' movement to take up special duty concerning labor movement work; (3) to strengthen the party's local organizations and transfer party members back from Moscow to take up the work. These two proposals were also accepted by the CCP central, and they prepared favorable conditions for the coming revolution.

Second in the same period, he propagated important theoretical propositions of Marxism-Leninism to fight Menshevik rightist ideas.

He pointed out that "Leninism is our weapon, and the October Revolution is our road. Let us practice our weapon, Leninism, and let us go towards our road, the October Revolution." That is to say that the national revolution in China should permanently go toward the socialist revolution.[2]

He also pointed out that "in the national revolution in China, *only* the Chinese working class is worthy to be the leader and *only* it can be the leader." "[T]he mission of the Chinese working class is definitely not limited to the national revolution, and definitely not limited to the elimination of imperialism and warlords; it has its greater mission and ultimate aim—proletarian revolution."[3] The ideas in this article, before its publication, had influenced Chen Duxiu and induced Chen to give up his previous idea that "class-collaborationist national revolution is at present necessary and feasible"[4] and to adopt the idea that "the main lesson we learn from the two decades of the movement for a national revolution is that among the various classes in society, only the last class, the proletariat, is the uncompromising class."[5] These correct ideas had often been publicly propagated in the party's organ and theoretical publications and had had constructive influences.

Third during the revolution, Peng Shuzhi continued with his propaganda and agitation for the practice of Marxism-Leninism and against Jiang Jieshi's counterrevolution. For example:

1. In response to the closure of the Shanghai General Union on September 20, 1925, Peng wrote an article in *Xiang Dao* (*The Guide*): "We had repeatedly said that the liberation of the Chinese nation from the yoke of imperialism and its tool, the feudal warlords . . . can be achieved only when the Chinese workers rise up in struggle and take up the leadership position." The several hundred thousand workers in Shanghai, "if they take one more step forward in the future, will go on the road of armed riot . . . will follow the example of the Petrograd workers, going from the February Revolution to the October Revolution."[6] This prediction was proved in less than six months, but the revolution was unfortunately betrayed by Stalin's opportunist policies.

2. To go on the road of the October Revolution, Peng wrote in early 1927 "Is Leninism not apt for China's so-called 'national conditions'?" which was published in *The Guide*. After a detailed analysis, his conclusion was that "it is proved that Leninist theories and tactics are particularly apt for China." He considered that "the present revolution in China is a national-democratic revolution. But this revolution is by no means limited to nationalism and democracy; it will inevitably quickly turn towards a socialist revolution." "Therefore, we should understand the meaning of 'permanent revolution,' and go from national revolution to proletarian revolution."[7]

3. Soon afterward the Chinese workers' and peasants' consciousness rose, the mass movement was growing, the Shanghai workers rose up, and the third uprising even established workers' power. At the same time, Jiang Jieshi intensified his counterrevolutionary activities. Peng Shuzhi published several articles on *The Guide* and pointed out the counterrevolutionary

tendencies and deeds of the "moderate faction" in the KMT represented by Jiang in an attempt to arouse high vigilance inside and outside the party to speed up the revolution and to stop the counterrevolution.[8]

4. During this period of revolution, Peng Shuzhi had striven organizationally in an attempt to change the false policies implemented by the CCP. They are:

   a. After Jiang Jieshi initiated the coup on March 20, 1926, Chen Duxiu and other leaders "proposed the preparation of an independent military force to confront Jiang Jieshi, and sent Comrade Peng Shuzhi as special representative of the party central to Guangzhou to discuss the plan with the Comintern representative, but the Comintern representative did not agree."[9] Peng Shuzhi as special representative of the party central showed that on this question he was in complete agreement with Chen Duxiu and had his trust. Although the Comintern representative did not agree, not daring to go against Stalin's will, Chen and Peng had had a correct proposition and had fought for it.

   b. To carry out the above proposition, Chen Duxiu and Peng Shuzhi, at the enlarged meeting of the Central Executive Committee in July of that year, formally proposed that the CCP withdraw from the KMT and that cooperation be transformed to that between two parties so that the CCP could independently lead the mass movement. This proposition was again rejected by the Comintern representative and the majority in the CCP central.[10]

   c. Around the occupation of Shanghai by the Northern Expedition Army in 1927, Peng Shuzhi, Luo Yinong, and Chen Duxiu considered that the central question was that if the strength of the proletariat could not defeat Jiang's military force, Jiang, directed by imperialism, would inevitably massacre the masses and induce the defeat of the CCP on a national scale. At that time Peng Shuzhi "went to Hankou to present their views and their plan to attack Jiang's army to the Comintern representative and the leaders of the majority of the party central."[11]

   The above three proposals (a, b, and c), had they been implemented, could have led to a totally different development of the subsequent events, and the revolution could possibly have been victorious. Although they were rejected, they showed that the main responsibility for the revolution's failure lay not with Chen and Peng; rather they had striven to prevent its failure.

5. When the Chinese revolution had been strangled by the KMT, the CCP central, headed by Qu Qiubai, ordered the Committee of the Northern Region to stage uprisings in Beijing and Tianjin in early December 1927. Peng Shuzhi, then secretary of the Committee of the Northern Region, refused to execute this putschist, adventurist order for the reason that the objective conditions were not yet ripe. Peng was dismissed from his position for refusal to carry out orders, but his refusal avoided the unjustified sacrifice of the local party members and militant workers.

Peng's ideas and activities in this period can be seen in published articles (mainly in *The Guide Weekly*), documents and minutes of meetings at that time (although they are generally unpublished), and in historical records. In the future when more historical materials are uncovered or publicized, some historical facts that are still controversial or questions that are recounted only from memory will be clarified.

2. 1929–49: LEADING THE CHINESE TROTSKYIST MOVEMENT

After the failure of the revolution, Peng Shuzhi, Chen Duxiu, and many other old leading cadres reflected on the reason for the failure of the revolution to learn lessons from it for the benefit of the workers and peasants of China and other countries. Trotsky's criticisms of the Chinese revolution, when they reached Peng and Chen, enlightened them and struck immediate resonance—Peng and Chen had already made some of Trotsky's criticisms, but for some others of them they had only a vague idea and had not been able to formulate them. Thus they readily accepted Trotsky's ideas and were prepared to fight for them. Although they were aware that their strength was limited and that they had to confront repression and persecution from various class enemies and political enemies, Peng and his comrades were fearless, uncompromising, and committed to fighting for the truth.

His thinking, activities, and contributions in this period can be summed up as follows:

First he carried out an ideologic and political struggle inside the CCP and introduced Trotsky's ideas and proposals concerning the Chinese revolution. His purpose was to gain the support of party members and cadres; change the putschist, adventurist policies at that time; and to fight for democracy inside the party. Although this struggle incurred repression by the party bureaucrats and the expulsion of Chen, Peng, and others from the party, they won the support of dozens of party cadres. For example, eighty-one people jointly signed "Our Political Position," an important historical document with theoretical and political significance, which was drafted by Chen Duxiu, Peng Shuzhi, and Yin Kuan. Later they also won the support of many important worker cells in Shanghai to leave the CCP and join the (Trotskyist) Left Opposition. These worker comrades played a significant role in the Shanghai workers' movement and led several important and successful strikes.

Second during the KMT white terror period, the Trotskyist organization was disrupted many times. When Peng Shuzhi was arrested and imprisoned for five years, he studied many Marxist-Leninist works. He had disagreements and polemics with Chen Duxiu (who was with him in prison), Liu

Bozhuang, and others on the questions of democratic struggle and the proletariat's seizure of power, the national assembly and the soviets, the theory of permanent revolution, and the national assembly. On these important political and theoretical questions, Peng applied Trotsky's position and method of permanent revolution and wrote several long articles and letters to point out the other side's mistakes, in particular those of Chen Duxiu. For example on the question of the national assembly, Chen believed that the proletariat should absolutely solve democratic tasks like the national assembly and the land question; Peng, on the other hand, believed that the land question was a task that must absolutely be solved, but the convening of the national assembly was only "probable." Chen argued that it was necessary only to fight for the national assembly and only to call on the masses to rise up and seize power to bring it into being; Peng's belief was that when the revolutionary tide came, the workers' councils (soviets) must be organized, and the slogan of the national assembly by that time would be "a subsidiary slogan" to help agitate the masses to support the soviets and take part in the insurrections directed by the soviets. These polemics had not only theoretical and educational significance but also practical political significance.

Third during the resistance war against Japan, in the Communist League of China, the basic position of the majority, led by Peng, was that China was a semicolonial country and Japan an imperialist country. Japan's invasion of China was extremely reactionary, and China's resistance against Japan's invasion was progressive even though the resistance war was later entangled with the U.S.–Japan imperialist war. The Trotskyists, like the worker and peasant masses of China, firmly supported China's resistance war against Japanese imperialism. They proposed that the land reform and the eight-hour workday be implemented, basic democratic rights such as freedom of speech and publication must be guaranteed, the livelihood of the workers and peasants must be fundamentally improved, and class struggle must be developed so that the worker and peasant masses could be mobilized to fight the resistance war to defeat Japanese imperialism decisively. At that time the Trotskyists actively committed themselves in the resistance war and conducted propaganda, agitation, and organization of the masses for the realization of the aforementioned demands.

On the one hand, Peng and his comrades supported the KMT government in its leadership of the war against Japan but criticized its false policies to prepare for its replacement by a revolutionary leadership. On the other hand, they criticized the CCP's class collaborationist policy, opposed the CCP's discontinuation of the land reform, and opposed its total subordination to the KMT, its readiness to fight for the KMT's Three People's Principles, and its liquidation of the soviet government and the name and designations of the Red Army, which was placed under KMT government command. Peng and those who agreed with him continued to conceive of the Soviet Union as a degenerated workers' state that should be unconditionally defended when it came under imperialist attack. In this position they agreed with Trotsky and the Fourth International's leadership.

At that time, Chen Duxiu proposed that unconditional support be given to Jiang Jieshi's KMT, and so he opposed criticism of the KMT in the Trotskyist journal. He considered the Second World War a war of the democratic countries against the fascist Axis countries, and so he abandoned defeatism for England, France, and others. He believed that the USSR was no longer a workers' state and no longer worthy of defense.

On the eve of the outbreak of the U.S.–Japan war, the minority in the Chinese Communist League considered that the resistance war would soon be "primarily transformed into a part of the war among the imperialist powers," and so they proposed a "revolutionary defeatist position" toward China's resistance war against Japan. Toward the Soviet Union, some of them considered it to be state capitalist, and some considered it bureaucratic collectivist, but none considered it as a degenerated workers' state.

At that time Peng, together with Liu Jialiang, conducted a blow-for-blow struggle against the minority's political views and defended the correct, marxist position. The documents they wrote for this purpose were almost all collected in a four-volume collection called *In Defense of Marxism*.

Fourth during the civil war, the Chinese Trotskyist organization headed by Peng Shuzhi first of all reunited Trotskyists who had been scattered in different places due to the Japanese occupation. The reorganized party conducted a struggle against the KMT dictatorship and for democracy. In Shanghai they put out two publications which helped greatly in that work. On the basis of a relatively developed organization, the third national congress of the Communist League of China was convened in August 1948. Peng Shuzhi drafted the party program, which was officially adopted after precongress discussion and amendments in the congress.

There has never been any political party or individual in history that has made no mistakes. When we objectively affirm the historical role and contribution of Peng Shuzhi, a revolutionary and leader of a political party, we should also make an appropriate evaluation of the mistakes that he and his organization made under his leadership.

We consider that the mistakes or weaknesses of the work of Peng and his organization in this period were first that there was no recognition that the CCP could successfully seize political power over the country. The civil war's objective revolutionary significance was thus underestimated. Second the slogan "both the KMT and the CCP should unconditionally stop the war," raised in public propaganda and agitation during postwar period when the KMT held power, was a tactical mistake, because it objectively equated the KMT with the CCP. The correct slogan should have been the demand for peace, for the KMT to immediately stop the war, and to oppose only the KMT's launching of the civil war. As for the KMT's extreme corruption and decay, arbitrariness, and dictatorship, build up of bureaucrat capital for the Four Families, and cruel exploitation of the workers and peasants, Peng and his party had seriously exposed and denounced them in their publications. Moreover in the resolution concerning the civil war in China, the basic attitude of supporting the CCP against Jiang's KMT was also expressed. Thus the mistake was not one of basic principle but of tactics.

Peng himself made a self-criticism of this mistake in his "Report on the Situation in China" to the Third World Congress of the Fourth International in November 1951.[12]

3. 1950–83: PROMOTING THE INTERNATIONAL TROTSKYIST MOVEMENT

Peng Shuzhi was forced to go abroad in early 1950. From 1951 to 1979, he was a member of the International Executive Committee of the Fourth International—except for the period from 1953 to 1962, the period of the split in the Fourth International, when he was responsible for leadership work in the International Committee. At the World Congress of the Fourth International in 1979, due to his old age, he was appointed a consultative member of the International Executive Committee. For more than thirty years, besides handling daily leadership work when he was in the Secretariat, he had also put forward his own ideas and proposals on many important international events and questions and helped define the political position and orientation of the international leadership. He had also conducted a serious ideologic struggle against some wrong political and organizational tendencies inside the international Trotskyist movement. Here are some examples:

In the early 1950s, Pablo (Michael Raptis), one of the leadership of the Fourth International, put forward ideas revising the Trotskyist assertions on the Soviet Union and its bureaucratic caste. He considered that the deformed workers' state could continue for several centuries and that the bureaucracy could reform itself. Peng believed that "degenerated or deformed workers' states definitely cannot last for several centuries; they can only be 'temporary and transitional phenomena' produced by specific conditions in the early stage of the transitional period from capitalism to socialism." Concerning the bureaucracy in the Soviet Union, Peng asserted that it cannot reform itself and that there was no substitute for a political revolution by the masses.[13] Besides Peng also opposed Pablo's identification of the CCP as a revolutionary marxist party and insisted that it be considered a Stalinist party.

On the question of the guerrilla warfare orientation in Latin America, Peng Shuzhi had insisted that rural guerrilla warfare cannot replace the traditional revolutionary road pointed out by Marxism-Leninism—the road of the October Revolution waged by the Russian proletariat. Without the rise and support of the masses, isolated guerrilla war will be defeated.

A more significant contribution was his effort for the reunification of the Fourth International, beginning in 1955. He wrote several long letters to the International Committee leadership and to the Socialist Workers Party in the United States, putting forward the necessity for reunification of the Fourth International. After a concerted struggle against the leaders of some organizations who opposed it, reunification was finally achieved in 1963, ending ten years of serious split (although some groups did not participate). Peng's effort indicated his faithfulness to the Fourth International.

In striving for reunification, Peng had opposed the Socialist Labour League in England for its organizational rejection of reunification and for its political sectarianism—it considered revolutionary Cuba not as a workers' state but as one of the various kinds of capitalist regimes. Peng defined Cuba as a workers' state because of its nationalization of property, and he defined the Castro regime as a workers' and peasants' government after its exclusion of the bourgeoisie.

On the important events that occurred after 1949, Peng Shuzhi had mostly made timely, unique analyses that were different from the opinion of many people at the time (including some people in the Trotskyist movement) and resisted the strong ideologic pressure of the CCP. Most of his analyses have stood the test of time. Peng used his profound understanding of Chinese history and politics to struggle against various adverse ideologic currents and strove to assist the Fourth International in establishing a correct position with respect to China. The following examples are an illustration:

Peng had listed important facts to prove that a privileged bureaucratic caste exists in China and that the CCP regime is a dictatorship of the bureaucracy and not a dictatorship of the proletariat in the Marxist sense. He considered that only by an antibureaucratic political revolution by the worker and peasant masses can a democratic socialist political system be established.

When the people's communes were being promoted in the Chinese rural areas, many people expressed their agreement with and support for the CCP policy. Peng Shuzhi on the contrary considered that the CCP's implementation of the policy was entirely by compulsion and command and was fundamentally against the peasants' will. Their character, as "large in size and collective in nature," also did not correspond to the productivity level and the material level in China at that time. Therefore he proposed that the peasants' will must be respected and that they must be allowed to withdraw from or reorganize the communes.

When the CCP launched the "Cultural Revolution," many people also supported it. Peng, however, considered that this "revolution" was Mao's purge of opposing factions in the party and Mao's seizure of the party leadership in order to implement his line and policy; therefore it had no progressive character. Later he further pointed out that the mass forces that emerged in the "Cultural Revolution" could break free of Maoist control and turn to oppose bureaucratic rule in its entirety. For this reason he also paid special attention to Chinese developments.[14]

Later in a series of interviews, Peng explained the significance and problems of events in China.[15]

After the 1976 events in Tiananmen Square, Peng explained in an interview that this demonstration was "obviously spontaneous" and was "a prelude to the political revolution against the dictatorship of the bureaucracy." He further characterized Deng Xiaoping as "a reformist and a compromiser."

In the last interview of which we are aware, he discussed the Chinese dissident movement. He saw in the rise of this movement the dawn of the future antibureaucratic political revolution waged by the Chinese workers and peasants. He had for many years firmly believed that the political revolution is necessary and will be successful in order to clear the primary obstacles on the road toward socialism.

On the basis of his entire political life, despite some mistakes and weaknesses, Peng can without question be considered a persistent proletarian revolutionary. Considering his long persistence in the political and organizational principles of Marxism-Leninism-Trotskyism, his firm adherence to correct traditional positions, and his uncompromising struggle with false tendencies and proposals, he is wholly worthy to be designated as a revolutionary Marxist militant. He had devoted his whole life to the communist movement, for which he was willing to give up everything else, and this showed his sympathy and love for the masses of people. For himself he had always led a difficult, arduous, and serious life. The events of struggle in his whole life indicate the contribution he had made to the cause of human liberation. He had a strong character but a kind heart. He has left many examples for us to follow and from which all revolutionists may learn. He will live in our hearts, and his cause will ultimately be successful.

Notes

1. See Qu Qiubai's *Polemics on the Chinese Revolution,* 716.
2. Peng Shuzhi's "The October Revolution and Leninism," published in *The Guide,* November 7, 1924. See *Selected Works of Peng Shuzhi,* Chinese edition, vol. 1, 166. The next five notes are also taken from this book. Besides, some information in this article has been taken from Peng Shuzhi's memory but has not been specified.

3. Peng Shuzhi's "Who Is the Leader of the National Revolution in China," first published in *New Youth Quarterly*, December 1924.
4. See Chen Duxiu's "China's National Revolution and the Classes in Society," published in *Vanguard* monthly, December 1923.
5. See Chen Duxiu's "Main Lessons of Twenty Years of the National Movement."
6. Peng Shuzhi's "The Closure of the General Trade Union in Shanghai and the Future Duty of the Shanghai Workers," published in *The Guide*, October 5, 1925.
7. See *The Guide*, January 21, 1927.
8. For example the articles "Rightist Danger of the Present Revolution" published on March 6, 1927; "The Compromise Between North and South" on March 12; and "On Jiang Jieshi's Speech of February 21" on March 18.
9. Chen Duxiu's "Letter to Comrades of the Whole Party." See Wang Jian-min's *History of the CCP*, vol. 2, 106.
10. Peng Shuzhi's "The CCP and a Short History of the Second Chinese Revolution," see *Selected Works of Peng Shuzhi*, Chinese edition, vol. 1, 73. At this enlarged meeting of the central committee, "Resolution on the Relationship Between the CCP and the KMT" was adopted, which stated that the formal relationship of the two parties would be a question at the next meeting; it also criticized the opinion of "some comrades" for withdrawal from the KMT.
11. Chen, *op. cit.*, 107.
12. See *Selected Works of Peng Shuzhi*, vol. 3, 64.
13. See Peng Shuzhi's "Evaluation of Pabloism."
14. Detailed discussions of these questions can be found in *Selected Works of Peng Shuzhi*, Chinese edition, vol. 3.
15. See the various interviews in *Selected Works of Peng Shuzhi*, Chinese edition, vol. 3.

22

In Memory of Proletarian Revolutionary Chen Bilan (1902–87)

THE EDITORIAL BOARD

Chen Bilan, an early leader of the Communist Party of China and a Trotskyist militant, died on September 7 at the age of eighty-five.

At the age of twenty, Chen Bilan committed herself to the cause of the liberation of humanity. For over sixty years, she persisted in her belief in communism. Like Peng Shuzhi, her life companion, she had fought all adversities and defied all enemies throughout her life.

Soon after the struggle of the May 4 Movement in 1919, Chen Bilan became a socialist. In early 1922 in the Hubei Provincial Teachers College for Women, where she was studying, she initiated and led a strike to protest the college's dismissal of progressive lecturers and to demand the resignation of the principal. The strike was the first victorious struggle of women students in Chinese history.

In April of the same year, while she was struggling in the student strike, she joined the League of Socialist Youth; six months later, she became a member of the Communist Party of China. In 1923 she was sent to study in the Social Sciences at Shanghai University. The next year she was sent to study at the University of the Toilers of the East in Moscow.

When the May 30th Movement of 1925 broke out, Chen Bilan, at the request of the CCP, returned to China to join in the revolution. In the autumn of 1923, she became secretary of the Department of Women of the Shanghai Regional Committee (Joint Provincial Committee of the Jiangsu, Zhejiang, and Anhui Provinces) and was a member of the Presidium of the Regional Committee. Soon afterward she was chief editor of *Chinese Women*, published by the Party Central. In July 1926 she was also acting secretary of the

241

Department of Women of the Party Central and took up practical leadership work in the revolution.

After the Guomindang strangled the revolution, Chen Bilan and many other comrades together tried to figure out the reason and to draw lessons from the failure of the revolution. Subsequently they came to learn of the differences between Trotsky and Stalin on the question of the Chinese revolution, and from their own experience, they knew that Trotsky's positions were correct and that Stalin's incorrect line and policy in guiding the Chinese revolution was the central subjective factor in the revolution's failure. Chen Bilan, Chen Duxiu, Peng Shuzhi, and others submitted their opinion to the Party Central, which requested that a general review be conducted throughout the party to discuss the reasons for the revolution's failure. It also opposed the putschist adventurism practiced at the time, and advocated the reformulation of a correct line and policy. However not only was their proposal flatly rejected, they were expelled from the party.

From 1929 onward Chen, as one of the founders, participated in the Chinese Trotskyist movement to continue carrying out revolutionary work and underground activity under the white terror of Jiang Jieshi's (Chiang Kai-shek) Guomindang. When Peng Shuzhi and others were arrested and imprisoned by the Guomindang regime under its massive repression, she had to bring up her children and make a living by writing journal articles and taking a job. The book *Essays on the Women's Question* was a compilation of articles she wrote for the journals under the pen name of Chen Biyun. In the preface written by Jin Zonghua, the author was referred to as "a woman who is genuinely devoted to the women's movement and has a profound understanding of women's problems."

Due to the eruption of the war against Japan, the Nanjing authorities released Peng Shuzhi and other Trotskyists. During the resistance war, Chen Bilan and Peng Shuzhi remained in Shanghai to lead underground revolutionary work. Their comrades were arrested by the Japanese occupation forces for leading workers' strikes, and they were the targets of arrest (Peng Shuzhi narrowly escaped from an ambush).

After Japan surrendered Chen Bilan and other comrades published two monthlies in Shanghai: Chen was the editor-in-chief of *Youths and Women* (later renamed *New Voice*), and Peng was editor-in-chief of *For Truth*. Through these publications political influence was spread and organizational strength was developed.

At the end of 1948, Chen and others knew that they would not be tolerated by the CCP, because the CCP had persisted in slander of and hostility to the Trotskyists and so they were compelled to go abroad. A few years later all Trotskyists in the country were arrested, and many were detained for a quarter of a century.

Chen Bilan, Peng Shuzhi, and Liu Jialiang went to Vietnam, and when Liu was murdered by the Vietnamese Communists, they feared for their lives and so went to Europe. Their lives in Vietnam and Europe were very difficult, and they had to do manual work for meager wages to make a living.

During their exile they participated more closely in the work of the Fourth International and frequently wrote articles analyzing developments in different countries, China in particular. In the first few years in France, Chen Bilan began to write *My Memoirs*, which recalls her experience in understanding of and opinion on the decades of struggle in which she had participated, in particular the 1925–27 revolution. (The book, 28 chapters, was printed in serial form in *October Review*, March 1981 to November/December 1984.) In the mid-1960s, Chen and Peng went to the United States.

The life of Chen Bilan is one of a proletarian revolutionary and feminist militant. Her dedication to the revolutionary cause manifests her virtues as an upright, kindhearted, strong, brave person. At the same time, the arduousness of her life manifests the oppression suffered by Chinese working women.

Chen has left us, three years after her partner, Peng Shuzhi. Yet, her example as a revolutionary militant will inspire the later generations, and her deeds will be remembered by history.

Index